"Are the Harry Potter books worthy of sustained scholarly attention? Yes, and then some, argues John Granger. 'Serious' thinkers who shun Harry Potter are denying themselves a serious intellectual and scholarly challenge. Christian thinkers who eschew the Potter series because they find it grates on their theology miss the opportunity to take up once again the daunting question of evil. Wisdom often comes through the eyes and thoughts of children and, in this case, 'children's books.'"

JEAN BETHKE ELSHTAIN
Professor of social and political ethics, the University of Chicago
Author of *Just War against Terror: The Burden of American Power in a Violent World*

"John Granger's thorough knowledge of classical literature, combined with a beguiling writing style, makes this study of Harry Potter's hidden themes not only enjoyable but persuasive. Parents will find here a useful tool, and any Christian curious about Harry will find much to think about."

FREDERICA MATHEWES-GREEN
Columnist for Beliefnet.com and author of *The Illumined Heart: The Ancient Christian Path of Transformation*

"John Granger calls upon his gifts as a classicist, a student of Scripture and Christian literature, a teacher, a parent, and a detective to answer the question, Why are the Harry Potter books so popular? He develops a thorough case that the Harry Potter books are essentially Christian fantasy, and their popularity can be attributed to human longing for the Christian truths that hide just beneath the surface of the stories. Mr. Granger presents a preponderance of evidence from the text itself, translates advanced literary concepts with ease, and addresses sensitive issues with forthrightness and clarity. Christians who love the Harry Potter books will love them more; Christians who oppose them will have a lot to think about."

CARRIE BIRMINGHAM, PH.D.
Pepperdine University

"John Granger has emerged in recent years as one of the most important voices in the literature concerning J. K. Rowling's Harry Potter series. *How Harry Cast His Spell* offers Granger at his most accessible and compelling. His careful analysis provides an exceptional guide to the content and meaning of the Harry Potter novels, as well as practical suggestions on how to approach the books in a meaningful way with children. Those who know and love the Harry Potter series will find that this volume adds a new dimension to their understanding and reading enjoyment. Those who are new to or undecided about the series will gain a great appreciation for what Rowling accomplishes in her novels and for the larger religious tradition that informs her stories. Granger writes with clarity and conviction, and his work is both a joy and an education for the reader. All of those interested in the ways that fiction and faith intersect owe it to themselves to read this book."

AMY H. STURGIS, PH.D.
Liberal Studies Program, Belmont University
Author of various books and articles, including "Harry Potter is a Hobbit: Rowling's Hogwarts, Tolkien's Fairy-Stories, and the Question of Readership"

"No one puts the case for Harry Potter better than John Granger. This book is full of wisdom and insight. . . . The Potter books are much deeper, and a great deal more wholesome, than the critics realize. If Granger is right, J. K. Rowling is writing in the same tradition as the Inklings. Probably millions of Rowling fans knew it all along, but even longtime readers of Harry Potter will find their appreciation deepened by this eye-opening analysis."

STRATFORD CALDECOTT
Author of *Secret Fire: The Spiritual Vision of J. R. R. Tolkien*

"John Granger says a 'Great Book' must do three things: (1) ask the big questions about life, (2) answer the questions correctly (in harmony with Christian tradition), and (3) support the answers artistically. According to these guidelines, the Harry Potter books can be celebrated as great fiction. Granger's engaging application of literature, language, and the logic of Christian belief in his book *How Harry Cast His Spell* may likewise be celebrated as great commentary. Readers will discover in these chapters the essential truth of J. K. Rowling's fictional world—that Love conquers all, even death!"

ROBERT TREXLER
Editor, *CSL: The Bulletin of the New York C. S. Lewis Society*

"Joanne Rowling is the greatest international 'smuggler' in history. She is smuggling thousands of pages of Christian theology into the hearts and minds of millions of people, both young and old. John Granger's book leaves no doubt whatsoever that this is the case. Will Ms. Rowling be unhappy that John has let the cat out of the bag?"

DON HOLMES
Retired Christian bookstore owner and distributor

How Harry Cast His Spell

THE MEANING

BEHIND THE MANIA FOR

J. K. ROWLING'S BESTSELLING BOOKS

JOHN GRANGER

SALT**RIVER**®

An Imprint of Tyndale House Publishers, Inc., Carol Stream, Illinois

This book is dedicated to my wife, Mary.

Visit Tyndale's exciting Web site at www.tyndale.com

TYNDALE is a registered trademark of Tyndale House Publishers, Inc.

SaltRiver and the SaltRiver logo are registered trademarks of Tyndale House Publishers, Inc.

How Harry Cast His Spell: The Meaning behind the Mania for J. K. Rowling's Bestselling Books

Designed by Luke Daab

Previously published in 2006 as Looking for God in Harry Potter under ISBN 978-1-1143-0634-6.

All Scripture quotations, unless otherwise indicated, are taken from the HOLY BIBLE, NEW INTER-NATIONAL VERSION®. NIV®. Copyright © 1973, 1978, 1984 by International Bible Society. Used by permission of Zondervan. All rights reserved.

Scripture quotations marked KJV are taken from The Holy Bible, King James Version.

Library of Congress Cataloging-in-Publication Data

Granger, John, date.
   How Harry cast his spell : the meaning behind the mania for J. K. Rowling's bestselling books / John Granger.
   p. cm.
   Includes bibliographical references.
   ISBN-13: 978-1-4143-2188-2 (sc)
   ISBN-10: 1-4143-2188-0 (sc)
   1. Rowling, J. K.—Criticism and interpretation. 2. Rowling, J. K.—Characters—Harry Potter. 3. Rowling, J. K.—Religion. 4. Potter, Harry (Fictitious character) 5. Spirituality in literature. 6. Christianity in literature.
7. Children's stories, English—History and criticism. 8. Fantasy fiction, English--History and criticism. I. Title.
   PR6068.O93Z6775 2008
   823'.914—dc22   2008015375

Printed in the United States of America

14 13 12 11 10 09 08
7   6   5   4   3   2   1

CONTENTS

ACKNOWLEDGMENTS

How Harry Cast His Spell is the fourth edition and third title of a book
I wrote in 2002 called *The Hidden Key to Harry Potter.* Way back then, my
thesis that Potter-mania was the product of the religious meaning and
Christian content of J. K. Rowling's books was considered a ridiculous
projection of my beliefs forced into the text. Rowling, however, has put
the question of my sanity, at least on this count, to rest. On her Open
Book Tour of the United States in 2007 after *Harry Potter and the Deathly
Hallows* had been published, she told a press conference that she
thought the Christian symbolism and meaning of the stories was "obvious" and that the scriptural passages in the last book "epitomized the
whole series."

I will always be grateful for the confidence Tyndale had in my arguments and for the editorial insights of Janis Harris and Lisa Jackson.

Kathryn Helmers of Helmers Literary Services, my literary agent, and
Robert Trexler, editor of *CSL: The Bulletin of the New York C. S. Lewis Society* and
at Zossima Press, also deserve special mention here. Ms. Helmers opened
the doors at Tyndale and has kept me from many more mistakes than I
care to admit here. Bob Trexler is the best friend and kindred spirit every

man needs and no one deserves. His example of the life in Christ is an everyday challenge.

I blog at www.HogwartsProfessor.com; I have taught classes at Barnes and Noble University online; I've been a keynote speaker at Harry Potter conferences in Orlando, Las Vegas, Los Angeles, Philadelphia, and Toronto; and I've communicated via e-mail with many people who read my books. (I welcome you to e-mail me; my address is at the bottom of this page.) The community of friends I have in Harry Potter fandom, consequently, has grown to the point that listing their names would constitute its own chapter. My Harry Potter friends and correspondents have been the best part of this seven-year adventure.

Last on this short list but first in my heart is my family. Thank you, Hannah, Sarah, Sophia, Methodios, Anastasia, Timothy, and Zossima for letting me share what were originally just our Potter conversations with the world. We've largely grown up together with Harry and friends since our Harry Potter adventure began in 2000, and I like to think our happiness is another demonstration of what I argue in this book.

John Granger
john@hogwartsprofessor.com

PUBLISHER'S PREFACE

Dear Reader,

Some may wonder why a publisher of distinctly Christian books would publish a book about the Harry Potter series, which, while phenomenally successful, has been criticized by some groups within the Christian community. The answer is really quite simple.

Millions of young people are reading the Harry Potter books, providing parents with a wonderful opportunity to use stories their children love to read to start discussions with them about Christian ideas and values—and about how to evaluate the worldview embedded in any piece of literature. We hope *How Harry Cast His Spell* will serve as a catalyst for such discussions and as a bridge to growth in faith and spiritual understanding.

THE PUBLISHER

INTRODUCTION

Imagine yourself walking in the park with your dog in the cool of the evening. Just like in the movies, a flying saucer descends from the skies and lands gently on the empty softball field behind the vacant warehouse. A little green man drops from a metal ladder under the craft and scurries toward you. You and the dog have seen this played out so many times on late-night television that you almost yawn.

The little guy doesn't threaten you or order you to take him to your leader. As you may have expected, the Dobby look-alike just wants to talk with you about Harry Potter. After all, doesn't everybody?

J. K. Rowling's seven Harry Potter novels sold more than 375 million copies and were translated into more than sixty languages between the publication of *Harry Potter and the Philosopher's Stone* (the original United Kingdom title) in 1997 and the end of 2007, the year in which *Harry Potter and the Deathly Hallows* was published. The first five Harry Potter movies each set records for opening box office, and the series as a whole had, by early 2008, already surpassed both the twenty-one-film James Bond series and the six Star Wars films as the most successful movie franchise of all time. The alien, like all good travelers, has done his homework about his planet vacation, and I'm betting that all the interplanetary guidebooks these days are urging earthbound tourists to talk about Harry with the natives this year. What else are they all sure to know about?

I first heard about Harry Potter and his friends in 2000. I was the homeschooling daddy to seven young children ages one to twelve years old, and I didn't want anything to do with the young wizard-in-training. From what I had heard from a coworker (whose judgment on literature I thought was not to be trusted), I assumed the books were serial schlock on the order of R. L. Stine's Goosebumps novels. Being something of a snob, I read the first Potter paperback just so I could explain to my oldest daughter why we don't read trash like this.

She calls it my "green eggs and ham" moment. Overnight, I was transformed from "I do not like them in a box; I do not like them with a fox" to reading the stories aloud to the younger children and discussing them at length with the older girls. I remember in that first week of Harry excitement when another colleague at work told me that Christians "as a rule" despised the books. You could have knocked me over with a feather.

What's Your Favorite Scene?

Back to the little green space guy in the park.

My bet is that the question his earth guidebook recommends he ask you is about your favorite scene in the books. Why would he want to know that? Because, besides being a great opening for conversation, unlike Earth's academics, our friend from outer space probably wants to learn something he can take back to the planet Zeno. I'm betting he wants answers to the big question, the only question that really matters about Harry Potter. He wants to know what it is about these books that has made them the "shared text" of children, parents, and grandparents on every continent and archipelago of the planet.

So why do readers young and old love Harry Potter? This is an important question, and the answer is a bit of a shocker. Before I share it with you, though, let me explain something I said earlier.

I said you could have knocked me over with a feather the day I heard Christians didn't like Harry Potter. You might recall that quite a few Christians in 2000 were, in fact, burning the books and asking that they not be allowed in public or school libraries funded with their tax dollars. Why was I so surprised by that? Because the reason I liked the Harry Potter books so much and the reason I was reading them to my children was the implicit, explicit, and very traditional spiritual, even Christian, content of the books, which I thought was as obvious as it was edifying.

I was interested enough in this subject that I gave a series of lectures on it at a C. S. Lewis Society gathering and at a local library. Before I knew it, ideas that had been floating around in my head found their way to book form. And in something like a Walter Mitty transformation, I morphed from Latin teacher to Harry Potter expert and media go-to source.

How Does Harry Cast His Spell?

Someday soon, folks who track this sort of thing to write about the intellectual history of popular culture will be sitting down to put together their notes on prevalent ideas about Harry Potter. What they will find, I'm pretty certain, is an arc of change much like the one described by J. B. S. Haldane: "Theories pass through four stages of acceptance: (1) this is worthless nonsense; (2) this is an interesting, but perverse, point of view; (3) this is true, but quite unimportant; (4) I always said so."[1] The historians of popular culture tracking how people understood Harry will discover that folks thought Harry Potter was (1) anti-Christian, even demonic; (2) anti-Christian in the sense of being an invitation to the occult; (3) not Christian, anti-Christian, or spiritual—just magic; (4) profoundly Christian, like C. S. Lewis ("I always knew it").

As broad as the always growing consensus about the depth of the Christian content of the Harry Potter novels now is—broad enough that in a recent documentary about her work, Rowling felt it necessary to deny at length that her purpose in writing was to convert readers to Christianity[2]—it bears recalling that even five years ago Christian critics of the series had convinced most people (and, it seemed, all journalists) that Harry was anything but Christian and that these books were dangerous for children to read.

How could they have gotten it so wrong? And why did readers believe them?

Answering the question "Why do readers young and old love Harry Potter?" explains the others because if they had gotten that one right, they couldn't have asserted what they thought about Harry and his author. The answer, believe it or not, is very simple, if frequently misunderstood. Readers love Harry Potter because of the spiritual meaning and Christian content of the books.

Let me explain what that doesn't mean before I jump into what it does mean.

First, it doesn't mean that the Harry Potter novels were written especially for Christians, with Christians in mind, or most important, for the sole purpose of evangelizing nonbelievers into accepting the Christian faith. None of those things are true, and none of them have anything to do with the answer to the important question of why we love Harry Potter.

Harry Potter is not the Left Behind series or even the Chronicles of Narnia in terms of being an in-your-face Christian drama or altar call.

Even now that J. K. Rowling has discussed the scriptural quotations in *Deathly Hallows*, I doubt that her readers would say they love her books because of their Christian meaning, especially her non-Christian readers in the United States, the United Kingdom, and around the world. My guess is that few if any readers, adults or children, responded to their first or last Harry Potter adventure with a whoop about the traditional Christian imagery or the literary alchemy that in many ways structures each story.

So how can the Christian content of the stories be the reason people love the books if they don't understand this content for what it is and if evangelization wasn't the author's point in writing the novels?

The answer to that question is pretty straightforward, but it takes a couple of steps to get into—and the rest of this book to explain in detail. Religion and literature have a long history, but almost none of us, even the English majors, studied that relationship in school. So let's start with an expert.

The argument begins with Mircea Eliade, a professor at the University of Chicago. In *The Sacred and the Profane: The Nature of Religion and the Significance of Religious Myth, Symbolism, and Ritual within Life and Culture*, Eliade explained that "non-religious man in the pure state is a comparatively rare phenomenon, even in the most desacralized of modern societies."[3]

Eliade's point is pretty simple. Human beings are spiritual by design, whether you believe that design is an accident of evolution or straight from God. By our very nature, humans resist an exclusively secularized world in which our faculties for perceiving a reality "saturated with being" have no play. It doesn't matter that schools, courts, and lawmakers have made the "G word" something taboo in education, government functions, and public discourse outside of presidential elections; human beings live on myth, religion, and spirituality because we're hardwired for it.

Modern and postmodern secular cultures that have driven the sacred from the public square are fighting the tide. Our world may be radically different from traditional, God-focused civilizations, but it is still crowded with religious elements. As Eliade wrote, "a small volume could be written on the myths of the modern man, on the mythologies camouflaged in the plays that he enjoys, in the books that he reads."[4]

Even the act of reading serves an important religious or mythic function:

> Even reading includes a mythological function . . . because, through reading, the modern man succeeds in obtaining an "escape from time" comparable to the "emergence from time" effected by myths. Whether modern man "kills" time with a detective story or enters such a foreign temporal universe as is represented by any novel, reading projects him out of his personal duration and incorporates him into other rhythms, makes him live in another "history."[5]

Accepting Eliade's premises that (a) humans are designed to experience the sacred and (b) humans will pursue this experience even in a culture that denies both a human spiritual faculty and a spiritual reality per se, answering the question about why we love Harry Potter is a slam dunk. The act of reading itself serves a religious function in a secular culture, but Harry gives us much more than that. Reading about Harry and the world of magic qualities is a respite from a universe without ennobling truth, beauty, or virtue. But more important, in image, character, and theme, these stories are the vehicles of spiritual meaning and specifically Christian artistry from the English literary tradition.

We love Harry Potter because we are designed for religious experience—and these books deliver religious experience the way coal trucks used to deliver fuel into people's basements: in a barely controlled avalanche. This isn't an evangelistic mountain slide meant to catch you off guard and force your conversion. It is the rhetoric of great storytelling with a host of religious and mythic hooks to catch on your Velcro heart, a heart designed to capture and resonate with these hierophanies, or intrusions of the sacred.

The business of this book is to peel away the layers of that rhetoric so you can understand the various symbols J. K. Rowling uses, the themes she develops, and the many traditional devices and structures she borrows from English "greats." Almost all these tools are Christian, but much more to the point, the English literary tradition in which she writes—twelve centuries of it, give or take a few hundred years—is exclusively Christian.

This bothers quite a few readers, so it is worth spending a moment to explain. Myth and archetype are okay to these readers, but once something becomes one specific religion, all their defenses go up. I don't know if it is fear of being converted or simply narrow-mindedness, but the heels go in deep against the idea that Harry Potter is written in religious language that is almost exclusively Christian. Even so, there's just no getting around this.

It is true that a phoenix, a unicorn, and a griffin are symbols found in cultures around the world. It is true, too, that these magical creatures are understood differently by different cultures compared to the way they are understood by English writers and readers. But in English stories, these symbols have specific Christian meanings (see chapter 9). Not knowing this meaning or insisting on a plurality of other meanings is not broad-mindedness or religious pluralism. It's just ignorance and, if I may be so bold, perhaps a little Christ-o-phobic.

If Rowling were an Islamofascist, Hindu Brahmin, or Buddhist ger dweller, when writing an epic adventure in English and within English traditions, her hands would still have been essentially tied to writing a Christian story. This huge monocultural sow that is the English literary tradition cannot be butchered in such a way that gets you Parliament of Religions bacon in slabs.

My job in *How Harry Cast His Spell* is to act as your guide through what I assume is already familiar territory, the seven Harry Potter books, and to point out all the religious and mythical elements specific to the tradition in which J. K. Rowling did her writing. Unless you're a very unusual reader indeed, this will be an eye-popping ride your first time through, so we give it a double pass to make sure you don't miss anything essential.

In the first ten chapters, we'll hit the high spots of alchemy, themes, and symbols, with a chapter-by-chapter introduction that takes a large view of the whole series, one subject at a time. We start, for example, with magic in literature because many readers don't see how that can be "religious" in any way when every revealed tradition forbids playing with magic. After that, we take similar long-range looks at the hero's journey, literary alchemy, and how symbols work. Then when we've made the first trip through and we understand what all the little marks on the Marauder's Map mean, we'll jump into the seven Harry Potter novels themselves one at a time to see what we can make of them. I'll explain the religious meaning and Christian content of each book, as well as why I think readers respond to them the way they do. Your job is to grasp what I explain and to see what I missed. This is the fourth edition of this book, and every update has been improved by readers who have written me to share something meaningful I missed.

Where Does This All Come From?

Before we dive in though, I am obliged to answer three questions I am inevitably asked at public talks I give:

❖ Do I really think Rowling intentionally gave the books all this meaning?

❖ Have I ever met Rowling? Has she confirmed that this was what she was doing?

❖ How did I figure all this stuff out?

DO I REALLY THINK ROWLING INTENTIONALLY GAVE THE BOOKS ALL THIS MEANING?

This is a polite way of saying, "John, could you be imagining all this?" I have three reasons for thinking J. K. Rowling is a profound writer who writes at several levels, some of which are well below the story line.

First, the woman has a first-rate education. Many readers familiar with the Cinderella story of her being a single mum on the dole when she wrote the first book imagine she was a welfare mother without a high school diploma who just got lucky. The truth is that she has an education and a degree equivalent to graduating from a prestigious American liberal arts college, say, Middlebury or Wesleyan, with a major in French and a minor in classics. She has said her stories come from the compost pile of books she has read, and I'm guessing this pile is several stories high.

Second, Rowling didn't dash off these stories. She claims she first thought of Harry Potter on a train in 1990. In the seven years before the first book was published and in the ten years it took to write and publish the seven books, Rowling planned, replanned, and filled notebooks with backstory she would never use in the published novels. "Planning" is her recommendation to all young authors, and it is the signature of her genius as a writer. There is nothing accidental or off the cuff about her work; if it's in there, she put it in there deliberately.

And third, the suggestion that Rowling didn't mean the books to be as profound as they are misses out on something essential. A lot of the most profound meaning of the books is in the formula of how the books are written, the things that happen again and again in every book. Harry's resurrection from the dead in the presence of a symbol of Christ could be accidental once, granted. But his doing it seven times without a variant is hard to scratch off as something unintentional. Rowling is, first and last, an accomplished storyteller—and the profound meaning of her writing is evident in the weave of the story fabric she creates.

HAVE I EVER MET ROWLING? HAS SHE CONFIRMED THAT THIS WAS WHAT SHE WAS DOING?

In words of one syllable, no, I have not met Rowling, and no, she has not told me one thing about her books. I think these questions are also polite ways of saying something completely different from the surface meaning. Folks who ask me this, as a rule, believe that only authors understand their books, and anyone else who interprets their fiction is just guessing. Having just written that Rowling is a very intelligent and very intentional, even formulaic, writer, let me rush to add that she would be an unusual writer (perhaps the first in history) if she understood her books' meanings comprehensively or even much better than very intelligent readers. She certainly does not have a monopoly on interpreting her books.

I like to think, in fact, as neat as it would be to talk with Rowling someday, that our conversation wouldn't be about the meaning of Harry Potter. From what I understand of such things from reading other authors, talking about her books' meaning would be just about the most insulting thing I could do.

In other words, asking Rowling what she meant in her stories is insulting; if what she meant is not discernible to a serious reader, I would be saying implicitly that she is a poor writer. And by restricting the meaning of the works to the author's intention and understanding of them, I would be suggesting that she as author is a god, fully conscious of her influences, prejudices, and meanings to every reader and aware of every valence and meaning of her stories' symbols.

I admire Rowling enough as an artist and a person that I do not to want to diminish her remarkable literary accomplishment or suggest she is something more than human. Two of the themes within the Harry Potter novels are that we respect people for who they are and that we struggle to come to terms with the limits of individual understanding. Let's avoid the celebrity school of interpretation that believes only writers understand their books; it leaves all the fun to the writers and insults them horribly in the bargain.

HOW DID I FIGURE ALL THIS STUFF OUT?

Here at last is an honest question! The answer will probably disappoint you. Not only have I not spoken with Rowling, we also grew up on opposite shores of the Atlantic Ocean. Not much common ground there, then, at least in a literal sense. Comparing and contrasting our worldviews and educations, though, I think it's fair to say that, despite significant differences, our ways of looking at the world have been calibrated with similar prescription eyeglasses.

Examples?

- ❖ Rowling grew up as something of a Hermione, a nerd who studied more than her share of classical and modern languages. I studied Latin, Greek, and German in high school and was certainly a geek.

- ❖ She chose to go to church (Anglican Communion) even though her parents and sister did not and sought baptism and confirmation on her own as an adolescent. I was baptized as an infant into the Anglican Communion (ECUSA), and when my family stopped going to church when I was in high school, I continued to attend and was confirmed alone among my siblings.[6]

- ❖ We both read and reread C. S. Lewis, Jane Austen, and the rest of the English greats because we loved the stories and the genius of the storytellers.

- ❖ I became interested in esoteric and literary alchemy while still in college and have continued to study its history and place in literature since. Rowling said in 1998 that she "read a ridiculous amount" about alchemy before writing Harry and that alchemy set the "magical parameters" and "internal logic" of the series.[7]

I could go on, but let's leave it at this. Both in interpreting what Rowling is saying and in the rather more bizarre field of guessing what she was going to write, my track record since 2002 has been good enough that I have been a keynote speaker at every Harry Potter conference of any size in the last five years, not to mention being interviewed by more than one hundred radio stations, the *Wall Street Journal*, the *New York Times*, and *Time* magazine. Odds are pretty good you've even seen my face as well, because I've been on national television to answer Harry questions on CNN and MSNBC, and for an A&E special that eventually became a DVD extra in the *Order of the Phoenix* movie package. I've taught online classes to international audiences at Barnes and Noble University, I blog daily on Harry subjects,[8] and I've written a book about how Rowling does what she does: *Unlocking Harry Potter: Five Keys for the Serious Reader.*

But to answer your question about how I figured all this stuff out, it always comes back to that fact that we share a similar eyeglasses prescription. Same church upbringing, same kind of classical education, same nineteenth-century dinosaur reading list, same interest in—can you believe it—alchemy.

Which brings us back again to our overarching question: Why does everyone love Harry Potter? Believe it or not, the answer is that it's the transcendent meaning of the books and, specifically, their Christian content, with which readers resonate. Go on to the next page and let's begin our trip through the mythical and religious meaning that drives Potter-mania.

1

MAGIC, FANTASY, AND TRANSCENDENCE

The magic in Harry Potter is traditional literary spellwork that acts as a counterspell to the materialism of our times.

More than any other book of the last fifty years (and perhaps ever), the Harry Potter novels have captured the imagination of the reading public worldwide. Hundreds of millions of copies have been sold to date. However, although the books have been wildly successful, no one as yet has been able to explain their popularity. The aim of *How Harry Cast His Spell* is to answer the question "Why do readers young and old love these stories?" The answer, believe it or not, is not great marketing, movie tie-ins, or product placement; it's the transcendent meaning of the books, and more specifically, their Christian content.

The Harry Potter books, in case you have lived on the planet Zeno since 1997 or have recently come out of a coma, recount the adventures of an English schoolboy as he advances from grade to grade at Hogwarts School. Hogwarts is no ordinary boarding school, however, and Harry Potter is no typical student—the former is a school for witchcraft and wizardry, and Harry is not only a wizard-in-training, but the target of attack by the worst of evil wizards, Lord Voldemort, and his followers, the Death Eaters. Each book ends with a life-or-death battle against Voldemort or his servants and enough plot twists to make you dream of saltwater taffy.

I am convinced that the fundamental reason for the astonishing popularity of the Harry Potter novels is their ability to meet a spiritual longing for some experience of the truths of life, love, and death that are denied by our secular culture. Human beings are designed for transcendent truths, whether they know it or not, and they pursue experience of these truths and some exercise of their spiritual faculties anywhere they can. Mircea Eliade suggested that modern entertainments, especially books and movies, serve a mythological or religious function in a desacralized world.[1] *That the Harry Potter stories "sing along" with the Great Story of Christ in the tradition of English literature is a significant key to understanding their compelling richness and unprecedented popularity.* We love these books because they satisfy our desire for religious experience in a big way.

Sound loony? I take hits from both sides of the Potter wars for this thesis—from Potter fans who are shocked by the suggestion that they have been reading "Christian" books and from Potter foes who are shocked by the thought that there could be anything "Christian" or edifying about books with witches and wizards in them. But like it or not, Harry's Christian content and the fact that he takes us out of our materialist mental prisons are what keep his readers coming back again and again.

As the magical setting of the books has caused the most controversy in religious communities and has the most important and obvious spiritual significance, I'll start with the setting and several formulas Rowling observes in every book to begin the discussion of what drives Potter-mania.

Magical Setting

Some Christians have objected to Harry Potter because Christian Scripture in many places explicitly forbids occult practice. Though reading about occult practice is not forbidden, these Christians prudently prefer (again in obedience to scriptural admonishments to parents) to protect their children because of the books' sympathetic portrayal of occult practice. These Christians believe that such approving and casual exposure to the occult opens the door to occult practice.

Reading the Harry Potter books myself has convinced me that the magic in Harry Potter is no more likely to encourage real-life witchcraft than time travel in science fiction novels encourages readers to seek passage to previous centuries. Loving families have much to celebrate in these stories and little, if anything, to fear. What they have to celebrate is the traditional, edifying magic of English literature—a magic that fosters a spiritual worldview that is anything but occult oriented.

I say this without hesitation because the magic in Harry Potter is not "sorcery" or *invocational* magic. In keeping with a long tradition of English fantasy, the magic practiced in the Potter books, by hero and villain alike, is *incantational* magic, a magic that shows—in story form—our human thirst for a reality beyond the physical world around us.

The difference between invocational and incantational magic isn't something we all learned in the womb, so let me explain. *Invocational* means literally "to call in." Magic of this sort is usually referred to as sorcery. Scripture of every revealed tradition warns that "calling in" demonic principalities and powers for personal power and advantage is dangerously stupid. History books, revealed tradition, and fantasy fiction (think *Dr. Faustus*) that touch on sorcery do so in order to show us that the unbridled pursuit of power and advantage via black magic promises a tragic end.

But there is no invocational sorcery in the Harry Potter books.

Even the most evil wizards do their nasty magic with spells; not one character in any of the seven books ever calls in evil spirits. Not once.

The magic by spells and wands in Harry Potter is known as incantational wizardry. *Incantational* means literally "to sing along with" or "to harmonize." To understand how this works, we have to step outside our culture's materialist creed (that everything in existence is quantitative mass or energy) and look at the world upside down, which is to say, God-first.

For some, the distinction between invocational and incantational magic is a new idea. I've been asked how prayer fits. "Isn't prayer invocational? Aren't we calling out to God with this concept—invoking his name—when we pray? How is this 'bad magic'?"

Calling out to God isn't bad magic, of course, and the reason helps to clarify the difference between sorcery and the "good magic" of English literature. It is the difference between the psychic and the spiritual realms.[2]

In a materialistic age such as the one in which we live, the distinction between the psychic and the spiritual is hard to keep straight, though it is an understanding all traditional faiths have in common. We struggle to hold on to this distinction because we have been taught that everything existent is some combination of matter and energy. Everything that's not matter and energy, consequently, is lumped together as "peripheral stuff" or "delusion." It's hard to remember the differences between things thrown together in the garbage can of ideas!

The distinction between the psychic realm and the spiritual realm is critical. The psychic realm—accessible through the soul and including the powers of the soul, from the emotions and sentiments to the reason and intellect—is home to demonic and angelic created beings and is predominantly a fallen place apart from God. The spiritual realm is "God's place"—the transcendent sphere within and beyond creation and the restrictions of being, time, and space.

Invocational magic is calling upon the fallen residents of the psychic realm. Prayer is the invocation of God's name that we might live deliberately and consciously in his presence within time and space.

Incantational magic in literature—a harmonizing with God's Word—is the story-time version of what a life in prayer makes possible. Invoking the powers of the psychic realm is universally forbidden in both literary and revealed traditions. However, calling on the spiritual realm and pursuing graces from it are the tasks for which human beings are designed, insofar as we are *homo religiosus*. One function of traditional English literature, of which Harry Potter is a part, is to support us in this spiritual life.

Christianity—and all revealed traditions—believes creation comes into being by God's creative Word, or his song. As creatures made in the image of God, we can harmonize with God's Word and his will, and in doing so, experience the power of God. The magic and miracles we read about in great English literature are merely reflections of God's work in our life. To risk overstating my case, the magic in Harry Potter and other good fantasy fiction harmonizes with the miracles of the saints.

C. S. Lewis paints a picture of the differences between incantational and invocational magic in *Prince Caspian*. As you may recall, Prince Caspian and the Aslan-revering creatures of the forest are under attack from Caspian's uncle. Things turn bad for the white hats, and it seems as if they will be overrun and slaughtered at any moment. Two characters on the good guys' side decide their only hope is magic.

Prince Caspian decides on musical magic. He has a horn that Aslan, the Christlike lion of these books, had given to Queen Susan in ages past to blow in time of need. Caspian blows on this divinely provided instrument in his crisis.[3] By sounding a note in obedience and faith, Caspian harmonizes with the underlying fabric and rules of the Emperor over the Sea, and help promptly and providentially arrives in the shape of the Pevensie children themselves.

Nikabrik the dwarf, in contrast, decides a little sorcery is in order. He finds a hag capable of summoning the dreaded White Witch in the hope that this power-hungry, Aslan-hating witch will help the good guys (in exchange for an opening into Narnia). Needless to say, the musical magicians are scandalized by the dwarf's actions and put an end to the sorcery lickety-split.

In the Narnia stories and other great fantasy fiction, good magic is incantational, and bad magic is invocational. Incantational magic is about harmonizing with God's creative Word by imitation. Invocational magic is about calling in evil spirits for power or advantage—always a tragic mistake. The magic in Harry Potter is exclusively incantational magic in conformity with both literary tradition and scriptural admonition. Concern that the books might "lay the foundation" for occult practice is misplaced, however well intentioned and understandable, because it fails to recognize that Potter magic is not demonic.

Perhaps you are wondering, *If Harry Potter magic is a magic in harmony with the Great Story, why are the bad guys able to use it?* Great question.

Just as even the evil people in "real" life are certainly created in God's image, so all the witches and wizards in Potterdom, good and bad, are able to use incantational magic. Evil magical folk choose of their own free will to serve the Dark Lord with their magical faculties just as most of us, sadly, lend a talent or power of our own in unguarded moments to the Evil One's cause. As we will see, the organizing structure of the Potter books is a battle between good guys who serve truth, beauty, and virtue and bad guys who lust after power and private gain.

Some fans of Lewis and Tolkien contrast those writers' use of magic with Rowling's, arguing that, unlike the world of Harry Potter, the subcreations of these fantasy writers had no overlap with the real world. They suggest that this blurring of boundaries confuses young minds about what is fiction and what is reality.

But Lewis and Tolkien blurred boundaries with gusto in their stories—as did Homer, Virgil, Dante, and other authors whose works regularly traumatize students in English classes. Certainly the assertion that Middle Earth and Narnia are separate realities is questionable, at best. Middle Earth *is* earth between the Second and Third Ages (we live in the so-called Fourth Age). Narnia overlaps with our world at the beginning and end of each book, and in *The Last Battle* is revealed as a likeness with earth of the heavenly archetype, or Aslan's kingdom. Singling out Rowling here betrays a lack of charity, at least, and perhaps a little reasoning chasing prejudgment.

That the magical world exists inside Muggledom (nonmagical people are called "Muggles" by the witches and wizards in Harry Potter), however, besides being consistent with the best traditions in epic myth and fantasy, parallels the life of Christians in the world. I don't want to belabor this point, but C. S. Lewis described the life of Christians as a life spent "in an enemy occupied country."[4] What he meant is that traditional Christians understand that man is fallen, that he no longer enjoys the ability to walk and talk with God in the Garden, and that the world is driven by God-opposing powers. Lewis's Ransom novels illustrate this idea.

Why do we love the magic of Harry Potter? I think we have three big reasons to be excited by it. First, we live in a time in which *naturalism,* the belief that all existence is matter and energy, is the state religion and belief in supernatural or contra-natural powers is considered delusion. The incantational magic in Harry Potter, because it requires harmonizing with a greater magic, undermines faith in this godless worldview. Harry's magic, even if only experienced imaginatively in a state of suspended disbelief, gives our spiritual faculties the oxygen our secular schools and the public square have tried to cut off. And by undermining the materialist view of our times, it can even be said that the books lay the foundation for a traditional understanding of the spiritual, which is to say "human," life.

Next, because there is overlap between the "magical" and "Muggle" worlds of Harry Potter, there is the edifying suggestion that the prevalent bipolar worldview of Americans, in which the world is divided by an arbitrary state versus church dichotomy, not to mention the secular versus sacred illusion, is just so much nonsense. The spiritual and traditional understanding of the world is a *sacramental* one, in which the spiritual suffuses the material (just as the human person is a psychosomatic unity with spiritual faculties). The breakdown of the Muggle/magic divide helps readers see that existence itself (in not being matter or energy) unites all reality and that "greater being" is found only in pursuit of the sacred, not the "scientific" and profane.

And third, we love the magic in Harry Potter because it helps us exercise those atrophied spiritual powers we have (as we identify with Harry and his friends), while at the same time encouraging us to be heroic and good alongside them. This is no small thing, and we'll be returning to it in the coming chapters.

Have you heard stories of children being sucked into witches' covens because they want to be like Harry? Reports of rising membership in occult groups since the Harry Potter books were published inevitably turn out to be generated by proselytizing members of these groups. People who track the occult for a living explain that, despite Buffy the Vampire Slayer and Harry Potter, membership in these groups in Europe and the United States are minuscule and are in decline despite a decade of Harry, Buffy, and occult milieu entertainment.[5] Children are far more likely to become Hare Krishna, gynecologists, or members of a Christian cult than real-world witches or wizards.

And even if children *were* being seduced into the occult because of their desire to do spells, I have to hope this would be understood by thinking people as a shameful, tragic aberration, more indicative of the child's spiritual misformation than a danger in the books. The Dungeons and Dragons craze in the sixties and seventies and its attendant occult paraphernalia sprang from an unhealthy fascination and perverse misunderstanding of *The Lord of the Rings*, an epic with clear Christian undertones. If we were to avoid books that could possibly be misunderstood or whose message could be turned on its head, incidents like Jonestown would logically suggest thinking people should not read the Bible.

What about the title of the first book in the Potter series? If there's no sorcery in these books, how come the first book and movie are titled *Harry Potter and the Sorcerer's Stone?* Well, because that isn't the title of the first book. Arthur Levine, under whose imprint the books are published by Scholastic in the United States, changed the title from *Philosopher's Stone* to *Sorcerer's Stone* because he was sure that no American would buy a book with *philosophy* in the title.

An Orthodox Christian bishop has noted that Harry haters "have missed the spiritual forest for the sake of their fixation on the magical imagery of the literary trees."[6] If there is anything tragic in this misunderstanding of Harry Potter by well-intentioned Christians, it is the tragedy of "friendly fire." Just as foot soldiers are sometimes hit by misdirected artillery fire from their own troops, so Harry has been condemned by the side he is serving. Because some Christians have mistaken fictional magic for sorcery, they have misconstrued what is a blow at atheistic naturalism as, of all things, an invitation to the occult.[7] If the "magical trees" in Harry Potter are of any help in retaking ground lost to those who would burn down the spiritual forest, then Rowling has done human communities everywhere a very good deed.

I receive e-mail from readers almost daily about the "problem" of reading Harry Potter in light of its transcendent meaning and specific Christian content. They insist that the symbols, themes, and meanings of the books are perfectly comprehensible without any reference to an imaginary Christian subtext that believers are projecting into the books.

The mistake these readers make when they insist that the symbolism of Harry Potter is not "exclusively" Christian is that they just don't understand a disturbing fact about English literature.

I have friends who teach and write about Saudi Arabia and Arabic culture in general. Their work is not restricted to Islam, certainly, but they wouldn't be experts in their field if they weren't aware of the tremendous influence of the Koran and the Islamic worldview on culture, politics, and everything Arabic. This, I hope, is a no-brainer.

Unfortunately, in a post-Christian era (culturally speaking), and one in which universities are in large part overly hostile to religious meanings (mine certainly was!), the simple, disturbing fact that English literature until the last fifty years was (ahem) "exclusively" a Christian field escapes people. Christian authors writing for a Christian reading audience—and writing books, plays, and poems that would edify them in their spiritual and workaday lives as Christians—was the rule of English letters until well after the first World War.

In explaining the popularity of the Harry Potter novels as a function of the response of a spiritually deprived world for edifying, transcendent experience (even experience limited to entertainment), I am frequently accused of proselytizing and forcing Christian meaning into the text. What a hoot! No one accuses my friends who are Saudi scholars of trying to convert people to Islam because their reports on Middle Eastern current events and trends are heavy on the place of Islam in Arabic culture.

If some Harry fans are uncomfortable because other readers, Christian or not, are interpreting the Potter books in a Christian light, I beg these readers to ask themselves where the problem exists. Reading books within a Christian literary tradition (if *not* for an exclusively Christian audience and *not* in a manner that is overtly Christian in any denominational or parochial sense) invites discussion of the Christian elements of the story and of the tools from the tradition the author uses. Literary alchemy, religious symbolism, and doppelgängers, for instance, don't make much sense outside of the tradition in which these books are written and in which these tools are used.

I have no evangelical cause or agenda here in discussing the Christian content of these books. My only hope is that readers will come to a greater appreciation of these works via the discussion of Harry Potter as traditional English literature, which, again, is an overwhelmingly Christian subject. William Shakespeare's plays and James Joyce's novels are impenetrable outside some appreciation of their spiritual context and the traditions of English literature. J. K. Rowling's stories are no different.

If readers want an exclusively secular view of the books—that is, a reading of them outside of the context and traditions in which they are written—this is probably not their book. English literature (Harry Potter is undeniably root-and-branch English literature) is as Christian as Tibetan culture is Buddhist and Saudi politics is Islamic.

Denying this is not "having a broad mind" but living in a fantasy. Likewise, refusing to see the Christian elements in Harry Potter and insisting it is demonic is not a greater piety or fidelity to the faith; it is just a reflection of not understanding the place of literature in the spiritual life, of not understanding the Christian tradition of English literature, and of not understanding the popularity of Harry Potter.

Let's move on from Harry's edifying incantational magic to the battlefield of good versus evil in these stories.

2

COSMIC WHITE HATS AND BLACK HATS

The Harry Potter novels revolve around the central conflict of good and evil.

However fascinating—and to some, distracting and disturbing—the magical backdrop is in Harry Potter, it is only a part of the setting and structure of these stories. A strong case could be made that the magic in these books is actually one of their less important aspects. Harry isn't an especially accomplished wizard (like the other Gryffindors—except Hermione—he is known for being a bit dull in the classroom), and his magical aptitude is never what saves him in his battles with the Dark Lord and his minions.

Having argued that the magic in Harry Potter is a big part of why readers respond to these stories with the enthusiasm they do, let's turn to the other parts of the setting that receive much less media attention than the magic to understand their transcendent or spiritual meaning and their Christian content, if any. In a simple list that will be the subject of the next several chapters, these parts include:

- ❖ Gryffindor/Slytherin opposition
- ❖ The hero's journey
- ❖ Alchemical "Great Work"
- ❖ Doppelgängers

One of the novelties of the Harry Potter books is that, while each book is an exciting story in itself, there is a larger story that is the context of these separate adventures. Every book lets the reader in on another part of the larger puzzle that clarifies the relationships of the major players. The relationship map on page 15 allows the reader to understand at a glance who is on whose side, who opposes whom, and who does not fit neatly into a relationship slot.

If you begin on the map's periphery, you see the founders of Hogwarts School: Salazar Slytherin, Godric Gryffindor, Rowena Ravenclaw, and Helga Hufflepuff. The two defining figures of this quartet are Slytherin and Gryffindor, whose disagreements and characters bleed into the remaining rings. Look for Gryffindor at the top and Slytherin at the bottom, just as their respective dormitory houses are in a tower and a dungeon.

The next ring in from the legendary founders, we find Albus Dumbledore and the Order of the Phoenix on the Gryffindor end of the ring and Lord Voldemort and his Death Eaters on the Slytherin end. Voldemort, we learn in *Harry Potter and the Chamber of Secrets*, is Slytherin's heir, and he and his Death Eaters labor to create a world ruled by pure-blooded wizards. Hagrid mentions in *Philosopher's Stone* that nearly all the wizards who joined with Voldemort were from Slytherin House.

Dumbledore is linked with Gryffindor by artifacts and personal history. He "owns" the Sorting Hat that belonged to Godric Gryffindor and the sword of Godric Gryffindor that Harry pulls from it in *Chamber of Secrets* ("sword-in-hat"—get it?). His office has a griffin door knocker, and more important, his life has been spent resist-

THE HOUSE OF GRYFFINDOR VERSUS
THE HOUSE OF SLYTHERIN

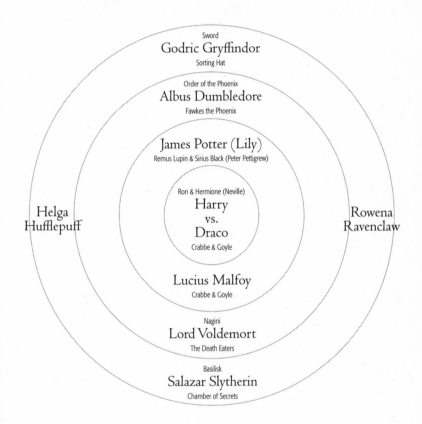

ing evil wizards, from the dark wizard Grindelwald in 1945 to Lord Voldemort in the present.

The Order of the Phoenix is a counterbalancing group of wizards under Dumbledore's influence (the "old crowd" he tells Sirius Black to bring together at the end of *Goblet of Fire* and whom we meet in *Harry Potter and the Order of the Phoenix*), offsetting the Death Eaters under Lord Voldemort. Dumbledore's glorious pet phoenix, Fawkes, is mirrored in a horrible contrast on the dark side by Voldemort's giant black snake, Nagini.

Moving toward the center, one ring in, we meet the parents of Harry Potter and Draco Malfoy. Lucius Malfoy, a loyal Death Eater and former member of Slytherin House, lines up, of course, on the Slytherin side of the map. I put Crabbe's and Goyle's names here both because we learn that their fathers are Death Eaters and for symmetry with the center ring (where they are inseparable from Draco Malfoy, the son of Lucius and Narcissa).

Harry's father, James, aligns with Gryffindor and Dumbledore. James was in Gryffindor House, lived in Godric's Hollow before his death, and had a close relationship with Dumbledore (close enough that after James died, Dumbledore acted as executor and protector of his son). His opposition to Voldemort, his murderer, is total. Though we learn in *Order of the Phoenix* that James was quite a jerk at fifteen, we know from the great respect shown to him by all but Professor Snape that he was a hero in the war against the Dark Lord.

James's two close friends from school, Remus Lupin and Sirius Black, join him in the ring with parenthetic inclusion of their sidekick and hanger-on, Peter Pettigrew. They balance Crabbe and Goyle and foreshadow Harry's close friends Ron and Hermione— with Neville Longbottom as their hanger-on, similar to Pettigrew (whom Neville resembles, at least in Harry's mind; see *Prisoner of Azkaban*, chapter 11).

In the center ring we find Harry Potter and his great rival, Draco Malfoy. Each lines up ring by generational ring with his respective parents, patron, and house founder. Each has friends who echo in number and character the friends of his parents. Each despises the other and lives for the pleasure of seeing the other fail. Their opposition becomes more open—and violent—with each book and reaches its redemptive conclusion in the series finale, *Harry Potter and the Deathly Hallows*.

The major characters, then, fall into place along the Gryffindor/Slytherin axis. The other characters? Hagrid, the Weasleys, and Professor McGonagall are in the Order of the Phoenix, and we have to suspect strongly that Ludo Bagman, the Minister of Magic, and Rita Skeeter (among others) are at least sympathizers, if not collaborators, with Lord Voldemort.

But there are a few question marks. Most important, on whose side is Professor Severus Snape? As the master of Slytherin House and an alumnus of the same; an open enemy of Harry Potter, his father, and his father's friends; and a Death Eater with the Dark Mark tattooed on his arm, isn't it obvious? No, not really. Snape haunts Professor Quirrell/Voldemort in *Philosopher's Stone* and does everything he can to keep him from winning the Stone. He saves Harry's life in the same book and has Dumbledore's trust because he acted as a double agent for the Gryffindor side in the last war with Voldemort. At the end of *Goblet of Fire* and all through *Order of the Phoenix*, Professor Snape returns to Lord Voldemort at Dumbledore's request and at obvious risk of his life.

Whose side is he on? We don't learn until the very end of *Deathly Hallows*, but he seems to be on his own side, which is to be on both sides of the map and neither side. Even after he seems to murder Dumbledore in *Half-Blood Prince*, there is good reason to doubt that Snape has shown his true colors. By not being able to place Snape, the map highlights his role as a critical or swing character. Does this Gryffindor/Slytherin opposition have a greater meaning than, say, the struggle between two football teams? Yep.

We need to note that the Slytherins are notoriously vicious and unapologetically focused on getting more power. The Gryffindors, though not incapable of some over-the-top behaviors and recklessness, do not torture Muggles for jollies or harass magical folk because they can. The battle between Gryffindor and Slytherin is a battle between good and evil—I will even argue, believe it or not, that it is a reflection of the battle between those who serve Christ and those who serve the Evil One.

You may have read Christian critics of the Potter books who

assert that Harry's world is morally ambiguous because the white hats need cleaning and the black hats demonstrate sufficient loyalty to one another not to be "jet black." This is just silly, frankly; some folks need to get out more. As W. H. Auden explained in his defense of Tolkien (yes, the author of *The Lord of the Rings* was charged with this type of ambiguity too), the difference between the good and bad guys in fiction comes down to the choices each makes.

Bad guys don't do the wrong thing after struggling with a decision; they almost automatically do what most advances their individual or group advantage without regard for principle. Good guys often are tempted to do the wrong thing—may even *do* the wrong thing—but they either choose the right or repent of their error in light of right and wrong.[1] This is exactly the situation between the Gryffindor white hats and Slytherin black hats. The Gryffindors (most often the lead players: Harry, Ron, and Hermione) choose to do the right thing—usually after some hand-wringing and soul-searching—though doing the right thing will probably mean their death. The Slytherins do the wrong thing without reservation or restraint.

The meanings of the house names, their respective house symbols, and even the title given to Lord Voldemort all point to this fictional division that defines Rowling's magical world being a deliberate parallel with Christianity and the spiritual realities of life on earth as described by Christian and other traditions.

Gryffindor is named for its founder, Godric Gryffindor, whose first name means "godly" or "worshipful." David Colbert, author of *The Magical Worlds of Harry Potter*, tells us that *Gryffindor* is French for "golden griffin" (griffin d'or) and that the griffin is commonly used as a symbol of Christ. Sound like a reach? Hardly. Remember from your fairy tales that a griffin is half lion and half eagle. Lions are considered the kings of the terrestrial animal world, and eagles are considered kings of the sky. An animal that is two-natured, one in essence, and king of Heaven and earth? More about symbolism and griffins in chapter 9, but the main point here is that the Gryffindor/Slytherin matchup is a lot bigger than a Cubs/Red Sox slugfest.

Oddly enough (on the surface at least), the house animal on the Gryffindor banners is not a golden griffin but a red lion. This is a clear tip of the hat to Lewis's Aslan, the Christlike lion of the Narnia books, although Lewis didn't invent this symbolism. The red lion as an emblem for Christ is part of traditional and alchemical imagery (see chapter 4). The phoenix, sometimes called the "Resurrection Bird," is also a symbol for Christ and a natural title for Dumbledore's (adult) army in *Order of the Phoenix*.

Not enough? Well, how about those Slytherin nasties, then? Their connection with the devil is remarkable. Their mascot is a serpent, their founder's name—Salazar Slytherin—is full of hissing serpentine sounds and suggests the motion a snake makes on the ground (slitherin'; see Genesis 3:14), and their leader is the *Dark Lord*. I don't think this is coincidental. That Voldemort's intimates are called "Death Eaters" is just icing on the cake. (The opposite of Death Eaters is "Life Eaters"—and those who eat the body and blood of God, who is the Way, the Truth, and the *Life*, are Christians.)

Readers familiar with the Bible will recognize Saint Paul's understanding of the world as being fallen (Romans 8:22) and ruled by the devil (2 Corinthians 4:3-4), against whom everything and everyone good is at war—and whose rule and corruption God became man to destroy (Colossians 2:13-15; 1 Corinthians 15:24-27, 54-57). Christians consciously battle against the principalities and powers (Ephesians 6:12) that subject all men who do not seek to know and resist the devil's thoughts (2 Corinthians 2:11). Rowling is creating a not-very-subtle parallel universe within Harry's magical world of a battle between the armies of Christ and those of Satan.

The central conflict of the Harry Potter books is the antagonism between the descendants of Godric Gryffindor and the descendants of Salazar Slytherin, a conflict that is consistent with the Christian view of the world as a battleground in the cosmic war between good and evil. Though there are ignoble Gryffindors and ultimately heroic Slytherins, the many clues in names and words in the stories point to Gryffindor House as being much like God's army and Slytherin House as being like Satan's servants. We learn more in each book about their battles inside and outside of Hogwarts and the eerie parallels across generations. My hope in this short chapter was to show that this central conflict is primarily spiritual and to suggest that this is why we respond to Harry with pom-poms and huzzahs and to the Dark Lord with boos and whistles. We are designed to have spiritual experiences and to long for the sacred—and not just any hierophany but something from the side of the angels. Given the many clues in names, words, and events that Rowling has given us to highlight Gryffindor House as God's army and Slytherin House as Satan's servants, it's pretty clear she wants us rooting for the King of Heaven and earth. As Perry Glazer of Baylor University has written, "Children need more than a set of virtues to emulate, values to choose, rules to obey, or even some higher form of reasoning to attain. They long to be part of a cosmic struggle between good and evil. And that's why children want to read Harry Potter."[2] I would only add, that is why Harry Potter is as popular as he is with children *and* adults; the books both satisfy and support our design for spiritual experience and our longing to resist evil and serve the good. Starved as we are for such stimulus in a desacralized city, Harry arrives likes water in the heart of a desert.

3

THE HERO'S
JOURNEY

*Harry's adventures take him through life,
death, and resurrection.*

The Harry Potter books are laid out according to a formula repeated in each story. This formula, used in stories from ancient epics to modern adventure novels, is known by many different names and has been attributed many different meanings.[1] As it is used in the Harry Potter books, the hero's journey or monomyth formula is a repeated snapshot in every book of Rowling's theme that love conquers death and that we will rise from the dead in a resurrection made possible by and in Christ.

No doubt you find this hard to believe. Let's start, then, just by describing the formula as shown in our second map and seeing what Harry's journey involves. The first six books begin and end in the same place and pass a series of landmarks that differ only in details. Here is a rough chart of the pattern as it appears in each of the first six books:

HARRY'S JOURNEY

	Sorcerer's Stone	Chamber of Secrets	Prisoner of Azkaban
START	Privet Drive	Privet Drive	Privet Drive
ESCAPE	Admission letters and Hagrid visit	Flying Ford Anglia	Knight Bus
MYSTERY	Stone's seeker and location	Chamber opening and Slytherin heir	Sirius Black's escape
CRISIS	Albus leaves	Ginny taken	Ron taken
DESCENT	Trapdoor	Bathroom chute	Under willow
COMBAT	Quirrell	Riddle	Black/Dementors
CHRIST SYMBOLS	Philosopher's Stone	Phoenix	Stag
RETURN	Albus, 3 days	Fawkes	Hippogriff
REVELATION	Snape OK, Quirrell = Voldemort	Dobby OK, Riddle = Voldemort	Black OK, Scabbers = Wormtail
FINISH	Platform 9¾	Platform 9¾	Platform 9¾

Harry's hero journey is a generic picture of each adventure Harry has taken.

❖ He begins at home on Privet Drive with his Muggle family, the Dursleys.

❖ He escapes to Hogwarts from his living death via the intrusion of extraordinary magic (Hagrid's birthday arrival, the flying Ford Anglia, etc.).

❖ Harry arrives at Hogwarts to find something mysterious going on.

❖ With help from Hermione and Ron, Harry tries to solve the mystery, which, inevitably, comes to a crisis demanding his immediate action (with or without his friends).

❖ He descends into the earth to face this crisis (except in *Goblet of Fire*, in which he portkeys to a graveyard, the surroundings of which have a resonant meaning with the underworld).

Goblet of Fire	Order of the Phoenix	Half-Blood Prince	Deathly Hallows
Privet Drive	Privet Drive	Privet Drive	Privet Drive
Floo powder	Rescue by Order	Dumbledore pickup	The seven Potters
Triwizard Tournament entry	Dreams/ Hogwarts takeover	Draco's suicide mission	The Deathly Hallows
Third trial	Sirius "kidnapping"	Draco's repair success	Harry's sacrifce in the Forest
Graveyard	Ministry of Magic	Into cave, from Tower	"Underground" King's Cross
Voldemort	Death Eaters/Voldemort	Inferi/Severus Snape	Harry/Voldemort
Phoenix song	Phoenix swallowing death curse	Dumbledore/Hippogriff	Harry Potter
Portkey	Portkey	Alongside apparition	Entering Hogwarts
Snape a hero, Moody = Death Eater	Dumbledore a human, Voldemort = Dream Weaver	Snape a Death Eater still?	Snape OK, Harry's lifelong protector
Platform 9¾	Platform 9¾	Dumbledore funeral	King's Cross

❖ Harry fights Voldemort or a servant of the Dark Lord and triumphs against impossible odds (in books 3, 4, 5, and 6 merely by escaping alive).

❖ He dies a figurative death, rises from the battlefield with the miraculous help of a Christ figure, and returns to the land of the living.

❖ Harry learns from Professor Dumbledore that a good guy is really a bad guy and a bad guy is really a good guy (along with the meaning and lesson of his adventure).

❖ Harry leaves us at Platform 9 ¾ to go home with the Dursleys.

Some friends have told me when I have shown them the second map that they feel cheated somehow. If this were just a mechanical formula, as in TV dramas, disappointment would be warranted. (Remember *The A-Team* television program? Same show every week with a different machine at the end to save the day?)

The Harry Potter formula, however, is anything but a scripting cookie cutter. While the story is a partial throwback to the heroes of old (Odysseus, Aeneas, Dante), these stories take quite a different turn. In the ancient and medieval epics, the heroes travel to the underworld to confront death (usually for information), entering and exiting without a trial much greater than the difficulties of the trip and the shock of what they see. Not so in Harry Potter.

Look at the chart again. What happens to Harry underground? Invariably he dies a figurative death.

- ❖ In *Philosopher's Stone*, Harry expires "[knowing] all was lost, and fell into blackness, down . . . down . . . down . . ." (chapter 17).

- ❖ In *Chamber of Secrets*, Harry is poisoned by the basilisk. "Harry slid down the wall. He gripped the fang that was spreading poison through his body and wrenched it out of his arm. But he knew it was too late. . . . 'You're dead, Harry Potter,' said Riddle's voice above him" (chapter 17).

- ❖ In *Prisoner of Azkaban*, a Dementor lowers his hood to kiss Harry. "A pair of strong, clammy hands suddenly attached themselves around Harry's neck. They were forcing his face upward. . . . He could feel its putrid breath. . . . His mother was screaming in his ears. . . . She was going to be the last thing he ever heard. . . . [When released, Harry] felt the last of his strength leave him, and his head hit the ground" (chapter 20).

- ❖ In *Goblet of Fire*, Rowling places Harry's seemingly hopeless battle with the risen Voldemort in a graveyard, so Harry is not only in an almost certain collision course with death, he is also already among the dead (chapters 32–34).

- ❖ In *Order of the Phoenix*, Harry is possessed by Voldemort to get Dumbledore to kill the boy. "And then Harry's scar burst open. He knew he was dead: it was pain beyond imagining, pain past endurance" (chapter 36).

❖ In *Half-Blood Prince*, the Inferi from the cavern lake grab
   Harry and begin to carry him into the Stygian depths.
   "He knew there would be no release, that he would be
   drowned, and become one more dead guardian of a fragment of Voldemort's shattered soul" (chapter 26).

Not much to recommend the books, though, if the hero merely
dies at crunch time, is there? Harry doesn't just die in these stories,
of course; he rises from the dead. And in case you think this is just
a "great comeback" rather than a Resurrection reference, please note
that Harry never saves himself but is always saved by a symbol of
Christ or by love. As you can see from the chart, in *Philosopher's Stone*,
it is his mother's sacrificial love and the Stone; in *Chamber of Secrets*, it
is Fawkes the phoenix; in *Prisoner of Azkaban*, it is the white stag Patronus; in *Goblet of Fire*, it is the phoenix song; and in *Order of the Phoenix*,
it is Harry's love for Sirius, Ron, and Hermione that defeats the Dark
Lord. Both Dumbledore and Buckbeak the hippogriff save Harry as
Christ figures in *Half-Blood Prince*. That he rises after three days in *Philosopher's Stone* is another obvious reference to the Resurrection.

Rowling begins her great departure from this formula at the
end of the sixth book, *Half-Blood Prince*. At the end of that book
Dumbledore is murdered, so there is no denouement with the
headmaster and Harry does not return to King's Cross or the Dursleys'. Harry vows that he will not be returning to Hogwarts for his
seventh and final year of magical education because he has a mission to destroy Horcruxes and vanquish the Dark Lord.

Oddly enough though, even if Harry's odyssey in *Deathly Hallows* does not conform to one or two details of Rowling's monomyth formula, it does conform to type on the important points.
Harry begins his adventure at Privet Drive after all, and there is a
magic escape featuring six of his friends pretending to be him à la
Polyjuice Potion. Harry, Ron, and Hermione, however, do not return
to Hogwarts. Instead, they go into hiding from the Dark Lord and
the Ministry while they search for Voldemort's Horcruxes.

On their adventures, they confront bad guys and go under-ground repeatedly—into the depths of the Ministry of Magic, the dungeon beneath Malfoy Manor, and the caverns miles beneath Gringotts Bank, most notably—to search for Horcruxes and to lib-erate the imprisoned and falsely accused. Incredibly, it turns out at story's end that all these trips underground, followed by resurrec-tions from the dead in the presence of a symbol of Christ, were just foreshadowing for Harry's sacrifice at the end of *Deathly Hallows* and his rising from the dead to defeat Voldemort—literally from King's Cross—*as a symbol of Christ himself.*

There's a lot more that needs to be said here about death, bereavement, and Christian symbols—which I'll get to in chapter 7, chapter 9, and of course chapter 17 on the events and meaning of *Deathly Hallows* itself—but for now let's leave the hero's journey for-mula with these two key points:

- ❖ The climax of Harry's hero journey invariably turns out to be a strong image of the Christian hope that death can be transcended by love and in faith and specifically that believers have reason to hope in their individual resurrec-tion in Christ.
- ❖ The answer these stories offer to the ultimate human problem—death—is always either love, Harry's great power, or the symbol of Love himself, Jesus Christ.

Why do people love these books? It's not because the author is especially shy about answering the big human questions in story form or because she doesn't point to specific enough answers! Every one of the seven Harry Potter novels and especially the last, *Deathly Hallows,* is built on the hero's journey story structure. Rowling has given a peculiarly spiritual and undeniably Christian finish in Harry's faux death and resurrection in the presence of or as a symbol of Christ. Readers don't need to be Christians, of course, to find this ending thrilling and satisfying, or even an image of their greatest hope. The greatest human fear is of death, and sharing in Harry's repeated and final victory over an enemy whose name means "willing death" brings readers back to the stories again and again for the vicarious pleasure of defeating death themselves. In a world largely stripped of the reality and inevitability of death, Harry Potter tackles the issue head-on in every story and gives a profoundly spiritual and specifically Christian answer: Love transcends death and defeats those who worship at death's altar. Those who love sacrificially have hope of a personal resurrection on the example and in the person of Jesus Christ. Whether readers accept this last part or not—there is no altar call, after all—the message of personal immortality and love's victory over death resonates in the human heart as a universal hope and explains in large part the widespread popularity of these books.

But there's more! Rowling, believe it or not, has another storytelling superstructure with a strongly spiritual message on which she builds these stories. Turn the page for an introduction to literary alchemy, Rowling's real magic for the transformation of her readers.

4

THE ALCHEMY OF
SPIRITUAL GROWTH

*The story cycles are built on the stages
of transformation.*

Maybe you think all this fuss about the hero's journey is wrong-headed. I mean, let's be serious. Going to school in the fall and returning home in the summer—where the destinations are always clearly understood and arrived at—may not seem like much of a journey. But there is another way to look at the Harry Potter stories that is much more exciting and unusual than the annual journey to even a magical prep school: alchemical adventures involving Harry's transformation from spiritual lead to spiritual gold.

Alchemy, though, is so misunderstood that saying the Harry Potter books are built on alchemical structures and imagery to many readers is not much different from saying the books aren't worth reading or that they're dangerous to read. So let's clear up this misunderstanding right away.

One of the first lessons in a chemistry class is that chemistry grew out of a kind of medieval voodoo called alchemy, a pseudoscience whose goal was to isolate a Philosopher's Stone that could turn lead (meaning base metals) into gold and bestow immortality on the alchemist. Alchemy has been called stupid chemistry, fraud, witchcraft, and even a path into the subconscious mind. But for our purposes, alchemy can simply be defined as the transformation of something common into something special. If historians of religion and sacred art are to be believed (most notably, Titus Burckhardt and Mircea Eliade), alchemy was a spiritual path within the great revealed traditions to return fallen man to his Edenic perfection.

Whether they are right or wrong, though, really doesn't matter. Alchemy, whatever it may have been, no longer exists except as a synonym for "magical transformation" and as a resource for artists and authors writing about personal change. Alchemical symbols are a large part of classic English literature. And if we don't understand the idea of alchemy, we can easily miss out on the depth, breadth, and height of plays by Shakespeare, poetry by Donne and Eliot, and the novels of Lewis and Tolkien.[1] Writing in the tradition of writers stretching from Chaucer to Joyce, Rowling uses alchemy in Harry Potter as a metaphor for change and as a resource for powerful imagery.

What is the connection between alchemy and literature that makes alchemical images such useful tools for writers?

I think the connection is probably most clear in drama. Many, if not most, of Shakespeare's plays, in fact, are written on alchemical skeletons and themes.[2] In a proper tragedy, the audience identifies with the hero in his agony and shares in his passion. This identification and shared passion is in effect *the same as* the experience of the event; the audience experiences catharsis, or "purification," in correspondence with the actors. Shakespeare and Benjamin Jonson, among others, used alchemical imagery and themes because they understood that the work of the theater in human transformation was parallel if not identical to the work of alchemy. The magic of alchemy and stage dramas is that through these external transformations, the alchemist's metals, the audience, and the actors onstage are all purified and transformed from leaden to golden hearts.

Alchemical language and themes are shorthand for transformation. The success of an artist following this tradition is measured by the edification of his or her audience. By means of traditional methods and symbols, the alchemical artist offers our soul delight and dramatic release through archetypal and purifying experiences.

That may be harder for some of us than believing that alchemy was once a sacred science. If you are like me, you grew up with the idea that reading was entertainment and diversion, and anything but life changing. This idea, really only in currency for the last seventy or eighty years, is a gross misconception. Anthropologists, historians of religion, and professors of literature will all tell you that the rule in traditional cultures, and even in cultures such as ours, is that story, in whatever form, is meant to instruct and change us.

In his book *The Sacred and the Profane*, Eliade argued that entertainments serve a religious function, especially in a profane culture. They remove us from our ego-bound consciousness for an experience or immersion in another world of greater being.

Alchemy is a great resource for writers because both the alchemical work and entertainments endeavor to transform the human person. It may not occur to most Christian artists to call their work "alchemical" because they aren't using traditional alchemical images and symbols in their writing. But that is exactly what films such as *Hoosiers* or *October Sky* and books such as the Left Behind novels and the Lord of the Rings series are designed to accomplish in their audiences: a real-life change triggered by the powerful experience of viewing a film or reading a book. The difference between these artists and Rowling is that she *does* use these images and symbols extensively and to great effect. As we'll see, she even talks about it.

Alchemy in Harry Potter

Rowling was asked in a 1998 interview if she had ever wanted to be a witch. She answered,

> "I've never wanted to be a witch, but an alchemist, now that's a different matter. To invent this wizard world, I've learned a ridiculous amount about alchemy. . . . I have to know in detail what magic can and cannot do in order to set the parameters and establish the stories' internal logic."[3]

Where is the alchemy in Harry Potter? In addition to the "magical parameters" and "internal logic," it's everywhere from the book titles to character transformations. Here are five areas in which alchemical imagery is especially evident in the Harry Potter books.

First, the book titles. The title of the first book is *Harry Potter and the Philosopher's Stone* and was only changed to *Sorcerer's Stone* because an American editor thought children wouldn't want a book with the word *philosophy* in the title. Creating the Philosopher's Stone is one of the more famous goals of alchemy, so this change obscured a pretty big pointer to Rowling's alchemical plan. And Warner Bros. has copyrighted the title *Harry Potter and the Alchemist's Cell* for use in any of their Harry Potter creations, from a possible Game Boy application to an amusement park ride at the proposed Harry Potter theme park.

Second, the alchemical characters. We learn early in the first book that Hogwarts' headmaster and Harry's mentor, Albus Dumbledore, is an alchemist of some renown and a partner of the famous alchemist Nicolas Flamel. Dumbledore is stripped of many of his honors in *Phoenix*, but we learn the only one that really matters to him is his chocolate frog trading card, where his alchemical accomplishments are listed. (Flamel was an actual famous alchemist who lived in fourteenth-century Paris.)

Hermione Granger's name has an obvious alchemical reference in it, too, as do several other names in the books. Hermione is the feminine form of Hermes, who, besides being the Greek messenger god (Mercury), was also the name of the great alchemist Hermes Trismegistos, in whose name countless alchemical works were written through the centuries. Harry's father is named James, the name of the patron saint of alchemists, and his mother is named Lily, a symbol for the second, purifying stage of the alchemical work.

Third, Harry's transformations from lead to gold. The alchemical work is about changing the soul from lead to gold, from failing to virtue; this is evident in the title character's transformations in each book.

In the first, *Philosopher's Stone*, the orphaned Harry lives in fear of his aunt and uncle, the Dursleys, and without any knowledge or delight in who he is. By the book's end, he shows himself a champion of remarkable courage and daring and has become reconciled both to his parents' death at the hands of the sorcerer Voldemort and to his own destiny as a wizard. In *Chamber of Secrets*, Harry begins the book as a prisoner both of the Dursleys and of his own self-doubts and self-pity. At the heroic finish, he risks his own life to liberate a young girl and vanquish the villain, who is an incarnation of selfishness and self-importance.

Harry blows up his Aunt Marge (like a balloon) because he cannot overlook her slights of his parents at the beginning of *Prisoner of Azkaban*. At the end, he rescues the man who betrayed his parents to Voldemort by offering his own life as a shield to him. He goes from unforgiving judgment to selfless mercy in a year. In the fourth book, *Goblet of Fire*, Harry is initially consumed by thoughts of what others think of him—his external person. By book's end, after trials with his best friend, the Hogwarts student body, and a dragon, he is able to shrug off a front-page hatchet job in the wizarding world's main newspaper, *The Daily Prophet*.

In *Order of the Phoenix*, Harry is consumed by a desire for news. He struggles to listen to the television, agonizes over the lack of reports from friends, and wanders his neighborhood in search of newspapers in trash cans. At the end, he is aware of his need to turn inward and to discover and strengthen his inner life. He knows that his dependence on the outer world and its events was his point of vulnerability, which Voldemort used to manipulate him, and the weakness that helped cause his godfather's death.

When Harry comes onto the scene in *Half-Blood Prince*, he is half asleep as he waits for Dumbledore to come for him. At this point he is very much in doubt about Dumbledore's arrival and even about Dumbledore's care for him. At book's end, Harry is vigilant and braced to take on the mission Dumbledore has given him, and he confesses to the Minister of Magic Dumbledore's presence with him, even though the headmaster is dead.

As with the hero's journey finale in *Deathly Hallows*, Harry's alchemical transformation in that book is the stunning ending to which all previous transformations turned out to be only pointers or foreshadowing. At the book's beginning, Harry's faith in the late headmaster and in himself as a "Dumbledore man" is all but broken by a series of revelations about Albus from Rita Skeeter and Dumbledore's contemporaries. Harry chooses to believe in the headmaster, however, after Dobby's death, despite his doubts and what he has learned, and Harry's great chrysalis into the Christ figure who rises from King's Cross begins with his statement of belief that he makes in Dobby's grave (again, see chapter 19 on *Deathly Hallows* for more on this). Harry's final transformation from doubter to believer and to vanquisher of both his internal failings and the external evil of Voldemort completes the seven-stage alchemical work.

Fourth, the design. Let me give you two quick examples of how the organization of the books parallels the alchemical work. First, let's compare the roles of sulfur and mercury in alchemy with the roles of Harry's friends Ron and Hermione in the books.

The alchemical work purifies a base metal by dissolving and recongealing the metal using two principal reagents, or catalysts. These reagents reflect the masculine and feminine poles of existence. Alchemical sulfur represents the masculine, impulsive, and red pole, while alchemical mercury, or quicksilver, represents the feminine and cool complement. Together and separately these reagents advance the purification of the base metal to gold.

Harry's two closest friends are Ron Weasley, the redheaded, passionate boy, and Hermione Granger, the brilliant, cool young woman. They are also living symbols of alchemical sulfur (Ron) and mercury (Hermione's initials are "HG," the chemical sign for mercury, her parents are both dentists, and in the *Deathly Hallows* epilogue we learn that years later she names her boy HuGo, making the Hermes-Mercury connection complete!). Together, and more obviously in their disagreements and separation, Harry's friendships with Ron and Hermione transform him from lead to gold. Sulfur and quicksilver are frequently called "the quarreling couple," an apt name for the always contentious Ron and Hermione.

The second example is the way the three stages of alchemy are illustrated in the cycle of each book. What has often been described as Harry's annual hero journey is actually the cycle of the alchemical transformation—and each stage of the work, in case you need a road sign, has a character named for it in the Harry Potter books. The first stage of the alchemical work is dissolution, usually called the *nigredo,* or black stage. In this black stage, "the body of the impure metal, the matter for the Stone, or the old, outmoded state of being is killed, putrefied, and dissolved into the original substance of creation, the *prima materia,* in order that it may be renovated and reborn in a new form."[4]

Harry's godfather, Sirius Black, is named for this stage of the work because the book that is the nigredo of the whole series features Sirius and ends with his death (see chapter 15).

The second stage is purification, usually called the *albedo*, or white work. It follows the ablution, or washing, of the prima materia, which causes it to turn a brilliant white. "When the matter reaches the albedo, it has become pure and spotless."[5] Albus Dumbledore (*albus* is Latin for "white, resplendent") is named for this stage of the work. Frequently used symbols of the albedo stage of the work include the moon and a lily. *Luna*, the Latin word for moon, is the name of one of Harry's friends in the fifth book, and *Lily* is the name of his mother, who gave her life to save his. *Half-Blood Prince* is the albedo novel of the series, which features the headmaster and ends with his death.

The third and last stage of the alchemical work is the recongealing or perfection, usually called the *rubedo*, or red stage.

> *The purified matter is now ready to be reunited with the spirit (or the already united spirit and soul). With the fixation, crystallization or embodiment of the eternal spirit, form is bestowed upon the pure, but as yet formless, matter of the Stone. At this union, the supreme chemical wedding, the body is resurrected into eternal life. As the heat of the fire is increased, the divine red tincture flushes the white Stone with its rich, red colour. . . . The reddening of the white matter is also frequently likened to staining with blood.[6]*

Rubeus Hagrid (*rubeus* is Latin for "red") might have been named for this stage. A common symbol of the red work and the Philosopher's Stone is the red lion. *Deathly Hallows*, as you'd expect, is the big crucible finish to the series and, sad but true, a character with "red" in his name dies in the battle for Hogwarts. But it wasn't the beloved Hogwarts gamekeeper!

Each book thus far is a trip through these three stages. The black work, or dissolution, is the work done in Harry at Privet

Drive by the Dursleys and in the Hogwarts classroom by Snape, the teacher who seems to hate him. The white work, or purification, occurs under the watchful eye of the white alchemist Albus Dumbledore during Harry's year at Hogwarts. This often occurs in combination with painful separation from Ron, Hermione, or both. The red work, or rubedo, is the climactic crucible scene, always underground or in a graveyard, in which Harry dies a figurative death and is saved by love in the presence of a Christological symbol.

The resurrection at story's end each year is the culmination of that year's cycle and transformation. The cycle then closes with congratulations and explanations from the master alchemist and a return to the Dursleys for another trip through the cycle.

And fifth and last, the curious images throughout the books.

Rowling weaves alchemical images here, there, and everywhere through the involved tapestry of her stories, and without a good dictionary of alchemical symbolism (I recommend Lyndy Abraham's from Cambridge University Press), it's easy to miss them all. Take the tournament tasks in *Goblet of Fire* as an example. Each of the wonderfully engaging events of the Triwizard Tournament and Harry's preparation for each trial by fire, water, or labyrinth in *Goblet of Fire* is from the alchemical work. A quick review of the tasks and search of guides to alchemical imagery in literature reveals the role of dragons, the egg, the prefects' bath and water trial, the labyrinth, and the graveyard resurrection and fight.[7]

Dragons: The first task in the tournament involves dragons, which are used in alchemy to represent "matter at the *beginning* of the work being resolved into philosophical sulphur and mercury" (emphasis added).

The egg: Harry and the other champions then have to solve the mystery of the egg, which appropriately is the name given to "the alchemist's vessel of transmutation in which the birth of the Philosopher's Stone takes place . . . also known as the griffin's egg" (i.e., from beginning to the place of the work).

The bath: Harry solves his egg puzzle in the prefects' bath/ swimming pool, a word used by alchemists to describe "the secret, inner, invisible fire which dissolves and kills, cleanses and resurrects the matter of the Stone in the vessel" (what makes the work proceed in the alchemist's test tube).

Water immersion/flood: The second task in the tournament is the trial underwater in the lake. Interestingly, one of the alchemist's maxims was "Perform no operation until all be made water."[8] Water immersion, it turns out, is "a symbol of the dissolution and putrefaction of the matter of the Stone during the black nigredo stage" (we're seeing some progress from preparatory dragons to the action of the first stage).

Labyrinth: The third task, which is supposed to be the end of the tournament, is a maze and is a metaphor for life in the world, or "the dangerous journey of the alchemist through the opus alchymicum. . . . While in the labyrinth of the opus, illusion and confusion reign and the alchemist is in danger of losing all connection and clarity" (we end with an image of the whole work).

Grave: All the alchemical images of Harry's Triwizard tasks are preparatory for and descriptions of the black stage of the Great Work, or nigredo, to come in *Order of the Phoenix*. (For more alchemical imagery, see the discussions of each book in chapters 11–19.) Rowling, following the lead of English dramatists, poets, and novelists from Shakespeare to C. S. Lewis, has written an alchemical tale to engage her readers and transform them alongside Harry.

Conclusion: Alchemy and the Popularity of Harry Potter

The following chart summarizes what we've learned about alchemy and Rowling's use of alchemical imagery in the Harry Potter novels.

The reason good authors use these alchemical images isn't from acute cleverness or chronic arcane-o-philia; it's because the three stages of the alchemical process and the whole "Great Work" of alchemy parallels the spiritual stages of transformation common to all the world's revealed traditions. As you can see in the chart below, the black stage represents repentance, humility, obedience, and renunciation. The white work is illumination and purification. The red work, rarely realized in this life but part of the human design nonetheless, is sanctity or perfection in God's glory through his grace.

Great writers in the English tradition have used alchemical imagery from the sixteenth to the twenty-first centuries because it works in grabbing hold of their readers' cardiac intelligence,

ALCHEMY AND THE POPULARITY OF HARRY POTTER

ALCHEMY	Stage 1	Stage 2	Stage 3
PROCESS	Lead or base metal	Action of contraries, purification process	Gold, Philosopher's Stone, Red Lion
COLOR (STAGES)	Black (Nigredo)	White (Albedo)	Red (Rubedo)
ACTION	Dissolution	Purification	Perfection
IN HARRY POTTER			
CHARACTERS	Dursleys, Snape, House of Black	Albus Dumbledore, Remus Lupin	Rubeus Hagrid
HARRY'S SCENES	Privet Drive, Potions class, Umbridge	Solving mystery at Hogwarts	Crucible scenes, denouement
CHRISTIAN PARALLELS	Repentance	Baptism	Sanctification
CHRISTIAN VIRTUES	Humility, obedience, renunciation	Illumination, purification, moral virtue	Theosis

the so-called "eye of the heart," and bringing them to an imaginative place of transformation. Just as with actors in Shakespearean drama, we identify with Harry, Ron, and Hermione, and, though we almost certainly miss out on the obscure hermetic references, we find ourselves sharing their agonies and their victories.

The alchemy works in connecting us in story form with the very real three-stage spiritual transformation of repentance, purification, and perfection common to the great religions. Be it by connection with psychological archetypes or with the realities of human spiritual design, this is so much a part of us that, though we have been in large part immunized to the message of repentance and purification or of spiritual reality of any kind by our culture and schooling, we respond as readers with joy and longing to the imaginative shadows of it in fiction.

Whence Potter-mania? I think a big piece of this worldwide phenomenon springs from our individual and collective response, largely unconscious, to Rowling's traditional alchemical artistry and the spiritual freight it carries. Go to the next page for more artistry from the English tradition, this time with a more explicitly Christian message.

5

ONE PERSON,
TWO NATURES

*Doppelgängers point to the struggle of dual
natures—and their resolution in the God-Man.*

I enjoy speaking with Rowling's readers, young and old, for a variety of reasons. To be honest, a great many in every Harry Potter audience I speak to—from schools and bookstores to churches and fan conventions—know the books' details much better than I do, so I always learn something. Then there's the fun of talking about a great story and its meaning (either to me personally or in the grand scheme of things) with thoughtful people; really, I live for those times.

What they tell me they get out of the talks, besides the kick they get out of reminding me again how to pronounce Hermione's name (you'd think I was Viktor Krum), is seeing the stories *diagonally*. By that I mean seeing the common elements of all the books rather than thinking of the stories in narrative sequences of event after event. Certainly the hero's journey and alchemical formula is a "wow" to them, but the biggest wow comes when we begin to talk about *doppelgängers.*

"Doppel-whatzits?" I feel a little bit like Hagrid with one of his nasty pets when I introduce that word. Anyway, it just means "double-goer" in German, and there really isn't an English equivalent. The term is used to describe a "shadow character." A doppelgänger is a character or creature's complementary figure or shadow, which reveals aspects of its personality otherwise invisible. Think of Robert Louis Stevenson's Dr. Jekyll and Mr. Hyde and Mary W. Shelley's Dr. Frankenstein and his monster. Rowling has created doppelgängers that, like Jekyll/Hyde, are in the same body, and at least one, like Frankenstein and monster, that is in separate bodies.

You might find one, maybe two, shadow characters in a common novel, but what makes this so important in understanding the books we're discussing is that almost every character in Harry Potter is something of a doppelgänger. Specifically, the Harry/Voldemort relation is key to understanding the meaning of the books and why they are so popular. Let's take a look first at how pervasive this idea really is in the books' characters and then take a close look at Harry and his dark shadow in order to get at the transcendent meaning of this character device in the stories.

Many of Rowling's characters, for instance, are *animagi.* These are masters of the magical subject of transfiguration who can change at will into an animal shape. The animagi we know of include James Potter (white stag), Sirius Black (black dog), Peter Pettigrew (rat), Minerva McGonagall (cat), and Rita Skeeter (bug). We know Albus Dumbledore was a Transfiguration Master, as well as being an accomplished alchemist. However, in *Half-Blood Prince,* he died without revealing if he was a white bumblebee animagus (his name means "white bumblebee") or the tawny owl that appears in several places throughout the series. And we don't learn anything about this in *Deathly Hallows* from his portrait or Severus's memories. We'll have to wait for Rowling's backstory encyclopedia.

This shape-changing stunt is not just a plot device or part of every magical novel's repertoire. The shape each animagus takes is a pointer to his or her hidden character; for example, Peter Pettigrew, who is a rat animagus, is the rat fink who betrayed the Potters to Voldemort. The animal figure is a shadow, or doppelgänger, that allows us to see more clearly the outline of the true person. Rowling, via this second figure or shape of the person, gives us a clearer look at what may not be so obvious from the first view.

A variant on animagi is the Patronus shape each character projects. The Patronus Charm, *"Expecto Patronum!"* produces an animal figure and is the only effective defense against the soul-sucking Dementors. Harry's Patronus quite appropriately is a white stag.[1] Cho Chang's is a swan, and Hermione's is an otter.[2]

Doppelgängers of the Jekyll and Hyde sort (meaning the shadow is an aspect within a person rather than another person) are often a simple matter of birth. Harry's world is populated with what Delores Umbridge hates: "half-breeds." Rubeus Hagrid and Olympe Maxime, for instance, are the children of giants and magical persons ("half giants"). Fleur Delacour's grandmother was a Veela (a beautiful woman who grows a beak and scaly wings when enraged). Then there are witches and wizards born from Muggle parents; Lily Evans Potter and Hermione Granger are the most notable Muggle-born characters, and Colin Creevy and his brother have to be the most fun.

Tom Riddle, aka Lord Voldemort, is a half-breed as well, because his mother was a witch and his father a Muggle. (That his own followers are unaware of this suggests he has concealed his double life.) Harry has an honorary membership to this club because, though both his parents were magical persons, his mom was Muggle-born, he grew up with Muggles, and for many years he was totally unaware of his magical heritage or abilities.

In addition to these half-breeds and shape-changers, we also have a category of shape-changers that do so because of their birthright or because of some tragic occurrence. Nymphadora Tonks is a *metamorphmagus* who is able to change shape at will, which is a handy trick for disguise in her work as an auror. Tonks's husband, Remus Lupin, much less fortunately, is a werewolf who is only able to control his dangerous transformations by way of difficult-to-brew and ill-tasting potions. Rowling has left clues in every book, some quite open, that suggest Severus Snape is a half vampire (though she has insisted in interviews that he is not a full-blooded vampire à la Count Sanguini). If this is not a MacGuffin or a red herring, then the "Half-Blood Prince," aka Severus Snape also has a meaningful shadow life, in addition to his being a double agent.

And there are more!

The books also include a host of "threshold characters" whom scholars call *luminal*, from the Latin word *limen*, which means "threshold" or "doorway." These folk stand in the doorway between two worlds, which amounts to their living in two worlds or so far to the periphery of their own world that they cannot fit into the usual categories (good guy or bad guy, insider or outsider, for instance). Severus Snape is a good example, half vampire or no. The Potions Master, as a former Death Eater and member of the Order of the Phoenix, lives and moves in both supposedly exclusive domains. Other threshold doppelgängers include the other Death Eaters and Dumbledore supporters (all of whom conceal their loyalties), the Dursleys, Dobby, Winky, Firenze, Peter Pettigrew, Neville Longbottom, the Squibs (Argus Filch and Arabella Figg), Mundungus Fletcher, and Percy Weasley.

And of course there is Polyjuice Potion. By means of this magical draught, Harry Potter characters can for a brief time transform into other characters. Ron and Harry become Crabbe and Goyle in order to visit the Slytherin common room in *Chamber of Secrets*, and Barty Crouch Jr. hoodwinks all of Hogwarts into thinking he's Alastor "Mad-Eye" Moody for the whole of *Goblet of Fire. Deathly Hallows* begins with Harry's escape from the Dursleys being disguised by six Polyjuice Harry Potters taking off in different directions from the real Harry.

I think the only Jekyll/Hyde folk I haven't mentioned are those who aren't "folks." Rowling's menagerie of magical creatures includes a host of half-breed, double-natured creatures. The centaurs, with the head and chest of a man and the body and legs of a horse, are a notable example, as are the merpeople, hippogriffs, and the sphinx (who makes a cameo appearance in *Goblet of Fire*). Though not exactly half-breeds, special mention should be made of the phoenix, thestrals, and unicorns in the Potter books, because they are not what they seem—namely, bird or horse or even bird/horse/dragon.

Now for the pairs. So far all the shadow characters or doppelgängers I have mentioned have been internal ones; that is, the mirrored aspects are within a single person or creature. It is just as common for there to be two persons, in which the one is a revealing reflection of the other (again, Dr. Frankenstein and his monster are a good example of this shadowing).

In Harry Potter, Rowling sets up quite a few such pairs for our consideration. Besides the obvious sets of twins (Fred and George Weasley, the Patil sisters), other notable Potter pairs include:

- ❖ Slytherin and Gryffindor (opposing houses)
- ❖ Hagrid and Grawp (giant brothers)
- ❖ Draco and Dudley (frequently paired in Harry's mind)
- ❖ Harry and Draco (generational leaders of opposing houses)
- ❖ Sirius and James (Harry's godfather and father)
- ❖ Ron and Hermione (friends with opposing personalities)
- ❖ Hagrid and Harry (two orphans at Hogwarts)
- ❖ Lily and Petunia (opposing mother figures)
- ❖ Peter and Neville (a cross-generational pair of look-alikes)
- ❖ Harry and Neville (joined by the prophecy)
- ❖ Grindelwald and Dumbledore

Rowling has paired these characters, be it through hatred, mutual delight, or historical accident, for a reason. While many authors use this writing device to highlight one conflict or draw the reader further into the drama, *Rowling uses it everywhere*. Look at the list above; have we left anybody out? The only people not animagi, half-breeds, characters living in the borderlands between communities, or pairs, are Nazis.

Not literally Nazis, of course. I mean witches and wizards, self-styled "purebloods" who hate Muggle-born magical persons and "half-breed" magical creatures. Dolores Umbridge personifies this spirit of eugenics in the magical community, in which the concern for purity of blood marks even families that don't openly support Voldemort and the Death Eaters. In *Deathly Hallows*, she leads the Ministry's witch hunt for all non-pureblood magical persons to take back the magical powers they cannot have acquired honestly (that is, by birth).

So what? I suppose the case could be made that everything in existence evidences some sort of polarity (male/female, tall/short, etc.). Maybe you can even screw yourself up into a knot and believe that *all* these pairings and doppelgänger figures in the Potter novels (and the central conflict between purebreds and half-breeds) are a remarkable coincidence or some sort of *idée fixe* on the author's part.

Except that the outcomes of the books hinge on the relation of Harry and Voldemort, a classic doppelgänger pairing. Understanding this specific relationship reveals why the rest of the book is cramped with half-breeds, outsiders, and orphans. The Harry/Voldemort shadow, the pivotal antagonism of the series, points to the duality in every human being; the way Rowling resolves it in the series finale uncovers why her good guys are all bipolar (in a manner of speaking) and why we identify with them rather than the purebloods.

The Harry/Voldemort Doppelgänger

Order of the Phoenix begins with three mentions of Harry's feeling that his skull has been split in two, and one has to imagine it must crack right down that jagged scar on his forehead. It turns out, as we learn by book's end, that Harry's head really is divided and he has an unwelcome guest. He isn't carrying a passenger like Quirrell, nor is he possessed as was Ginny in *Chamber of Secrets*. Rather, Harry has a double nature, or shadow, in his link to Voldemort—and his inability to turn inward and confront this shadow is the cause of the tragedy in *Order of the Phoenix*'s battle royal.

Harry's literal schizophrenia or double-mindedness with Voldemort really evidences itself in *Order of the Phoenix*, but each of the preceding books hints at it. Harry's scar—the mark he received from the curse that failed to kill him as an infant—always burns, for instance, when Voldemort is in a rage. Harry has the ability (known as *Parseltongue*) to speak to snakes from Voldemort via the curse. And quite a few times Harry has been able to see the goings-on in Lord Voldemort's surroundings in his dreams (as in the opening to *Goblet of Fire*). *Order of the Phoenix* just marks the first times that the Dark Lord took advantage of his tie with Harry to manipulate his thinking.

We also learn in *Order of the Phoenix* that Harry and Voldemort were initially joined by a prophecy. It had been foretold just before Harry's birth that "the one with the power to vanquish the Dark Lord approaches" and that either the Dark Lord or his prophesied vanquisher "must die at the hands of the other."[3] Harry, it seems, must kill his ugly relation or be killed. Because Rowling had guaranteed that there would only be seven Harry Potter novels, a lot of fans were concerned when the prophecy was revealed that Harry's future looked dim.

As I argued in chapter 2, Harry and Voldemort, besides being doppelgängers, are both representatives of the primeval Gryffindor/Slytherin feud. Though it is never spelled out in the books, Rowling has left clues in each book that Harry is also the Heir of Gryffindor. We learn in *Chamber of Secrets* that Voldemort is certainly the Heir of Slytherin. Voldemort has a split history, but his blue blood comes through his magical mom (who died at his birth).

We will interpret names further in chapter 10, but it will help here to recall that Voldemort is not the Dark Lord's given name. His real name is Tom Riddle, which, because *Thomas* comes from the Aramaic word for "twin," is a pointer to how important the doppelgänger structure is to these stories. Voldemort's given name means "twin enigma."

The *riddle* we have to solve, then, is what meaning, if any, is there to this doubling or *twin* motif in Harry Potter? Alchemy helps unwrap the riddle. As you'll recall, the principal activity of alchemy is the chemical marriage of the imbalanced "arguing couple": masculine sulfur and feminine quicksilver. These two qualities have to be reconciled and resolved ("die" and be "reborn") before they can be rejoined in a perfected golden unity. Opposites have to be reconciled and resolved for there to be a new life. *One part of a pairing or both must die for there to be new life.* Alchemists frequently cited Christ's words: "Verily, verily, I say unto you, except a corn of wheat fall into the ground and die, it abideth alone: but if it die, it bringeth forth much fruit" (John 12:24, KJV). Alchemists took this verse and their hope of eternal life in Christ's death and Resurrection as scriptural confirmation that their doctrines were correct.

Remember that Christianity and most of the great revealed traditions differ from conventional ideas of what a human being is. The biology textbooks we grew up with offer a strictly naturalist or materialist idea, which, to risk simplification, restricts explanation of everything about the human being to his or her body. The "mind" is just chemical reactions in the brain, and "life" itself is about genetic programming and biochemistry.

The great religious and philosophical thinkers disagree. They argue that the human person isn't just a body with invisible aspects but a body-soul (psychosomatic) unity, in which the soul or spirit is the prior or greater part. Death to these thinkers is not natural, but an effect of the corruption of the soul, usually attributed to the fall of man. "Carnal-mindedness," one's soul being tied to the body and personal advantage, is death, according to Saint Paul; "spiritual-mindedness," or focusing on the greater, transcendent qualities of life, is "life and peace" (Romans 8:6, KJV).

This duality in every human person and the contrary tendencies to be more about individual ego than love and the spirit is the reality that every revealed tradition explains and attempts to transcend. Christianity has the seeming impossibility of uniting opposites like soul and body right at its heart, hence the virgin mother you meet right at the beginning of Christ's story, and Jesus himself being simultaneously perfect God and perfect man.

Back to Harry's shared nature but different essence with Voldemort and all the doppelgängers that populate the pages of the Potter epic.

Rowling makes the two-being-one connection joining Lord Voldemort and Harry all but explicit in chapter 21 of *Order of the Phoenix*. Harry has just witnessed while dreaming (through his mind link with Voldemort) the snake attack on Arthur Weasley. He tells the tale to Dumbledore and, while waiting for magical transit to Grimmauld Place, watches the headmaster do a smoke augury.

The smoke auguror puffs out some smoke, which takes the shape of a serpent's head, mouth wide open. Dumbledore murmurs, "Naturally, naturally" and asks, "But in essence divided?" The smoke serpent answers in the affirmative by neatly splitting into two snakes.

Interpreting the smoke snake augury works on two levels. As Rowling has said, the scene in the headmaster's office shows us Dumbledore "playing through his own theory about what's happened and his theory is, of course, correct. That Voldemort, as summed up by the snake, [is] divided [via Horcruxes]."[4] But the scene is more than confirmation of Dumbledore's theory that Lord Voldemort has divided his soul. It's at least as much about Harry's ability to see through Nagini's eyes. Dumbledore's first question to the auguror was about Harry's assertion that "I was the snake. . . . I saw it all from the snake's point of view." The question Dumbeldore asks the auguror was, perhaps, "Is there a shared nature here between Voldemort and this young man?" The single smoke-serpent form suggests the answer from the auguror is, "Yes, there is! They share a serpent nature."

Then Dumbledore asks, "But in essence divided?" Again, a "yes" answer. *One nature, two essences.*

This confirms that Nagini is a Horcrux (though Dumbledore does not list Nagini with any certainty as a Horcrux in *Half-Blood Prince*), but again, it is also about Harry as a Horcrux. Perhaps the phrase "One nature, two essences" doesn't make you sit up and slap your forehead. Folks don't kill each other anymore (or as often, at least) over who Jesus is, so I guess that's understandable. But when they did, the fight was often about the nature and essence of Christ.

The first great heresy in Christianity was the Arian heresy, in which a priest named Arius argued that Christ was not God in essence and that he had only a human nature. The heretics tended to square off by reducing Christ to *either* a divine nature but not really human *or* a human nature but not really divine. The Church insisted (Council of Chalcedon, AD 451) that Christ has two natures, *both* fully divine *and* fully human. In his divine nature, he was able to conquer sin and death and rise again; in his human nature, Christians believe they are able to share in his Resurrection and inherit eternal life: *one divine essence, two perfect natures.*

Back to Harry and his bad twin, Tom. When Dumbledore gets the message from the auguror that Harry and Voldemort are one in nature and two in essence, what are we supposed to make of that?

First, we can see that Harry and Voldemort are a doppelgänger pair, something like mirrored images of the other. They have the same nature certainly—the *fallen* nature Christians believe we all have as a result of the sin in the Garden. Second, we can see that Harry is moving toward resolution of this struggle of two natures by choosing life, not death; spiritual-mindedness, love, and sacrifice rather than his own advantage, physical comfort, or power. Tom Riddle has the same fallen nature but has chosen the way of death—an essential difference.

This difference is only made clearer by the revelations of Lord Voldemort's pursuit of immortality via the creation of six Horcruxes, in which he inserts a piece of his soul into an object after murdering another human being. This path of death has made Lord Thingy into something hardly human. Harry's choice of life and what is good, in contrast, has made him even more clearly an image of his "father in heaven" and what Dumbledore calls "pure in heart" (compare to Matthew 5:8) and "a soul that is untarnished and whole."[5]

We learn at the end of *Deathly Hallows* that Harry actually has one of Voldemort's soul fragments, courtesy of the curse that failed to kill him as a child. Because he used Harry's blood to reconstitute his body at the end of *Goblet of Fire*, Lord Voldemort has forged a bond with Harry (and the sacrificial love of Lily, Harry's mother) in his body. As Dumbledore explains to Harry at King's Cross, the soul fragment in Harry protected Voldemort from death as long as Harry was living, and the Bond of Blood in the Dark Lord's body meant that Voldemort was reciprocally Harry's life insurance policy. "Lord Voldemort doubled the bond between you when he returned to human form."[6]

The answer to this seeming endless loop? One or the other of the Harry/Riddle pair has to sacrifice himself to the other to eliminate his enemy's faux immortality. Harry, of course, having already died to himself several times in the series, lets Voldemort kill him in the Forbidden Forest at the end of *Deathly Hallows,* and the soul fragment is destroyed while Harry survives. The evil within him having been destroyed and having been saved again by the sacrificial love of his mother, Harry goes on to vanquish the external evil, the remnant of the evil already destroyed.

In other words, Harry and Voldemort, with their mirrored and magically joined bodies and souls, are reflections of the body-soul unities we all are and of the choice each of us makes between carnal- and spiritual-mindedness. For whatever reason, call it the Fall, if you like, our hearts are dark, and this choice isn't easy. But making the hard, right choices, we can die to that evil within and, having won the interior battle, the exterior enemy is defeated when we choose to confront him.

And all the other characters with doppelgänger issues?

Their duality isn't the straight-up Jekyll/Hyde, good/evil polarity of shared fallen nature (soul-soul fragment) and different essence consequent to their different choices, as Harry and Voldemort are. Their contrary cores are like the body-soul aspects that make up every human person. The answer to their internal issues, though, is resolved the same way Harry destroys his interior and exterior Voldemort. By making the hard choices for the good, the loving, and the sacrifice of self, they transcend this interior duality and become androgynes like the alchemists—and Christians, who in the sacrificial love of the Nazarene are "neither Jew nor Greek, slave nor free, male nor female, for you are all one in Christ Jesus" (Galatians 3:28).

In our world of Republicans and Democrats, rich and poor, hawk and dove, Rowling puts her finger on the issues of body and soul that concern us all. She points to the spiritual resolution of our troubles as the necessary inner victory and the beginning of the answer to the external conflicts and contrary ideologies that separate us. As we'll see in the next chapter, this concern about prejudice is one of Rowling's biggest themes, and she has set the stage of her alchemical drama with her cast of mixed breeds, doppelgängers, and purebloods to teach us a remarkable lesson in story form.

6

DON'T JUDGE,
LEST YOU BE JUDGED

*Surprise endings suggest a remedy for the
evils of prejudice.*

How Harry Cast His Spell is not *The English Major's Guide to Harry Potter.*[1]
This book lacks, consequently, discussions of narratological perspective, three-dimensional theme work, and the all-important
influence of previous writers. By choosing to focus on the spiritual content of English literature, in which context the Harry Potter
books have been written, to answer the question "Whence Potter-
mania?" I have had to leave out a lot of stuff.

Which is, of course, as it should be. (Buy a book on polar bears,
you don't want to find out it's really a treatise on the geometry
in Gothic cathedrals.) I do, however, need to discuss the principal
themes of the books. Their transcendent meaning that lights up
our hearts and spirits is relatively self-evident; the trouble is keeping people in the room when you use the word *themes.*

Briefly, here's how I decide if a book is a "classic" or not. My
"Great Book" test has three parts:

❖ Does it address the big questions of human life?

❖ Does the artistry of the work support the answers given to these questions?

❖ Are the answers about edifying relationships with God, man, and the world? (This last, in light of historic English literature being almost exclusively by Christians for other Christians, can be rephrased more simply, "Are the answers Christian?")

The Harry Potter books are classics—and not just as "kid-lit" but as classics of world literature. The tales are masterfully told, at least in terms of how carefully the books and series have been structured, and they carry a mother lode of meaning. Which brings us to what English teachers call themes.

Themes are just the questions authors try to answer in story form. The larger the question and the more important it is for us to understand the answer is a decent gauge of whether the book is worth reading. We know the Potter books have been ingeniously plotted and are engaging enough to have sold more than 375 million copies; the subject for discussion, then, is what is in these beautiful, best-selling wheelbarrows?

In them, we find the answer to four principal questions:

❖ How are we to treat one another?

❖ What is the answer to the mystery of death?

❖ When are we to embrace change or flee change?

❖ What makes a human being good or bad, or even human?

Teachers give these questions "theme" titles like Pride and Prejudice, Death and Bereavement, Personal Transformation, and Choice. And these are the four overarching themes in the Harry Potter novels. In the next three chapters, I will look briefly at each before discussing the Christian meaning of Rowling's answer.

Rowling has special sympathy for the victims of prejudice and ill treatment. Her favorite writers are Jane Austen and Charles Dickens, who champion the downtrodden and underdogs in every one of their books. Before her writing career took off, Rowling worked professionally on behalf of the helpless at Amnesty International, the worldwide advocacy arm and voice of political prisoners and the unjustly persecuted and tortured everywhere. Closer to home, Rowling experienced the agony of losing friends who avoided her during the degenerative illness of her mother. She also endured the public shaming of single mothers during the Margaret Thatcher/ John Major years. Since her success, her largest public gifts have been to causes supporting single mothers, those with AIDS, and the children of Eastern Europe via the Children's High Level Group. Her heart and her money go to underdogs on the periphery of society. No surprise, then, to find out that prejudice—its cause, effect, and cure—is a primary focus in the Harry Potter novels.

As is evident in the chart on page 56, every one of the Harry Potter books reveals a prejudice against another downtrodden group of people who are different from "normal" wizards or Muggles in big ways and small.

Rowling doesn't just lay out a black-and-white world where the good guys aren't racist and the bad guys are. Only Dumbledore seems free of prejudice. Hagrid doesn't trust foreigners or Muggles, though he himself is hated by magical folk because he is a half giant. Ron, despite his insecurities about being poor, has a host of wizarding prejudices from giants to werewolves (though he only knows—and likes—one of each) and is always the first to point his finger at someone he doesn't like. Harry's "age-old prejudice," as Lupin puts it, against Severus Snape and Draco Malfoy is his heroic flaw, and it is the only prejudice explored in *Half-Blood Prince* that prepares us for Harry's struggle in the final chapter.

And the prisoners of prejudice, mostly the Slytherins, seem so unhappy in their sarcasm and meanness that they are more to be pitied than despised.

What is remarkable about the magical world of Harry Potter,

PREJUDICE IN HARRY POTTER

Book	Prejudice Against	Origin	Object
Sorcerer's Stone	Abnormal or magical folk	Dursleys	Harry & Hagrid
	Nonmagical folk (Muggles)	Slytherins	Muggles
	Poor	Malfoys	Weasleys
	Clumsy, awkward, stupid	Draco	Neville
Chamber of Secrets	Mudbloods (Muggle parent)	Slytherins	Hermione & others
	Squibs (magic-born Muggle)	Magic folk	Argus Filch
	Ugly, unpopular	Olive Hornby	Moaning Myrtle
	The Nearly Headless	Headless ghosts	Nick
Prisoner of Azkaban	Prisoners	Everyone	Sirius Black
	Werewolves	Almost everyone	Remus Lupin
	Hippogriffs	Ministry of Magic	Buckbeak
	Intelligent women	Boys & teachers	Hermione
Goblet of Fire	Young people	Fleur	Harry
	Giants	Magic folk	Hagrid & Maxime
	Foreigners	Hagrid	Triwizard guests
	Unprejudiced	Death Eaters	Albus & Weasleys
Order of the Phoenix	Harry supporters	Ministry of Magic	Order & Harry's friends
	Alternative press	*Daily Prophet*	*Quibbler* & Luna
	Centaurs and half-breeds	Umbridge	Firenze
	Giants	Everyone	Grawp
	Nonconformists	Teaching establishment	Fred/George & Trelawney
Half-Blood Prince	Severus Snape	James Potter/Sirius Black/Harry Potter	Severus Snape
Deathly Hallows	Mudbloods	Ministry of Magic	The Cattermoles
	Resistance fighters	*Daily Prophet*	Harry Potter
			Albus Dumbledore

then, is not so much the incredible creatures, structures, and enchantments as it is the fact that the wizards and witches are as unloving and self-important as the Muggles many of them despise (and all patronize). Good thing the magic folk have an enlightened government and a free press to stand up for the oppressed!

Ha! Pardon my sarcasm. The *Daily Prophet* is the television news and newspaper media conglomerate for wizards and witches. Every book chronicles the way it spreads half-truths and misinformation as gospel wisdom "hot off the press." In *Goblet of Fire*, though, we learn that these are not just the inevitable mistakes from rushing news to print. Meeting Rita Skeeter, star reporter for the *Prophet* and other wizarding publications (*Witch Weekly,* for one), we realize that errors that might have been caused by incompetence or negligence are the result of plain and simple wickedness.

Take a look at Rita's name for a clue as to what she's about: *Rita* = "read-a," *Skeeter* = "squito, mosquito, or bloodsucking-disease-carrying-parasitical-bug." And Rita is equal to her name. Rather than exposing the unjust and prejudiced in defense of the down-trodden, Ms. Skeeter, an illegal "beetle bug" animagus, does everything she can to make life miserable for those in positions of responsibility or who are somehow different. She loves to create hardship for the Ministry, of course, but saves her special venom for individuals she dislikes. In *Goblet of Fire* she writes unflattering, unkind, and rude pieces, several of which she makes up whole cloth, about Dumbledore, Hagrid, Hermione, and Harry, who is misrepresented once and cruci-fied another time on the morning of the last Triwizard task.

Thus the media in the magical world (I think we are meant to ask, "Unlike our own?") is not about the life-supporting mission of exposing prejudice and uplifting those beaten down by it. As we learn in *Order of the Phoenix,* the newspaper instead actively and inten-tionally creates or fosters prejudice against individuals and groups in toadying service to the government. Cornelius Fudge wants Harry and Dumbledore discredited? The *Daily Prophet* is there to package the news daily for weeks on end—and on a different cue from the Ministry, tells a story saying the complete opposite without a blush for the lies and distortions of the previous months.

The reading public acts on cue from the shadow casters and either attacks or passively agrees to thinking less of the misrepre-sented. Remember how Hermione is treated by Mrs. Weasley after the *Witch Weekly* article portrayed her as a scarlet woman? And Har-ry's reception at Hogwarts in *Order of the Phoenix* after a summer of innuendo that he is a braggart and show-off in need of attention? Even the good and wise have their opinions made to order and prejudices confirmed by the popular media. Only media-savvy Hermione figures out how to manipulate the system by having Harry's interview printed in the alternative press. The media in Harry Potter's world is key in attacking the downtrodden and furthering prejudice (just as it often is in our own world).

The Ministry of Magic (MOM), one assumes from its initials, is supposed to be the protector of the helpless and a force for good against evil in the world. However, the Ministry (I think we are again meant to ask, "Unlike our own government?") is anything but maternal or heroic. Rowling consistently represents them as a gaggle of self-important airheads busying themselves with laughable trivia (cauldron bottom reports) or international bread-and-circus functions like the Quidditch World Cup, while neglecting to take care of even their own. Just how long was Bertha Jorkins missing before the Ministry sent out a search party?

But the Ministry is worse than bumbling and distracted. In *Chamber of Secrets*, in response to pressure and the need to appear active, Minister of Magic Cornelius Fudge has Hagrid imprisoned in Azkaban, though he knows Hagrid is innocent. In *Goblet of Fire*, Sirius Black reveals that his life sentence in Azkaban was handed down just for the appearance of acting with strength. Stan Shunpike's imprisonment under the new law-and-order regime of Rufus Scrimgeour in *Half-Blood Prince* shows us the Ministry has learned nothing about how to resist evil effectively. Azkaban is a psychic concentration camp where few survive. The Ministry, it turns out, had been torturing those imprisoned in Azkaban through the guards, the Dementors, who lived by sucking everything good and beautiful from their souls. These guards return to Lord Voldemort's service on his return and are rapidly reproducing, as we learn in *Half-Blood Prince*, causing all of Britain to fall into a joyless depression. The name of the prison itself is a magical turn on Alcatraz and gulag-rich Soviet republics such as Uzbekistan.

The Ministry has its comic front, then, but a gulag back. Ambitious ministers fiddle with inconsequential matters and act in response to pressure generated by the rich and the media. The ministry is incapable of passing the Muggle Protection Act or of policing wizards practicing dark magic and Muggle baiting. Those who press for this sort of "social good" legislation are demoted for lacking "real wizard pride." And beyond its failure to protect the innocent, in its nightmarish prison and zeal to incarcerate the innocent, the Ministry becomes the agent of discrimination and persecution of the defenseless. The modern Orwellian regime with MOM's face!

It is a great disappointment but little surprise when the Minister of Magic, in the dark hour at the end of *Goblet of Fire*—a time requiring decisiveness and courage to combat the risen Lord Voldemort—shows himself an impotent coward and fool. In a world (unlike our own?) ruled by prejudices and stereotypes, a world whose thoughts and feelings are guided by a self-serving media, and a world whose government maintains order by fear of torturous imprisonment, don't look for public figures of the stature of Winston Churchill. *Order of the Phoenix* is a dark novel, not because the bad guys are so bad—they are largely invisible—but because the supposed good guys have black hearts, which makes the life of the truly virtuous a catacomb nightmare. Though Fudge acknowledges in the *Daily Prophet* at the end of *Order of the Phoenix* that the Dark Lord is back and the magical world is ready to oppose him, little has changed. The new Minister of Magic, Rufus Scrimgeour, whom we meet in *Half-Blood Prince*, is a get-tough politician who resembles Churchill in appearance but who rearranges deck chairs while Albus Dumbledore is effectively researching and resisting Lord Voldemort.

In *Deathly Hallows*, Lord Voldemort easily takes over the Ministry by installing Pius Thicknesse as his puppet Minister of Magic, and the entire machinery of magical government serves his dark purposes openly. To show how low the Ministry has gone, Rowling makes flushing toilets the point of entry for all Ministry officials. Gone is the golden delusion visible in the Fountain of Magical Brethren; the atrium of the Ministry is filled with ebony stone statues of an enthroned witch and wizard over the statement "Magic is might."

These are kids' books? Hardly. The message of Harry Potter is clear: Poisonous prejudice is everywhere, and only constant vigilance and resistance to the regime of ideas (whose government and media authorities foster and codify this hatred) will free us of it. The Harry Potter books encourage readers to take a step back from the world and recognize what an unloving place it is. This stepping back to appreciate the satirical picture of our world drawn in story is the first step necessary to any spiritual life. The ladder of divine ascent in every revealed tradition requires recognizing the fallen world for what it is and, in Christian language, deciding to be "in the world" but not "of the world" (John 17:13-16).

Look again at the chart listing the prejudices of the wizarding world and the persecuted individuals and groups who live there. Only in *Order of the Phoenix* do we learn (in the House of Black, looking at the Black family tapestry) how inbred and insular the leading magical families have become over the generations and how far their narrow belief in eugenics, or "good breeding," to overcome the world's ills had taken them—that is, into the Dark Lord's service. We can see this same thinking reflected in modern society. It is responsible for the Soviet gulags, Nazi camps, and abortion clinics, and it's this same thinking that continues to drive our culture of death (euthanasia, abortion, self-sterilization, etc.).

But why do we get so much out of hearing such a difficult message in the pages of Rowling's Harry Potter novels? Adult and child readers who rarely read 800-page novels are reading the 4,100 pages of these seven novels repeatedly, and I mean again and again and again. There has to be a reason such a painful message about our times is much more than reader-friendly. I think there are two reasons.

First, the hook. Nothing is worse than being preached at in a novel (okay, there are a lot of things worse than that, but among reading headaches, a writer on a philosophical or theological hobby-horse is way up there). Rowling lulls one almost to sleep with all the persecuted groups and individuals with double natures and how wicked she makes the bad guys. Yawn! The good guys are the victims of prejudice, the bad guys are all proud and prejudiced, what's to keep one awake?

The revelation to come is that *we readers* are the prejudiced ones. Every Potter novel ends with an Agatha Christie surprise. These surprise endings make the dullest reader slap himself in the forehead and say, "Duh! What was I thinking? I should have known that bad guy was a good guy! Why was I so sure he was a bad apple?"

This gives Rowling's prejudice theme a third dimension: the dimension above the page and in your heart. It's one thing to hate Draco along with Harry and his gang because of his Nazi-like snobbery—it's another thing entirely to learn that *you're* as bad as Draco for having assumed that the bad guy was good and the good guy was bad (which Rowling tricks us into doing in almost every book, and especially in *Half-Blood Prince*, in which we are tricked into believing Severus Snape is a murderer and once again that Albus Dumbledore is only an angel, and Harry's guardian angel at that).[2]

The second reason we respond to the agonizing problem of prejudice in the world is more to the point. We read and reread the books because they offer the right answer. That answer is love. Prejudice or a rush to judgment is a failure in love. We recognize in these stories the desire to see what makes us feel best about ourselves even if it means being unkind or dismissive of others. The Sorting Hat, Hermione, and Dumbledore all make pleas in *Order of the Phoenix* for students to overlook their differences for the greater good—pleas for love which mostly fall on deaf ears. Though it has prevented him from being the Dumbledore man he imagines himself to be, Harry's hatred for Severus Snape—his prejudice—is what largely defines him at the end of *Half-Blood Prince*. Harry's ability to defeat the Dark Lord in *Deathly Hallows*, of course, is consequent to his learning and accepting that it was Severus's love for and loyalty to Harry's mother, Lily, that has kept him alive all these years. Confronted by his core prejudice, Harry is able to sacrifice himself in love for his friends because he has the darkness within himself.

That love as the solution to prejudice so dominates the story line of a book written in a tradition of Christian literature should not be a surprise. Love is supposed to be the defining mark of Christians: "By this shall all men know that ye are my disciples" (John 13:35, KJV). One of the few explicit commandments given by Christ to his followers is the love of God and neighbor (Mark 12:30-31). Another commandment, really an application of the commandment to love, is the prohibition against judging our brother's sins (Matthew 7:1-5). This is not a prohibition of discernment and virtuous discrimination, but the warning against identifying our neighbor by his sins and the pretense of being without sin ourselves.

Just as the sacrificial love and spiritual-mindedness of the God-Man was the answer to the "twin riddle," so Christ is also the answer to the prejudice nightmare. Christ is Love himself, and as much as he lives in our heart, like him we stand with the underdogs of society, resist the Pharisees and forces of this world, and are called to love others as ourselves, that is, unconditionally and sacrificially. Christ never conformed to the prejudices of his times or shrank to being a respecter of persons or position. His disciples are called to a no less heroic position—and the Harry Potter books, in their satire of worldly institutions and exposure of our own rush to judge and condemn, point to this selfless life of love.

But being against prejudice and for love is a little bit like being against drunk driving. Christians are against drunk driving, but so are sentimental nihilists and Christian-baiting communists. In the theme and treatment of death, and in the means to transcend death, the Potter books move from implicit support of the Christian understanding of the world to almost explicit statements of doctrine.

7

THE TRIUMPH OF LOVE
OVER DEATH

*The mystery of death meets the
ultimate answer.*

The Halloween murders of James and Lily Potter can be taken as
the starting point of the Harry Potter stories, and death is never
far from the reader's line of sight from *Philosopher's Stone*'s opening
chapters to the epilogue of *Deathly Hallows*. As we've already discussed, Harry dies a figurative death in each book. *Goblet of Fire, Order
of the Phoenix*, and *Half-Blood Prince* feature the violent deaths of characters readers have come to love. Harry struggles with the meaning
of death at the end of *Phoenix* and *Prince*, and all of *Deathly Hallows*—
from the Aeschylus and Penn quotations that serve as frontispiece
to the duel to the death in the Great Hall in the last chapter—is one
long exploration of love and death.

It's safe to say, consequently, that Harry Potter is about love and
death, but if I had to choose one over the other, I'd say the books
are about death. Why am I so sure? Well, on this subject, Rowling
has been very open. She has said, "In fact, death and bereavement

and what death means, I would say, is one of the central themes in all seven books."[1] Can't be much plainer than that. Why would a young woman in the bloom of life write a series of books about death and bereavement? The best guess I've read is the common-sense one: she has experienced the death of loved ones and has something to say.

Every book develops the theme of love trumping death. Let's stroll through the books with Harry and see how he is learning that love is the power that defeats death—and how the Dark Lord is missing this lesson.

Death in *Harry Potter and the Philosopher's Stone*

Albus Dumbledore, the greatest wizard of the age and headmaster of Hogwarts, has two heart-to-heart talks with Harry during his first year at Hogwarts. The first is after Harry has discovered the Mirror of Erised, and the second is at book's end after Harry defeats Professor Quirrell in front of the Mirror. Harry learns from Dumbledore that he has destroyed the Stone. This shocks Harry because he knows that Dumbledore's friends, Nicolas Flamel and his wife, are only alive because of the Elixir of Life they get from the Stone. Dumbledore explains to Harry that "to the well-organized mind, death is but the next great adventure."[2]

This definition of death—how to think of it rather than fear it—is the only part of this conversation repeated word for word in Harry's account to Ron and Hermione later. Harry then asks how it was possible for him to defeat Professor Quirrell, whose hands burned at the touch of Harry's skin. Dumbledore tells him it is love.

> "Your mother died to save you. If there is one thing Voldemort cannot understand, it is love. He didn't realize that love as powerful as your mother's for you leaves its own mark. Not a scar, no visible sign . . . to have been loved so deeply, even though the person who loved us is gone, will give us

some protection forever. It is in your very skin. Quirrell, full of hatred, greed and ambition, sharing his soul with Voldemort, could not touch you for this reason. It was agony to touch a person marked by something so good."[3]

In the opening book of the seven-book series, then, Rowling offers explicit teaching of what death is, and the importance of the love of those departed that continues to protect us even in their absence. Especially when this love was a *sacrificial* love.

Death in *Harry Potter and the Chamber of Secrets*

Harry's meetings with Dumbledore in the next book include a short discussion in the headmaster's office and another after Harry fights the young Voldemort and his pet basilisk. Neither talk is about death. Harry does have a near-death scene, however, in *Chamber of Secrets*. He was wounded by the basilisk as he killed it, and Voldemort/Riddle taunts him as he "dies."

As it turns out, Harry is saved by the healing tears of the phoenix Fawkes, Dumbledore's pet. Harry, facing certain death in combat with an older and wiser wizard, not to mention his giant, poisonous pet basilisk, triumphs through loyalty to Dumbledore and the graceful help of Fawkes. Believe it or not, this is an implicit, symbolic teaching on how to escape death through love, which I'll discuss at some length in chapter 12 on *Chamber of Secrets*.

Death in *Harry Potter and the Prisoner of Azkaban*

The title of *Prisoner of Azkaban* is meaningful, but it might have been titled *Harry Potter and the Dementors* because so much of it turns on Harry's meeting with these soul-sucking monsters. The Dementors raise in their victims their most painful memories in order to sap them of joy and hope; for Harry that memory is a reliving of his parents' murders. Harry fears this replayed experience more than he does Lord Voldemort; the pain of seeing his parents die again is worse than facing his own death.

Harry spends much of the book, consequently, with his teacher/ analyst Professor Lupin, learning how to conjure a Patronus Charm that will protect him from the Dementors. Not surprisingly, Harry's Patronus is very much about his late father.

His meeting with Dumbledore after the bizarre climax of *Prisoner of Azkaban* is a return to the discussion in *Philosopher's Stone* of death and our relationship with the dead who loved us. Harry admits to Dumbledore that he thought he saw his dead father save him from the Dementor's kiss. Dumbledore's response is that the dead we love never "truly leave us" and that James Potter "is alive in you, Harry, and shows himself most plainly when you have need of him."[4]

We return here to the lesson we learned about love and death through Dumbledore at the end of the first book: that the love of the departed lives on in us as a protecting grace, and in this, the dead are never truly "departed." This is an echo of the Christian belief that in Love, which is Christ, the saints are a "cloud of wit-nesses" ever encompassing those joined with him in his Church (Hebrews 12:1).

Death in *Harry Potter and the Goblet of Fire*

We see a picture of this theme again in Harry's combat with Lord Voldemort at the end of *Goblet of Fire*. Lily and James Potter, via the "Priori Incantantem" effect, appear as shadowy echoes out of Volde-mort's wand (in the company of his other victims). Harry's dad coaches him and comforts him and after explaining to Harry how to escape, gives him the cue to go, attacking Voldemort with the other shadows in order to buy Harry the time he needs to get away. Not bad for a dead man who is not even a ghost.

But the end of *Goblet of Fire* is mostly about how to grieve. Cedric Diggory is murdered in Voldemort's black resurrection, and the community is stunned. Dumbledore puts on his Elisabeth Kübler-Ross hat and insists that Harry talk through his ordeal right away. He offers the answers that Harry needs in order to accept and recover from his experience, and then Dumbledore publicly acknowledges the heroism of the dead student in the Leaving Feast so the community has its closing ritual. (We learn how *not* to grieve from the house-elf Winkie, who chose to drink herself into oblivion and not share with anyone that her master, Barty Crouch Jr., was alive.)

Death in *Harry Potter and the Order of the Phoenix*

Alastor Moody shows Harry an old photo of the original Order of the Phoenix. In a spirit of nostalgia he relates how those pictured were almost all murdered by Death Eaters and Voldemort—and though he doesn't retell the story of their deaths, "Mad-Eye" Moody is sure to show Harry his dead parents. Harry is revolted by Moody's tactlessness. In the same chapter, while Moody watches, Harry sees Mrs. Weasley grieve for all her children and family (including Harry) when a Boggart reveals to her a vision of her worst fear: their deaths.

Moody's plan? I assume it was to remind the boy-man that a war must have casualties. Certainly Harry was temporarily sobered. He was in no way prepared for Sirius Black's death when it came, of course. And nothing Dumbledore said at the end of *Order of the Phoenix* made Black's death less of a senseless, agonizing loss to Harry. We are left reeling with Harry about the seeming arbitrariness and meaninglessness of death. (See chapter 15 for a discussion of the deliberate darkness of *Phoenix*.)

Death in *Harry Potter and the Half-Blood Prince*

The death of Albus Dumbledore—the beloved Hogwarts headmaster, Harry's mentor, and the greatest wizard and alchemist of the age—is the climax of *Half-Blood Prince*. We learn in the series finale that Dumbledore's death had happened before the action of *Half-Blood Prince* began and that his murder was staged to deceive the Dark Lord. What we knew even before these revelations in the Pensieve was that the headmaster, Harry's best example in life, left

him in *Prince* with the best example of how to die. The headmaster
dies a death that is simultaneously:

❖ Heroic—He rushes to the Astronomy Tower when he sees
the Dark Mark, despite knowing he is at death's door.

❖ Merciful—The headmaster uses his last strength to reveal
gently to Draco Malfoy a lifesaving mercy and love unlike
anything the boy could have expected from a man he was
trying to kill.

❖ Selfless—Dumbledore, as he dies on the Tower turret,
labors to help Draco, Harry, and Severus—and he does
not make any effort to save himself. Even those former
students, now Death Eaters, who have come to kill him
are challenged and edified by his grace while dying.

❖ Fearless—The great alchemist clearly does not fear death,
because he is both courteous to those taunting him and
insistent on their good behavior. He acts as their host and
teacher—and remains "upright" as long as possible—while
he awaits his execution.

❖ Sacrificial—Albus could escape but allows Severus to "push
him over the edge" to save Snape's life, which otherwise
would have been lost because of the Unbreakable Vow.

Coupled with his actions in the cave (discussed in chapter 16),
Albus Dumbledore's death is a loving, fearless, sacrificial death that
testifies to life. Harry has a Christlike standard to take with him in
his coming confrontation with Lord Voldemort.

Even before Harry's choices in *Deathly Hallows*, we readers, like
Harry at the end of *Half-Blood Prince*, can find a lot to hope for in
Dumbledore's death and in the message of these books; namely,
that death is not the end, that a soulless existence is worse than
death, and that death can be transcended by love and the bond of
blood. Let's look at these one at a time.

Death is not the end. Death is no joke in Harry Potter, certainly.
Dumbledore tells us in *Goblet of Fire* that "no spell can re-

awaken the dead," and so far, everyone who has bought the farm, on or off stage, has stayed dead. Harry tries to find a way to bring Sirius back as a ghost, but Nearly Headless Nick assures him at the very end of *Order of the Phoenix* that Sirius "will have . . . gone on." Only cowardly wizards like Nick, afraid of death, choose "to remain behind" as an "imprint of themselves."[5]

This shatters Harry—until he is reminded by Luna that they have evidence of an afterlife. In the Department of Mysteries (situated below the Ministry of Magic—which is already far underground) is the Death Chamber. At the center of a sunken theater-in-the-round with tiers of descending stone benches is a raised stone platform on which stands a broken, ancient stone archway. "The archway was hung with a tattered black curtain or veil, which, despite the complete stillness of the cold surrounding air, was fluttering very slightly as though it had just been touched."[6]

Harry and Luna hear voices behind the veil, though there is no one visible on the other side. When Sirius is killed in battle with Bellatrix Lestrange in the Death Chamber, he literally "passes through the veil," a traditional English idiom for dying. Luna reminds Harry that, yes, death is final, but the fact that they hear voices on the other side of the veil means there is good reason to hope for an afterlife.

A soulless existence is worse than death. If there is one single difference between Harry Potter and Voldemort, it is that Harry thinks there are worse things than dying. Voldemort reminds his supporters at his rebirthing party at the end of *Goblet of Fire*: "You know my goal—to conquer death." He claims to have taken "the steps" to "guard [himself] against mortal death" and "to have gone further than anybody along the path that leads to immortality."[7] As Voldemort shouts at Dumbledore in their wand-to-wand combat in *Order of the Phoenix,* "There is nothing worse than death, Dumbledore!"[8]

Voldemort, fearing death, pursues personal immortality through his horrible Horcruxes. He creates reservoirs in material objects for the splinters of his soul that have separated from the whole in the act of murder. The Dark Lord is merely a cartoon of fallen man; he asserts and seeks his advantage before others (a shadow of murder) and invests himself in temporal things and ideas (modern idolatry and material-ism) to flee death and imagine himself immortal. Such a self-focused, unloving existence ironically separates him from the love of others and ultimately from the Love that defeats carnal-mindedness and death. Fleeing a human death, Volde-mort becomes its nonliving, inhuman incarnation.

In contrast, when given Dumbledore's choice between what is good and what is easy, Harry always chooses the good—even though it means the probable loss of his physical life. He does so at the moment of crisis in every book.

What could be worse than death? A selfish life without truth, love, and beauty—a life on the Dark Side, chosen in fear of physical death, a life that is not really life at all. A physical life without a soul is what happens to a Dementor's victim, as Professor Lupin explains to Harry in *Prisoner of Azkaban:* "You'll just—exist. As an empty shell. And your soul is gone forever . . . lost."[9]

The war between the forces of good and evil, Death Eaters and the Order of the Phoenix, that defines the final three nov-els of the series is largely between those who think physical life (existence) and advantage or power are the greatest goods and those who think what gives life meaning (the soul's ability to love and laugh) is more real and important than just what is visible (namely, continued physical existence). Again, "to be carnally minded is death; but to be spiritually minded is life and peace" (Romans 8:6, KJV). Harry (like Saint Paul) knows that physical death is not the greatest evil; living a soulless existence in fear of death is the true death of the human spirit and the greater evil.

Death is transcended by love and the bond of blood. Death may not be anything at all. I don't mean to be cute. *Evil,* as defined by philoso-
phers and many Christian thinkers, is not something existent in
itself; rather, it's an absence or a negation. Death as an evil is life
turning up missing from where it should be. How do we protect
ourselves from this chasm? How do we transcend death?

As we have seen, Dumbledore tells Harry at the end of *Philosopher's Stone* and *Prisoner of Azkaban* that his parents, through
their love for him and his for them, are still alive in him. We
learn in *Order of the Phoenix* that the sacrificial love of his mother
is what has protected him from Voldemort his whole life, and at
his King's Cross meeting in *Deathly Hallows* with Harry, Dumbledore explains that Voldemort had unwittingly doubled his bond
to Harry by using his blood (and Lily's) in recreating an adult
body for his soul fragment.

Dumbledore calls the "ancient magic" he uses to protect
Harry from Voldemort consequent to Lily's sacrifice "the bond
of blood." He places Harry with Lily's sister because her home is
a place where Harry's mother's blood dwells. As Dumbledore
puts it, "Her blood became your refuge."[10]

Dumbledore is not talking about a refuge in family blood,
clearly; the Potter books (as shown in the previous chapter)
deal extensively with the evil in families who think they deserve
special privileges because of the purity of their blood. The refuge of blood Dumbledore is talking about is possible because
of the sacrificial love of Harry's mom.

Does this idea of a refuge in blood sound familiar to you?
It is probably because the idea of a blood refuge echoes in

story form Christ's promise to his apostles that "whoso eateth my flesh, and drinketh my blood, hath eternal life; and I will raise him up at the last day" (John 6:54, KJV; see also Matthew 26:27-28; 1 Corinthians 11:24-25; Ephesians 1:7; and Hebrews 13:12, 20). Christians believe that Christ's divine essence and sacrifice for us are necessary for human salvation and victory over death. Harry has the imaginative equivalent: freedom from death through the "bond of blood"[11] magic that resulted from the loving sacrifice of Lily Potter.

Why does Harry need such a refuge? We learn in *Order of the Phoenix* that a boy of Harry's description was prophesied before his birth to be the coming vanquisher of the Dark Lord: "He will have power the Dark Lord knows not."[12] Voldemort learns of the prophecy, rightly or wrongly believes it is about Harry, and hunts him down. Lily Potter's sacrifice saves Harry as an infant and protects him in his first meetings with the Dark Lord and within the refuge of his aunt's home. But Voldemort hunts on.

Which brings us to the power Harry has that "the Dark Lord knows not." When Voldemort tells Dumbledore there is nothing worse than death, the headmaster tells him he is wrong. "Indeed, your failure to understand that there are things much worse than death has always been your greatest weakness."[13]

Perhaps you scratched your head at this point in the story and asked yourself, "What could be worse than the absence of life?" Rowling tells us (through Dumbledore) that what is worse than an absence of life is an absence of love—and that love trumps death just as light overcomes darkness. Dumbledore describes the power of love as a transcendent force within Harry that is sufficient to vanquish the Dark Lord:

> *"There is a room in the Department of Mysteries," interrupted Dumbledore, "that is kept locked at all times. It contains a force that is at once*

more wonderful and more terrible than death, than human intelligence, than forces of nature. It is also, perhaps, the most mysterious of the many subjects for study that reside there. It is the power held within that room that you possess in such quantities and which Voldemort has not at all. That power took you to save Sirius tonight. That power saved you from possession by Voldemort, because he could not bear to reside in a body so full of the force that he detests. In the end, it mattered not that you could not close your mind. It was your heart that saved you."[14]

Harry and friends had tried to force this door with Sirius's knife in their adventure in the Department of Mysteries—but the force behind the door had melted the knife. Over Luna's objections, they choose to try another door and leave the power to save them all behind—until, as Dumbledore points out, Harry expels the possessing Voldemort by recalling his beloved Sirius. Voldemort, like Quirrell in *Philosopher's Stone*, burns and flees. Love is behind the door, love is the power that Voldemort cannot understand or endure, and it is love, the sacrificial love that saves Harry, which permeates Harry's heart and gives him a reflected part of its power.

Death and the Transcendent Meaning of Harry Potter

Rowling has told us a central theme of her books is death. Can we say that the largely spiritual, even religious, treatment of this theme is a big part of the overwhelming and still largely unexplained popularity of these books? I think we can. Before we talk about Harry's victory over death in *Deathly Hallows*, let's match up what Christians know about death with Rowling's story line.

The purpose of the Incarnation of God as Jesus of Nazareth was to destroy death by death. Love himself became a man, lived sinlessly, sacrificed himself in love for his creations, and blew a hole through the veil, figuratively speaking. With his death "the veil of the temple was rent," literally speaking (Matthew 27:51, KJV), and he opened for human beings passage to eternal life with him in God's eternal glory (also called his love and his mercy).

How do humans of body and soul participate in Christ's Resurrection? How do individuals share in Christ's victory over death? First, by living in love. All the moral virtues we have and good deeds we do are trash unless we have love, specifically his love (1 Corinthians 13). To use Rowling's language, when we take "refuge" in the bond of blood"[15]—which Christians know as the sacrificial blood of Christ on the Cross—we are fortified in Love himself against death.

Paul teaches that "the wages of sin is death" (Romans 6:23). Death, in other words, is the life spent in selfish pursuit of advantage rather than with the God who is Life and Love himself. This pseudolife apart from God is a death worse than a physical death because it promises an eternity in darkness outside the glory of God. Human beings experience true life when they choose against death and accept a life of love in resistance to selfishness and evil, spent in pursuit of communion with God, in victory over death made possible by the life and the death-destroying Resurrection of Christ.

Harry Potter doesn't lay out Christian doctrine about death explicitly until *Deathly Hallows*, but Dumbledore comes close. Death, he tells us in *Philosopher's Stone*, "to the well-organized mind is just the next great adventure." Life is not a value to be pursued in itself; what value it does have we create by our choices—for the good over what is easy. Those who love us live on in us after their death because of this love, a love which is their immortality and which protects us—the Love which Christians recognize in Christ. Dumbledore teaches Harry not to fear death as much as a life without love, which is the real death.

The *wow!* of Rowling's presentation of this theme is our vicarious experience of dying heroically in resistance to evil with Harry in every book, then rising from the dead with him to talk with Dumbledore and those we love. This shared resurrection in *Philosopher's Stone*, in case you resist the Easter parallel, comes after three days.[16] Rowling has us share in the spoils of a life spent in love and resistance to darkness by this cathartic death and resurrection—and it is the great joy, relief, and lesson of each book. Death is not final. Death has been overcome by Love himself.

And *Deathly Hallows?* I don't want to discuss the meaning of the great finish to the series both here and in the chapter devoted to that book (see chapters 17–19), but let me just say this: Rowling finishes the way you would expect, with love's victory over death and a pointer to what seems to be a specifically Christian answer to the question. Three quick references from *Deathly Hallows:*

❖ We start out with a quotation from William Penn, a notable Christian nonconformist, and a passage about the immortality and omnipresence of departed loved ones.

❖ In a critical scene in a church graveyard, Harry reads two headstones' Scripture quotations, one from the Sermon on the Mount ("Where your treasure is, there will your heart be also," Matthew 6:21, KJV) and the other from Saint Paul ("The last enemy that shall be destroyed is death," 1 Corinthians 15:26, KJV). Hermione explains to Harry that it s about "you know . . . living beyond death. Living after death."[17] Rowling said this in an Open Book Tour interview in 2007: "I think those two particular quotations he finds on the tombstones at Godric's Hollow, they sum up—they almost epitomize the whole series."[18]

❖ Harry offers his life as a sacrificial lamb to defeat the Evil One, and he walks the Via Dolorosa into the Forbidden Forest in the company of his mother and a trinity of friends. He winds up at King's Cross but returns to the Forest, where Narcissa's "nails pierced him."[19] He feigns death but reveals himself at the rising of the sun and vanquishes the Dark Lord with the truth, with an invitation to repentance, and by turning his own death curse upon himself. Harry's holly and

phoenix-feather wand is restored so he can put away the
buckthorn and hawthorn sticks he's been using.

That would mean an ending featuring a loving sacrifice, King's
Cross, nails, thorns, and a resurrection from the dead that defeats
an incarnation of death.

Maybe that's not transparent enough for some readers, but
it isn't especially opaque. MTV even commented in the interview
mentioned above that the Scripture passages and Hermione's
explanation were "the central foundations of resurrection theology." Rowling ends the Potter epic with something of a parallel Passion gospel in story form. "O death, where is thy sting? O grave,
where is thy victory?" (1 Corinthians 15:55, KJV). Love has won its
victory over death.

The great mystery of human existence is death. Rowling has
given what seems to be a profoundly spiritual and Christian answer
to this question throughout the Harry Potter series and especially in
its finale. The enthusiastic and uniformly positive response outside
of the most contentious of academic ghettos and fundamentalist
cults points to this answer fitting what Pascal called the God-sized
hole in human hearts, even—perhaps especially—in hearts immunized by school and state against the presence of Light and Love
himself.

8

THE QUESTION
OF IDENTITY

Harry defines himself through choices,
change, and destiny.

Choice is the human ability to decide between two options.[1] If this faculty is well trained, a person is able to discriminate or choose well between options of good and evil, right and wrong, advantage and disadvantage. In each of the Harry Potter stories, we're able to see just what constitutes "good choosing."

The first dimension of choice is the implicit level. Harry makes two types of choices in every book—about what sort of person he is and about what to do in a crisis—and he consistently chooses what is right over what is easy.

Let's look at the choices Harry makes—choices that will define who he is. In each decision, Harry has the option of loyalty to a high and difficult standard versus personal advantage. He chooses (with one exception that has heavy consequences) loyalty to the good.

- ❖ In *Philosopher's Stone*, Harry asks not to be put in Slytherin House, though Draco Malfoy and the Sorting Hat point to Slytherin as his path to power.
- ❖ At the same time, he chooses to be friends with Ron and Hermione—one poor, the other unpopular and of questionable lineage, despite being advised (again by Draco) to avoid hanging out with "riffraff."
- ❖ In *Chamber of Secrets*, Harry professes his loyalty to Dumbledore at the risk of being murdered by Riddle/Voldemort, Dumbledore's enemy.
- ❖ In *Prisoner of Azkaban*, Harry chooses to spare Pettigrew, who betrayed Harry's parents to their murderer, out of loyalty to his understanding of what his father would have wanted.
- ❖ In *Goblet of Fire*, Harry refuses to reconcile with Ron, despite loneliness and friendship for Ron, in loyalty to the truth.
- ❖ Later in the same book, Harry withstands persecution by the media, unabashed again because of his commitment to standing with what is true over what others think.
- ❖ In *Order of the Phoenix*, Harry chooses the easy way (*not* to study Occlumency with Snape and before bed), and the consequence is Sirius's coming to the Department of Mysteries to rescue Harry—and dying in battle.
- ❖ In *Half-Blood Prince*, Harry chooses to ignore Dumbledore's unqualified trust in Severus Snape and Ron and Hermione's skepticism about Draco being the youngest Death Eater in favor of his "age-old" prejudice against the Slytherins. The consequences of this surety in his opinions play out painfully in *Deathly Hallows*.
- ❖ In *Deathly Hallows*, Harry chooses to pursue Horcruxes in obedience to Dumbledore's direction rather than try to find the Deathly Hallows. He does this despite doubts in Dumbledore's goodness and out of loyalty to Dobby's sacrificial example.

These internal choices are significant, and they are paired in each book with a life-or-death decision. Each choice occurs as the result of a crisis in which Harry must choose between what is safe and easy for him versus resisting evil at risk of his life. He chooses each time to do the right, dangerous thing. Consider the following life-or-death decisions:

❖ In *Philosopher's Stone*, Harry chooses to pass Fluffy and enter the trapdoor in order to keep the Stone from Snape and Voldemort.

❖ In *Chamber of Secrets*, he opts to search for the Chamber in order to find Ron's sister Ginny, and in the Chamber he elects to fight Riddle against all odds.

❖ In *Prisoner of Azkaban*, Harry dives in front of Peter Pettigrew, saving him from Lupin and Black, who have wands drawn to kill him for betraying Lily and James Potter to Voldemort.

❖ In *Goblet of Fire*, Harry chooses to warn Cedric of a giant spider about to attack him (though that would have cleared his way to victory—and the spider turns on Harry!). He also chooses to resist and attack Voldemort in the graveyard—again, against all odds.

❖ In *Order of the Phoenix*, Harry "learns" in a dream that Sirius is being tortured by Death Eaters and rushes to his rescue.

❖ In *Half-Blood Prince*, Harry learns almost simultaneously of the mission to find the cave Horcrux and of a man who is celebrating in the Room of Requirement, which he rightly assumes is a sign that Malfoy has completed his assign-ment. Harry chooses to go with Dumbledore—and to "call up" Dumbledore's army to patrol the castle in their absence.

❖ In *Deathly Hallows*, Severus's memories reveal to Harry that he must die if Voldemort is to be defeated and that he must die without fighting back. Harry walks into the Forbidden Forest and lays down his life voluntarily.

Harry's choices deliver the implicit message "Do the hard, right thing; don't take the easy, advantageous route." What does Dumble-dore teach us about choice in his discussions with Harry and others? You guessed it: "Your choices are what matter" and "Choose what is right over what is easy."

In *Chamber of Secrets*, Harry is confronted repeatedly with suggestions that he is somehow akin to the Dark Lord. He learns at the end, from both Voldemort and Dumbledore, that there is some truth in that. Harry then asks Dumbledore if he should have been put in Slytherin House, where (Harry believes) the Sorting Hat thought he belonged. Dumbledore responds that while Harry has much in common with Voldemort and the Slytherins, he is different from the bad guys largely because he *asked* not to be put in Slytherin House. "It is our choices, Harry, that show who we truly are, far more than our abilities."[2]

Dumbledore reemphasizes the relative importance of our choices compared with our birthright in *Goblet of Fire*. Confronting the stuffed-shirt Minister of Magic, he bares Fudge's prejudice by pointing to the fate of Barty Crouch Jr. "Your Dementor has just destroyed the last remaining member of a pure-blood family as old as any—and see what that man chose to make of his life!"[3]

Your life is of value only if you choose the good over what is easy and evil. Dumbledore drives this point home in Churchill-like cadences to the assembled Hogwarts student body in the conclusion of his tribute to Cedric Diggory when he says, "Remember if the time should come when you have to make a choice between what is right and what is easy, remember what happened to a boy who was good and kind and brave, because he strayed across the path of Lord Voldemort."[4]

So we have the *implicit* treatment of choice in what choices Harry makes, and we have the *explicit* dimension in Dumbledore's talks on choice. Harry is often forced to make these difficult choices during the scenes of greatest drama, when we are most engaged in the story. In this way, we identify with Harry and make the choice with him, usually amazed at our own virtue.

In her treatment of choice Rowling engages us not in the choosing per se (as it was when "dying" with Harry) but in *the goodness we experience as we choose the harder, virtuous, self-sacrificing option with Harry.* C. S. Lewis called this "training in the Stock Responses" and thought it the responsibility of the better writer. Rowling stands with Lewis in using her art to assist our growth in virtue. And her readers like that. A lot. We participate imaginatively with the characters when they make good choices—and this reading experience positively influences the decision making in our own lives. Sort of like vitamins for the soul.

Choices aren't that big a deal, of course, except in the context of change or personal transformation. Dumbledore chides Fudge for not understanding that it is choice, not blood, that shapes the human person—and Draco Malfoy is always telling Harry the same thing.[5] Even the bad guys understand that your choices shape who you become. Choices we make both reflect the character we have and shape the character we will have. This is the same idea as keeping your house clean; it reflects the value you give order, and it shapes and confirms this priority in your life.

Now that we have discussed choice in Harry Potter, let's move on to a look at the consequences of our choices, that is, what we become: our changes and transformations.

Change in Harry Potter

Transfiguration is a required course in the Hogwarts curriculum. *Transfiguration* comes from the Latin *trans*, meaning "across" (hence "motion, change"), and *figura*, meaning "form, appearance, shape"— in other words, "shape changing." Young wizards and witches at Hogwarts are taught from the first year on the basics of turning beetles into buttons, up to the advanced magic (not with teacher approval, it seems) of "turning [your] friend into a badger."[6] Even though the Transfigurations Masters we meet in the stories are usually good guys, not all shape-changers are good!

There is, for example, a rather nasty creature called a Boggart that we meet in *Prisoner of Azkaban* that takes on the appearance of what a person fears most. It can be dispersed by a Riddikulus Charm and laughter—humor is a valuable weapon in fighting fear and evil.

One of the more poetic aspects of transfiguration is that those who take the shape of animals become animals that are metaphors for their human characters. When Moody punishes Malfoy for attacking Harry when his back is turned, the sneaky and rodentlike Draco becomes a ferret that Moody bounces up and down with his wand. Hagrid tries to turn Dudley into a pig but only succeeds in giving him a curly pig's tail because, as he explains, Dudley is "so much like a pig there wasn't much left ter do."[7] The obnoxious and nosy reporter Rita Skeeter, of course, becomes a bug for the purpose of eavesdropping as an (illegal and unregistered) animagus.

If Harry's choices are good and good choices mean good changes, then we should see Harry changing via his choices and experiences from a child to a more mature, in-control, self-monitoring "human animal" (if you will) over the course of each year at Hogwarts. Not as exciting as watching Malfoy change into a ferret perhaps (if his choices seem to be confirming him in that role), but Harry's changes should be almost as dramatic. In fact, they are:

❖ When we meet Harry in *Philosopher's Stone* he is a victim of his step-family's abuses and seemingly has no heritage. He has become, by book's end, a victor in battle against the Dark Lord and the heir of his family's legacy. How? It is through his heroic choices, in which he chooses the good over his personal gain.

❖ *Chamber of Secrets*, too, opens with Harry literally and figuratively a prisoner; the Dursleys have locked him in his room, and he is moored in his own self-doubts and self-pity. He saves Ginny from her enchantment by the Dark Lord and escapes the Chamber at the end of the book on the wings of a phoenix, in every sense a free man. This transformation from prisoner to liberator is again a function of his choosing what is right rather than what is easy.

❖ In *Prisoner of Azkaban*, Harry's transformation is more profound than in any other book in the series until *Order of the Phoenix*.

Prisoner of Azkaban opens with Harry not at all in control of his passions. Vernon Dursley's sister, Aunt Marge, patronizes Harry as an unwelcome burden on his brother and at last insults him and his parents as an example of bad blood and poor breeding. Marge is a bulldog fancier, and given her name and the bulldog's being to Britain what the eagle is to America, I have to suspect she is a rather transparent caricature of Margaret Thatcher and her uncharitable opinions about dole recipients.

Harry's response? He tries some self-control techniques to ignore her but of course fails. He has too many unresolved feelings and unanswered questions about his parents' death and especially about his dad to suffer Aunt Marge gladly. In a rage (and without a wand), Harry makes this woman, so full of herself, into a three-dimensional picture of her character by "blowing her up"—not as a bomb blows up, but as a balloon. Aunt Marge and her bulldog point to Margaret Thatcher and John Bull patriots who Rowling believes were self-inflated monsters.

Harry experiences the death of his parents again and again in *Prisoner of Azkaban*, courtesy of the Dementors and a Boggart. He learns from his analyst, "Dr." Lupin, how to fight off the depression and despair brought on by these nasties. When he learns in the Shrieking Shack of Pettigrew's Judas-like betrayal, he has been changed so much by his choices in therapy and his consequent enlightenment that not only does he refrain from attacking Pettigrew, but he risks his own life to save Wormtail.

Harry has transformed from a passionate child rushing to judgment and punishment on Privet Drive to a young adult capable of great discernment and semidivine mercy. Both Dumbledore and Black comment that at last Harry is "truly [his] father's son."[8] He has become not really an orphan but a living image of his father.

❖ Harry begins *Goblet of Fire* as a boy understandably concerned about what others think and say about him. His experiences and choices following a fight with Ron and an article in the *Daily Prophet* transform him into a mature young man more interested in "being" than "seeming." His personal integrity and emotional maturity allow him to rise above popularity concerns or fear of slander.

When Rita Skeeter's second article about Harry in the *Daily Prophet* appears on the morning of the last Triwizard task (titled "Harry Potter: Disturbed and Dangerous"), Harry shrugs off her portrayal of him as a troubled mental defective. "'Gone off me a bit, hasn't she?' said Harry lightly, folding up the paper."[9] This accomplishment is in a way more remarkable than his successes in the Triwizard Tournament tasks and is the foundation of his ability to fight Voldemort to a draw at the Dark Lord's rebirthing party. The primary characters in Harry Potter, although mostly children, are never especially childish; by the end of *Goblet of Fire*, Harry has transformed into a real he-man of sacrificial virtue and is nearly a superhero.

❖ In the opening of *Order of the Phoenix*, Harry is a caged animal who looks outside himself for his bearings. He digs in garbage cans for newspapers and fights to listen to the evening news for some word about Voldemort's return. By the end of the book, the exterior world has stripped Harry of everything about himself because of the choices he makes to speak the truth and be loyal to his friends. Though he never learns the introverted skill of Occlumency, his losses through the year (and especially the death of his godfather, Sirius) turn him inside out from year's start. By the end of the book, Harry has learned to look to his heart for his bearings and to the world for very little.

❖ When we meet Harry in *Half-Blood Prince*, he is half-asleep, "looking through a glass darkly," waiting for Dumbledore, and very much in doubt that Albus will come (though the headmaster had written in no uncertain terms that he would come). Harry testifies to Scrimgeour at story's end, after Dumbledore's funeral, that he is "Dumbledore's man, through and through" and that he feels his mentor's presence in death more nearly than he did while living.

❖ Harry's faith in Dumbledore comes under sharp attack in the opening of *Deathly Hallows*, and it is an effective attack. At a low point he tells Hermione that Dumbledore never shared the truth with Harry and that the headmaster didn't love him.[10] By book's end, however, the headmaster explains to him that Harry is "the better man"[11] because of his selfless choices and sacrifices made despite his doubts.

One aside here. As we talked about earlier, much of the imagery of change in the Potter novels springs from the tradition of alchemical symbolism in English literature. Every Potter book ends with a superheated crucible scene, or rubedo, in which the characters reveal themselves and transform into greater or lesser people (see the chapters on individual books for more on this). Dissolution, purification, and perfection, the three stages of the alchemical Great Work (and of changing the human soul from lead to gold), are reflected in Harry's transformations.

Perhaps the formula of "good, hard choices make good people" strikes you as a little simplistic, leaving out as it does both ideas of fate or destiny and even the seeming arbitrariness of who is born into which families (the big "Sorting Hat"). This "fate or free will" question hangs over English literature. As it is often posed, the fate/free will question goes something like this: God sees all and knows all—past, present, and future—so in what sense can human beings be said to act freely? If all human action is foreordained in God's knowledge, this contradicts the idea of human freedom and God's revelation that he longs for our freewill decision to live in communion with his divine will. In less theological language, the question has been posed as a matter of our programming. Are we simply programmed machines of matter and energy, designed to reproduce our specific programming? From this perspective, even acts of self-sacrifice are understood as defenses of the local gene pool; free will and altruism are fictitious concepts, no more, no less.

This is no small matter. You read every day or hear from friends about how circumstances outside someone's control (read "fate," "destiny," or even "providence") *determine* a person's actions and character. Perhaps they grew up poor in a bad neighborhood or with parents who neglected and beat them. The Harry Potter books have a different, sobering emphasis. Whereas our popular culture often excuses people based on their circumstances, these books raise the question of responsibility for our actions and point out that our choices have moral significance.

The Harry Potter books take aim at the "you're as good or bad as your programming" position. Again and again, we see that it's our choices that shape us; if we make the good, hard choices against evil, we will become a better person.

But it's clear that even Rowling's characters are born with a destiny. As hinted strongly in the first books and revealed outright in *Order of the Phoenix*, Harry has been born with the mother lode of responsibility. In three stages, we've come to think of Harry as more than the sum of his choices.

First, it was the King Arthur references. From the opening of *Philosopher's Stone*, the parallels with the legend of King Arthur are remarkable. Harry and Arthur are both orphans hidden and protected by grand wizards. Harry's being shown respect by the chess king in *Philosopher's Stone* points to his innate royalty. Even the magical sky ceiling above the Great Hall at Hogwarts is an exact copy of the enchanted ceiling above the round table at Camelot. And just as Arthur pulls a sword from a stone to show he is the rightful heir to the throne, so Harry pulls the sword of Godric Gryffindor from the Sorting Hat in *Chamber of Secrets*. Harry's love for (and romance with, in *Half-Blood Prince*) Ginny Weasley, whose first name is "Ginevra," a variant of "Guinevere," is just icing on the Arthurian cake.

Second, we have the Heir of Gryffindor references. Besides Harry being called "a true Gryffindor" by Dumbledore at the end of *Chamber of Secrets* and the red and gold sparks that fly from Harry's wand involuntarily when he's angry,[12] the Gryffindor/Slytherin opposition throughout the books points to Harry as Heir of Gryffindor.

Both Harry and Voldemort are not from pureblood families. Both Harry and Voldemort grew up as orphans in painful living situations. Both have qualities in common: "Parseltongue—resourcefulness—determination—a certain disregard for rules."[13] Tom Riddle says, "We even *look* something alike."[14] Harry and Voldemort are mirror-reflection doppelgängers; the apposition of Harry with Voldemort, the Heir of Slytherin, throughout the books suggests Voldemort knows Harry is Heir of Gryffindor. Gryffindor means "golden griffin" (golden eagle/lion) and is a pointer to Christ, the King of Heaven and earth (see chapter 9). Harry, as Heir of Gryffindor, is clearly more than your average boy wizard or just the product of his environment and choices.

Third and last are the revelations of the prophecy in *Order of the Phoenix*. We've already seen that Harry (and/or Neville) was prophesied before his birth to be the coming vanquisher of Voldemort, complete with a power the Dark Lord "knows not." The vanquisher's life is not one he can choose to disregard; the prophecy says in detail that the Dark Lord and his vanquisher have a kill-or-be-killed relationship that isn't to be ducked. Like King Arthur, Harry—as Heir of Gryffindor and prophesied vanquisher of the Dark Lord—is a boy with a remarkable "career track"!

So the question, now that we know that Harry was born into this giant-sized destiny, is how important are his choices after all? Wasn't he born to his difficult, heroic choices the same way Malfoy was born to his nasty Slytherin decisions? Isn't his seeming free will just a function of his predestined programming?

Rowling takes aim at this view, both in interviews (as she gave at the publication of *Half-Blood Prince*) and in the narrative of *Half-Blood Prince* itself. In this book, Dumbledore's big teaching moment comes before the adventure in the cave and the Astronomy Tower. He enlightens Harry about the difference between fatalism—that is, a future predetermined by God or circumstances to which one is resigned—and human freedom, which is choosing as best as one can to meet one's destiny heroically. Here is Harry's reaction:

> He understood at last what Dumbledore had been trying to tell him. It was, he thought, the difference between being dragged into the arena to face a battle to the death and walking into the arena with your head held high. Some people, perhaps, would say that there was little to choose between the two ways, but Dumbledore knew—*and so do I,* thought Harry with a rush of fierce pride, *and so did my parents*—that there was all the difference in the world.[15]

Harry's conviction that making the choice himself makes all the difference is, of course, put sorely to the test in *Deathly Hallows,* in which book all the romance of being "the Chosen One" rubs off, leaving Harry alone and chosen seemingly only for an ignominious death.

If the reader wants to believe in an existential fatalism, something like Harry sitting at the window staring into the darkness and doubting the arrival of his deliverance, rather than in moral virtue and heroic choice of the good, that reader is fighting the tide of Rowling's message. The human heart thrills in resonance to Harry's heroic decisions—decisions made (until Dumbledore's revelations at the end of *Order of the Phoenix) without knowledge of his destiny* and throughout *Deathly Hallows* without much hope that his destiny was any help to him at all. Readers around the world share his programming, it seems, to the tune of more than 375 million copies of Harry's stories being sold. If this is only a matter of programming, there seems a prevalent programming in the human person for sacrificial, altruistic, loving service that loyalty to the local gene pool does not explain. Why do readers thrill to Harry's choices if they're just a function of his being the boy born to be "king"?[16]

The answer to this question brings us to the spiritual meaning of choice and change in Harry Potter. Harry, it turns out, has a larger-than-life destiny (vanquish Voldemort; save the world) but he can realize this destiny only by making the right choices and becoming the sort of person—an embodiment of love, the power the Dark Lord knows not—able to defeat the Dark Lord. He has to transcend his ego concerns, even his inherited prejudices and the doubts he knows are meaningful reasons not to believe or obey.

Yes, Harry has a destiny, but his freewill choices are what will make the difference between his realizing his prophesied end or not. Why do readers' hearts around the world thrill to this message? Because human beings everywhere know that they, too, have a prophesied end in which their choices every day, choices for or against their becoming more loving people and more like God, are the deal makers or breakers. Christians tell us that every person is born as an image of God, created for an eternal life in his presence. We have a choice, however, because of the free will given to us by him; we can become images in the *likeness* of God by choosing love over death and sharing in the Resurrection of Love himself—or we can choose the easy road of advantage and personal comfort (a metaphor in our hearts for immunity to pain and death). It is our daily choices that make this difference: image or likeness? Love or death?

Reading Harry Potter is an edifying lift and support for human beings, be they believers looking for a "spiritual supplement" or nonbelievers whose only spiritual experience comes from the mythic or religious experiences they have from books and movies. As *homo religiosus*, we have faculties of soul only exercised and satisfied by experiences pointing to and confirming our beginnings and endings in realities that transcend time, space, and mortal concerns. By reading these books and identifying with the hero's good choices, readers get a boost via their imaginations to do the right thing in difficult circumstances themselves. Our circumstances may make these choices relatively hard or obvious, but Harry's choices point us to the ones we must make in order to realize our prophesied destinies as children of God and heirs of the *real* Golden Griffin.

Ever wonder what a griffin symbolizes or why story symbols are such a big deal? Just make the hard, right choice to keep reading and watch as your understanding is transformed!

9

EVIDENCE OF
THINGS UNSEEN

*The symbols in Potterdom are powerful
pointers to spiritual realities.*

Do you groan when you read the word *symbolism?* If so, I bet I know why. You had a high school English teacher like mine who made sure you "got" the symbolism in everything you read—from the great White Whale in *Moby Dick* to the all-seeing billboard eyeglasses in *The Great Gatsby.* Problem was, she never explained how symbolism worked or why these supposedly great writers were spending so much time hiding what they meant behind silly images and metaphors. I figured it was just another adult game for writers and literature teachers to enjoy.

Boy, was I wrong. I will go so far as to say that this chapter on symbolism is the most important chapter in this book in terms of our ability to understand the popularity of Harry Potter, to understand the specifically Christian meaning of the books, and even to understand the *right* reasons for parents to object to stories their children are reading. Once we understand symbols we can better understand what it means to be human. As Christians who believe we are creatures made in "the image of God" (Genesis 1:26-27), we have to take seriously the idea, at least when studying English literature, that we are indeed three-dimensional symbols, in time and space, of the Trinity.

The world we live in is incomprehensible except in light of symbols. As Martin Lings, tutorial student and friend of C. S. Lewis, wrote:

> There is no traditional doctrine which does not teach that
> the world is the world of symbols, inasmuch as it contains
> nothing which is not a symbol. A man should therefore
> understand at least what that means, not only because he has
> to live in the herebelow but also and above all because with-
> out such understanding he would fail to understand himself,
> he being the supreme and central symbol in the terrestrial
> state.[1]

Symbolism, it turns out, is not just an English major's thing—it's a human thing.

Let's start by ridding ourselves of some of the mistaken ideas we may have been taught about symbolism. Symbolism is not something "standing in" for something else, a tit-for-tat allegory. An allegory is a story or word picture in which something exist-ing on earth is represented by another earthly character or image. Some critics, for example, have written that *The Lord of the Rings* is an allegory of the Second World War, with Sauron and the forces of darkness standing in for the Axis powers while the Fellowship of the Ring and other white hats represent the Allies. As readers, we don't interpret allegories as much as we translate them; allegories, unlike symbols, are just a translation of one story into another lan-guage or story. Neither are symbols simply signs, or at least they are not like street signs, which are simple representations for earthly instructions or things (such as Stop or Deer Crossing).

Literary characters and stories are not necessarily symbolic. Great novels like *The Pilgrim's Progress* are allegorical both in regard to their characters and story line. Christian's journey in *Progress* is a detailed picture of events and people met on every Christian's earthly journey. The men that he meets—I think immediately of "Mr. Worldly Wiseman" (a great stand-in for television talking heads!)— are cardboard cutouts of people we meet every day who support or obstruct us in our passage to the heavenly Kingdom.

Many stories that are symbolic, however, are often mistakenly explained (and dismissed) as allegories. Please note that little else disturbed C. S. Lewis and J. R. R. Tolkien as much as critical explanation of their fiction as "allegorical" (as in the WWII analogy). The reason their books touch us so deeply and have endured in popularity as long as they have is because of their symbolic meaning.

Symbols, rather than analogies for other earthly events, are transparencies through which we see greater realities than we can see on earth (see 1 Corinthians 13:12 and 2 Corinthians 3:18). The ocean as it stretches to the distant horizon is a symbol of the infinite power and breadth of the spiritual reality human beings call God. In seeing the one, we can sense the other. The ocean as a body of water has no power in itself to stir the heart; it's just an oversized bathtub. But as a symbol of God, a way of seeing the unseeable, it can take our breath away or bring tears to our eyes.

Symbols are windows, too, through which otherworldly realities (powers, graces, and qualities) intrude into the world. As Lings wrote, this is the traditional understanding of Creation— that all earthly things and events testify to "the invisible things of him from the creation of the world" (Romans 1:20, KJV). This testimony includes the power of natural beauty and grandeur (think of mountain ranges, a field of flowers, or a lion on the savanna). It also includes sacred art, architecture, and liturgy, which are by definition symbolic in their portrayal of greater than earthly realities.[2]

Christ, of course, speaks in story symbols, too, through his parables. He knows we cannot understand the truth as it exists, so he wraps these truths in edifying stories or windows we can look through in order to experience some likeness of truth. "These things have I spoken unto you in proverbs: but the time cometh, when I shall no more speak unto you in proverbs, but I shall shew you plainly of the Father" (John 16:25, KJV). Until we see things "face to face" (1 Corinthians 13:12), though, we have symbols to understand ourselves and Creation.

The great revealed traditions teach that man, as an image and likeness of God, is a living symbol—both in the sense of transparency through which we look and of an opening through which God enters the world. Mankind is created in the image of God so that the world will reverence the God who cannot be seen (see 1 John 4:20 and the sequence of the Great Commandments in Mark 12:30-31). Humanity also is designed to be a vehicle of God's grace, power, and love intruding into the world of time and space. The tragedy of man's "fall" is that, because most people no longer believe they are symbols of God, shaped in his likeness, it is more difficult to see God in our neighbor, and the world is often denied access to God through his chosen vessels.

We are still moved, however, by the symbols in nature and the symbols that we experience in story form. This is the power of myth: that we can experience invisible spiritual realities and truths greater than visible, material things in story form. Tolkien described Christianity as the "True Myth," the ultimate intrusion of God into the world through his Incarnation as Jesus of Nazareth. Tolkein's explanation of this idea was instrumental in C. S. Lewis's conversion to Christianity; it is this understanding of the purpose and power of story that gives his fiction its depth, breadth, and height.

Symbols in stories, just as the symbols in nature, sacred art, and edifying myths, are able to put us in contact with a greater reality than what we can sense directly. They do this through our imagination. The power of Lewis's and Tolkien's writing is found in their profound symbolism; *The Lord of the Rings* is not a strained allegory or retelling of WWII but a dynamic symbol of the cosmic struggle between good and evil of which WWII was also but a real-world representation.

What This Means for Understanding Harry Potter

Knowing that symbols are points of passage between this world and the greater world "above"—and "within"—us explains a lot about Harry Potter and Potter-mania. Magic, for example, is not demonic or contrary to Scripture when used (as it is in Harry Potter) as a symbol of the miraculous power of God that men as images of God are designed to have (see John 14:12 and chapter 1 of this book).

Books that are rich in symbolism necessarily support a transcendent worldview. The difference between believers and atheists or agnostics is that the secular crowd does not believe that anything exists beyond what can be sensed or measured. Everything is a this-worldly quantity. Christians and other believers understand the world to be a shadow of the reality of its Creator and that this greater reality—God—is rightly the focus of our lives. Symbolic literature requires—and celebrates—this otherworldly perspective that magically undermines the worldly, atheistic, and materialist perspective of our times.

This explains, too, why books that are rich in specifically Christian imagery and symbols are as powerful and popular as they are. Tertullian said that "all souls are Christian souls" and Augustine echoed him in writing that "our hearts are restless 'til they rest in Thee." Tertullian was not making a sectarian argument contra Islam or Buddhism in saying "all souls are Christian souls." Instead, he was pointing out the universal human end in the God who is Love. Since we as human beings are designed for the experience of this God, stories that retell the Great Story of our greater life in the Spirit satisfy the longing we are hardwired to feel and answer.

Unlike most contemporary novels, which portray realistic morals or earthbound allegories, Harry Potter is very much a myth pointing to the True Myth. Take, for instance, lead characters Harry, Ron, and Hermione. I already explained how Harry's two friends are ciphers for the "quarreling couple" of alchemy, but there is a more profound symbolism the trio, Snape's "Dream Team," make up.

What's great about this usage is that you've seen it before. Take a look at this chart:

Work	Body (Desire)	Mind (Will)	Spirit (Heart)
Fyodor Dostoyevsky's *Brothers Karamazov*	Dmitri Karamazov	Ivan Karamazov	Alyosha Karamazov
C. S. Lewis's *Narnia Chronicles*	Edmund Pevensie	Peter Pevensie	Lucy Pevensie
J. R. R. Tolkien's *Lord of the Rings*	Smeagol (Gollum)	Sam Gamgee	Frodo Baggins
Gene Roddenberry's *Star Trek*	Bones	Spock	Kirk
George Lucas's *Star Wars*	Han Solo	Princess Leia	Luke Skywalker
J. K. Rowling's *Harry Potter*	Ron Weasley	Hermione Granger	Harry Potter

Writers as different as Dostoyevsky and Tolkien, television producers and moviemakers, have all used this particular symbolism—because it works. Man is most obviously an image of God in that his soul is three parts; it has three faculties or powers symbolizing the three persons of the Godhead.[3] We call these powers "belly," "head," and "chest," or more commonly "body," "mind," and "spirit."[4]

Rather than try to show how these three principal faculties respond to situations as a sum in every character, artists can create characters that represent *one* of these faculties and show in story how these powers of the soul relate to one another. Every one of the original *Star Trek* television shows, for example, was a psychic drama of Kirk (spirit) leading Spock (mind) and Bones (body) against some outer-space adversary.

Harry, Ron, and Hermione can easily be connected with their corresponding faculties. Ron is the physical, comfort-focused complainer; Hermione, the thinker; and Harry, the heroic heart that leads the company.

So what? To understand the purpose and power of this literary model, take a moment to think of Harry, Ron, and Hermione's relationships—when they work and when they don't. Harry is clearly in charge. Hermione is the best thinker. Ron is the cheerleader and flag-waver (in his best moments). When they follow Harry's lead in line—Harry, Hermione, Ron—all goes well. Think of their assault on the obstacles leading to the Philosopher's Stone in the first book or their teamwork to get to the Chamber of Secrets: amazing work for preteens.

But when the team breaks down and the players don't play their roles or won't play them in obedience to Harry, things go wrong in the worst way. In the first six books, this happened twice, both times because Ron, low man in the hierarchy of faculties, takes the wrong role, and both of these times were pointers to his defection in *Deathly Hallows*.

In *Prisoner of Azkaban*, Ron takes the lead position. He gets into a bitter fight with Hermione about her decision to tell Professor McGonagall about Harry's broom and then about her pet cat's seeming to have made a meal of his pet rat. As Hagrid points out, a broom and a rat are hardly reason to throw off a friend, especially a friend in need; but no matter, Harry follows Ron's passionate cues and stops speaking to Hermione. Harry also decides to go to Hogsmeade on Ron's advice and against Hermione's pleas—and narrowly misses being expelled. Lupin shames Harry; Ron comes to his senses, apologizes to Harry, and they reconcile with Hermione—with Ron again in a place of service to his friends.

In *Goblet of Fire*, Ron breaks entirely with Harry out of jealousy and meanness of spirit when Harry is chosen by the Goblet to be a school champion. Ron is pathetic on his own, and Harry misses his friend terribly, but he learned his lesson in *Prisoner of Azkaban:* the heart following selfish, spiteful passions gets you nowhere good, fast. Ron returns to the fold after the first Triwizard task, the danger of which seems to have jerked him back into remembrance of his rightful place in Harry's service.

These two misadventures and reconciliations were only foreshadowing for Ron's leaving Harry and Hermione in *Deathly Hallows* and his spiritual purification on his return in the Forest of Dean (see chapter 17's discussion of "The Silver Doe"). As with the previous split and makeup, the trio and readers are in agony about the betrayal and longing for the return of order.

We should remember that it is Hermione who almost has nervous breakdowns during her time apart from Harry and Ron and during Ron's breaks with Harry and with her. This is not feminine weakness, but rather a picture of the fragility of an intellect that is disembodied and heartless. Part of Hermione's brilliance is her determined dependence on her friends; she understands that her jewel intelligence is glorious in its right setting and almost inhuman on its own (remember Hermione at the beginning of *Philosopher's Stone?*). Her difficulty in accepting Ron's return in *Deathly Hallows* speaks to her greater injury in his absence.

In *Order of the Phoenix*, Harry is separated from Ron and Hermione by virtue of their being selected as house prefects. Ron and Hermione both flourish as they take on responsibilities independent of Harry—and at the same time, their appreciation for him and their friendship grows apace. The trio's love for one another and our identification with them makes their hard times with each other the most painful parts of the stories—and their reconciliation the most joyous. We become aligned in this identification—spirit to mind to body—and feel strangely upright and all right for the change.

Good literature trains us in the "stock responses" and lets us see and pattern ourselves after the right alignment of the soul's powers. When our desires are in line with our will, and both will and desires are obedient to directions from the heart or spirit, we are in operation the way we were designed to be, "spirit side up," if you will. Turn this upside down, though, so that will and spirit answer to the desires (as the commercials in our desire-driven culture would have it), and you have a wreck-in-the-making. The human person isn't designed to be belly-led, as Scripture, history, and experience all testify (see Romans 16:18 and Philippians 3:19, and visit any one of the addiction recovery programs in your neighborhood for verification).

Mythical Beasts in Harry Potter

For most of us, the connection between an animal and its symbolic quality is pretty clear. A dog embodies and radiates the virtue of loyalty; a cat, feminine beauty and grace; a lion, power and majesty; an eagle, freedom; and a horse, nobility.

The animals in Harry Potter, though, are not your conventional domestic pets or zoo beasts. Rowling has a rich imagination and a special fascination for fantastic beasts; she has even written a Hogwarts "schoolbook," *Fantastic Beasts and Where to Find Them,* cataloging her favorites, A–Z. Are these products of her imagination symbols in the way eagles and lions are symbols?

Yes and no. No, I don't think a fictional lion (say, the one that occurs throughout the Potter books on the banners of Gryffindor House or the lion Aslan in Lewis's Chronicles of Narnia) has the same power to suggest "majesty" as a real lion on the savanna. One works through the sense of vision and the other through the imagination. But, yes, if the fictional beast is capably depicted, both contain the quality that makes the lion regal and stirs the heart.

Many of the animals in Harry Potter are Rowling's own inventions (although the acromantula reminds Tolkien fans of the giant spider Shelob and of the den of spiders in *The Hobbit*). However, let's focus on traditional symbols from European and especially English literature because of the wealth of references that support the interpretation of their supernatural qualities. If there is a single giveaway of the transcendent and specifically Christian meaning in Harry Potter, it is in the uniform meaning of the symbols. The magical creatures and figures we will look at more closely are the griffin, the unicorn, the phoenix, the stag, the centaur, the hippogriff, the Philosopher's Stone, and the red lion. Each is a traditional symbol of arts and letters in the English tradition used to point to the qualities and person of Christ.

THE GRIFFIN

I've found only two mentions of a griffin per se in the Harry Potter books, and they are details mentioned in connection to Dumbledore's office. Professor McGonagall is bringing Harry there in *Chamber of Secrets* after he has been discovered next to the petrified forms of Justin Finch-Fletchley and Nearly Headless Nick: "Harry saw a gleaming oak door ahead, with a brass knocker in the shape of a griffin."[5] The password keeper on the stairs leading to Dumbledore's office that Harry passes twice in the last chapters of *Deathly Hallows* is also a griffin.

The griffin is described in *Fantastic Beasts* as having "the front legs and head of a giant eagle, but the body and hind legs of a lion."[6] It is an important symbol in the Potter series, though only mentioned at Dumbledore's office entrance, because "Harry's House, Gryffindor, literally means 'golden griffin' in French (*or* is French for 'gold')."[7] So spell it "Griffin d'or." As Harry is considered a "true Gryffindor" in Dumbledore's estimation,[8] you can put a bet on there being great significance in the meaning of golden griffin for the identity of Harry Potter.

How does a beast that is half lion and half eagle symbolize Jesus Christ? Two ways. First, Christ is the God-Man, so double-natured symbols are a natural match for him. More important, though, is that the two natures here are the lion and eagle. A beast that is half "king of the heavens" (eagle) and half "king of the earth" (lion) points to the God-Man in his role as King of Heaven and earth.[9]

THE UNICORN

Harry first meets a unicorn in the Forbidden Forest under the worst of conditions. The unicorn is dying or dead; Voldemort, as something like a snake, is drinking its blood, which "tonic" curses the drinker but keeps him alive.[10] Unicorns pop up again in Ms. Grubbly-Plank's and Hagrid's Care of Magical Creatures Classes.[11]

I remember as a young boy being taken to the Cloisters, a New York museum of medieval art in an authentic castle brought stone by stone from Europe. The highlight of the trip was the tapestries—specifically the unicorn tapestries. The guide told us that the unicorn was the symbol of Christ preferred by the weavers of these giant pieces. Though I was a child of no special faith (or sensitivity), I was moved by the images of the unicorn being chased, captured, and resting its head on a virgin's lap.

A check in *Strong's Concordance to the Bible* reveals mentions of unicorns in the Old Testament books of Deuteronomy, Numbers, Job, Psalms, and Isaiah.[12] One Harry Potter guidebook comments that "these references, to some scholars, indicate that the unicorn is actually a symbol of Christ."[13] Scholars of symbolism as diverse as Carl Jung and Narnia expert Paul Ford confirm this interpretation of the pure white animal whose single horn symbolizes the "invincible strength of Christ."[14]

As we'll see in the chapter on *Harry Potter and the Philosopher's Stone*, the unicorn as a symbol of Christ is essential in understanding the meaning of the dramatic scene in the Forbidden Forest during Harry's detention with Neville and Draco.

THE PHOENIX

My flat-out favorite beastie in Rowling's menagerie is Fawkes the phoenix, Dumbledore's pet. Harry meets him in *Chamber of Secrets* on a "dying day" when Fawkes bursts into flame and rises as a chick from his own ashes.

Given Fawkes's role in the defeat of the basilisk in *Chamber of Secrets,* Harry's draw with Voldemort in *Goblet of Fire* in the cage of phoenix song and light, and that Dumbledore's adult army in opposition to the Dark Lord is called the Order of the Phoenix, this symbol is central to any interpretation of the books or understanding of their power and popularity. How is the phoenix a symbol of Christ? In the Middle Ages the phoenix, because of its ability to "rise from death," was known as the "Resurrection Bird." Like the griffin, it was used in heraldic devices and shields to represent the bearer's hope of eternal life in Christ.[15] A sure pointer to this symbolism comes in the climactic battle between Dumbledore and Voldemort in *Order of the Phoenix.* Voldemort has managed to get the drop on his headmaster nemesis and shoots out the death curse, *Avada Kedavra.* Fawkes the phoenix dives between Dumbledore and certain death, swallows the death curse in his place, explodes into flames, and rises from the dead on the spot. The phoenix here, of course, portrays not only the Resurrection of Christ but also the Christian belief that he has intervened for humanity and taken the curse of death upon himself.

THE STAG

Lupin and Black explain to Harry in the crucible of the Shrieking Shack that his father, James, was an animagus. Harry discovers later that night what form his father took: a majestic stag with a full rack of antlers. His nickname at school, Prongs, came from these antlers, which are the stag's weapon and defining characteristic.[16] That Harry's Patronus likewise takes the shape of a stag gives this already powerful symbol even more importance.

Narnia fans recall that the Pevensie children in *The Lion, the Witch and the Wardrobe* only return to Earth from their Narnia kingdom because, as kings and queens of Narnia, they pursue the White Stag into a thick wood. Lewis points to their search for Christ as the cause of their return, because Christ is to our world what Aslan is to Narnia. The stag can be described as "a beast, the quest of great hunting parties, who was said to grant wishes to his captors. Lewis, as a student of the Middle Ages, would know of the *symbolism of the stag for Christ*"[17] (emphasis added). Maybe you don't see how a big deer can link our world and the Christian creative principle.

It's simple, really. The power of the symbolism comes from the antlers. Just as the phoenix is the "Resurrection Bird" because it can rise from its own funeral pyre, so the noble stag "came to be thought of as a symbol of regeneration because of the way its antlers are renewed."[18]

The stag's antlers break off and grow back, tying the animal symbolically to the tree of life and the Resurrection. Given this correspondence, it is no accident that when Harry first sees the stag Patronus who saves him from the Dementor's kiss—the living, soulless death worse than death—he sees it "as a unicorn."[19] The stag in Harry Potter, like the unicorn, is a symbol for Christ.

THE CENTAUR

Fawkes is great, but my favorite character in literature may be a centaur out of Narnia because of his last words. In *The Last Battle*, the centaur Roonwit—literally "he who knows the ancient languages"[20]—reveals to King Tirian the signs that calamity is about to strike Narnia. The king sends him on a dangerous mission, and Roonwit is shot by the archers of invading Calormenes he has been sent to spy on. But he sends this edifying, otherworldly message as he expires: "Remember that all worlds draw to an end and that noble death is a treasure which no one is too poor to buy."[21]

C. S. Lewis, renowned classicist and medieval scholar of Oxford and Cambridge, was certainly familiar with the conventional interpretations and uses of the centaur as symbol. His centaurs in the Chronicles of Narnia are often of this reveling type, but in Roonwit's case the centaur is heroic and sacrificial in service to the King. In Harry

Potter, similarly, we have passionate centaurs and one heroic example, Firenze, who saves Harry from Voldemort in *Philosopher's Stone.*

The centaur is first and foremost a symbol of man. It has the
head and chest of a man and the body of a horse. The head and chest
of a man are man's will, thought, and spirit; the horsey bottom is his
desires or passions. The centaur is a comic picture of a man's dual
nature as angel and beast. When man is right side up, his angelic part
tells the horse desires what to do, as a rider directs a horse; when the
beast is in control, however, the belly of the horse drags the chest and
head where it wants like a runaway pony.[22] We see the donkey centaurs in *Half-Blood Prince* and *Deathly Hallows* where the herd in the Forbidden Forest refuses to help Harry and fight the Dark Lord until they
are shamed by Hagrid and by seeing Harry's seeming corpse. Then
they come to themselves, man over donkey, and lead what seems a
suicidal charge on the Death Eaters and the Dark Lord.[23]

The heroic centaurs Roonwit and Firenze and these repentant
champions in *Hallows* are all symbols of Christ because, as carica-
tures of men, they are also imaginative "images of God." Through
these characters, Lewis and Rowling refer to a tradition that links a
man on a passionate beast with heroic, sacrificial, and saving actions:
Christ riding into Jerusalem in triumph on a donkey.

The traditional Christian explanation of why Christ rides in triumph into Jerusalem on a donkey rather than a noble steed is that
he wanted to show the hosanna-shouting assembly on the sides of
the road a three-dimensional icon or symbol of the obedient man.
Thus the donkey (certainly a picture of willful, stubborn desire)
serves his master, Spirit and God incarnate, in cheerful obedience.
Roonwit and Firenze give us this scriptural image of the God-Man
and the rightly ordered soul . . . another symbol of Christ.

THE HIPPOGRIFF

I confess to initially thinking that Buckbeak the hippogriff was
another one of Rowling's mythological innovations—and a hoot.

I had certainly never heard of one. Turns out, it is the creation of a sixteenth-century Italian court poet named Ludovico Ariosto in his *Orlando Furioso*.[24] The original hippogriff, of whom Buckbeak must be a descendant, is a griffin/centaur cross. "Like a griffin, Ariosto's hippogriff has an eagle's head and beak, a lion's front legs, with talons, and richly feathered wings, while the rest of its body is that of a horse. Originally tamed and trained by the magician Atalante, the hippogriff can fly higher and faster than any bird, hurtling back to earth when its rider is ready to land."[25] The hippogriff is "a kind of supercharged Pegasus, a blend of the favourable aspects of the griffin and the winged horse in its character as the 'spiritual mount.'"[26]

Hippo is the Greek word for "horse" (a hippopotamus is a "river-horse"), and *griff* takes us back to the griffin. A *hippogriff*, then, is a combination horse/lion/eagle, or a centaur with a lion/eagle "top." We have already learned how the griffin in Gryffindor is a symbol of Christ as King of Heaven and earth. As a griffin/centaur, the hippogriff, too, suggests Christ's divine conquest of the passions, as evidenced by his donkey ride into Jerusalem.

Hagrid describes hippogriffs to his students as "proud," but they are not proud in the sense of conceit or vanity. They are great-souled and aware of their virtue, which the ignoble misunderstand (Hagrid loves them dearly; he knows!). The noble—even supernatural— Buckbeak in *Prisoner of Azkaban* pecks the disrespectful and shameless Malfoy, is persecuted by the godless Ministry, and is almost executed by the Death Eater McNair. He escapes death at the hands of a world that cannot understand him (and that chooses to hate and fear him) to serve as Sirius's salvation. As with the griffin's and centaur's double-natured symbols, Rowling uses the hippogriff as a symbol of Christ, the God-Man.

THE PHILOSOPHER'S STONE

The end result of the alchemical Great Work was a stone that produced the Elixir of Life (an elixir often called "the red lion"). This magical object, known as the Philosopher's Stone, gave its owner immortality (as long as the owner drank the elixir) and infinite wealth. Touching any leaden or base metal object to the Stone would make it turn to gold.

Historians of science, religion, and literature agree on very little, in my experience. However, they do agree that the Philosopher's Stone is a symbol of Christ.[27] There isn't anything else in the Western spiritual tradition that promises eternal life and golden (that is, incorruptible or spiritual) riches except Christ, so the connection is transparent. The end product or aim of alchemy is life in Christ; English authors and poets of many centuries have used this symbol of Christ, consequently, to dramatize the search for an answer to death and human poverty of spirit. Harry Potter is no exception, as we will see in chapter 11 on *Harry Potter and the Philosopher's Stone*.

THE RED LION

Narnia fans have told me they do see Aslan, Lewis's Christ figure from the Chronicles of Narnia, in the Gryffindor House lion symbol. I think that is a reasonable link, especially in light of the symbolic meaning of Gryffindor and its opposition to the Slytherin serpent. This idea, however, hasn't been "lifted" from Lewis—the lion, and specifically the red lion, has been a symbol of Christ from the first century.

Saint John the Evangelist had no need to explain this usage in the book of Revelation: "Weep not: behold, the Lion of the tribe of Judah, the Root of David, hath prevailed" (Revelation 5:5, KJV). It is a theme of Christian literature and heraldic signs, consequently, throughout the Middle Ages. Lewis draws from this tradition both for Aslan (Persian for "lion") and Aslan's devotees in Narnia. Remember Peter's shield? "The shield was the color of silver and across it there romped a red lion, as bright as a ripe strawberry at the moment when you pick it."[28] The seven Harry Potter books are full of alchemical imagery, and even if Lewis was unaware of it (the silver and red in Peter's shield makes me doubt his ignorance), we can assume Rowling knows what the "red lion" means to an alchemist.[29] The "red lion" is the Elixir of Life coming from the Philosopher's Stone, a symbol of the blood of Christ received in Communion. The Stone in the first Harry Potter book, in case we missed this point, is described as "blood red."[30] The red lion, then, is still another symbolic point of correspondence between Christ and the world of Harry Potter.

The following chart recaps the eight symbols of Christ we've examined:

Symbol	Meaning	Therefore
Philosopher's Stone	Transforming lead to gold = Immortality Fount of Elixir of Life = Communion	Christ
Red Lion	Life-giving alchemical elixir; Aslan Revelation 5:5	Christ
Gryffindor = Golden Griffin	Eagle/Lion = Kings of heaven/earth = God/Man = Two natures of Christ	Christ
Unicorn	Biblical references: Numbers, Psalms, Job Christian tapestry & literary tradition	Christ
Phoenix	Resurrection Bird; immortal life Medieval literature theme	Christ
Stag	Tradition: "Tree of Life" in antlers Regeneration of antlers = Resurrection	Christ
Centaur	Perfect man in control of passions Christ riding donkey into Jerusalem	Christ
Hippogriff	Eagle/Lion/Horse, Heaven/Earth, God/Man Two natures of Christ	Christ

Does it seem odd that there are so many symbols of Christ? There is a big difference between symbols and allegorical figures. Allegories are stand-ins or story translations of a worldly character, quality, or event into an imaginative figure or story. There can be only one figure representing the other, consequently, or it's difficult to translate; I cannot have two Hitler figures if I'm writing an allegory of the Second World War, or the allegory fails.

Symbols, in contrast, can be stacked up. If I am telling a fantasy story with a transcendent meaning, even a Christian message, I can include characters and beasties and events that all point to the various qualities, actions, and promises of Christ. Rowling, depicting Dumbledore's suffering in the cave and in his death on the Astronomy Tower in *Half-Blood Prince*, is writing in story form of Christ's death on the Cross at Calvary.[31] If the symbols correspond with these qualities, even if they are not consciously understood as Christ symbols, they open us up to an imaginative experience of those supernatural qualities. A variety of these symbols woven into a story that itself echoes the Great Story will powerfully stir even the unconscious or spirit-denying soul because the heart of *homo religiosis* is tuned to these specific spiritual frequencies that cannot be totally shut down. Our cardiac intelligence radios are always tuned to the frequency of spiritually laden symbols transmitted through story.

The Harry Potter stories, in their formulaic journeys that end every year with love's triumph over death in the presence of a Christ symbol, find their power and popularity in the resonance they create in our hearts. We connect with them because they point toward the True Myth that lifts us above our mundane ego concerns. So much of Harry Potter—the symbols of Harry, Ron, and Hermione; the drama of the soul's faculties in action; the imagery of the many beasts; the windows into Christ's role in the Great Story; and the stories themselves—all foster a Spirit-first perspective by "baptizing the imagination."[32] Even neglecting the transparent Passion narrative at the end of *Deathly Hallows*, a powerful symbolic message about the spiritual realities celebrated in the Christian tradition has rarely, if ever, been smuggled into the hearts and minds of readers so successfully and profoundly.

Now that we have examined the formulas, themes, and symbols of the books, we have only to detour briefly to decipher the secret names many Harry Potter characters have before jumping into the stories themselves.

Ever wondered what *Neville Longbottom* means? Keep reading.

10

FUN WITH NAMES

The character names are delightful puzzles
with hidden spiritual meanings.

I confess to enjoying one aspect of Harry Potter's magical world more than all the others: the names of the characters. Rowling has said that she collects names for both their sound and their meaning, and no doubt she has made up a few to suit her purposes.

In this, we can see a tip of the hat to Charles Dickens, whose novels are peppered with names rich and often comic, both in the way they strike the ear and in what they reveal about the so-named person.

As much as I love Dickens, I think the names used in Harry Potter are as good as, and more often than not, better than Dickens's best. Take, for example, the three chasers on the Gryffindor Quidditch team in the first four Potter books: Alicia Spinnet, Katie Bell, and Angelina Johnson.

The Gryffindor team is something of a team of destiny, struggling to win the Quidditch Cup after years of dominance by the

Slytherin thugs. The Gryffindors seem to have a higher calling, as suggested by the fact that its chasers' names are church pieces: *spinnet* is an organ, *bell* is what it is, and *angelina* is a decorative angel, wooden or stone, that was commonplace in older English churches. Olive wood, which is the preferred material for church devotional carvings, is reflected in the Gryffindor House's "flying chapel." And who replaces one of the Weasley twins as a Beater in *Order of the Phoenix?* A boy named Kirke, the German word for church![1]

Not *all* the names have two or three layers to them. Some are evidently there just to cue us in to the ethnic diversity you'd expect at a twenty-first-century school in the United Kingdom. Cho Chang, Padma and Parvati Patil, Lee Jordan, Justin Finch-Fletchley, and Seamus Finnegan represent the minority members from the periphery of the old Empire who are rapidly becoming the majority (except for the blue-blooded Finch-Fletchley). Lee Jordan's name takes on a biblical meaning in *Deathly Hallows* when his radio alias is given as River Jordan.

Some names, too, are references to historical magical figures and tips of the hat to Rowling's favorite writers. Minerva McGonagall, Cassandra Vablatsky, and Sibyll Trelawney all have names that point to magical mythology, and Vablatsky is, no doubt, a pointer to the founder of the modern Theosophical Society, Helena Blavatsky.[2]

More fun are the characters from Rowling's favorite writers. Mrs. Norris, Argus Filch's peculiar cat, is no stranger to friends of Jane Austen; Mrs. Norris walks on the stage of *Mansfield Park* with the same aplomb as her feline namesake does at Hogwarts. Robert Louis Stevenson gets a nod or two (Trelawney and Flint are the names of major characters in his adventure novels), the Death Eater Dolokhov echoes Tolstoy, and the Irish representative on campus, Seamus Finnegan, is a probable pointer to the egghead pick for greatest novelist of the twentieth century, James Joyce, and echoes his *Finnegan's Wake.*

My favorite literary reference is to C. S. Lewis. Paul Ford in his

Companion to Narnia explains that the Digory Kirke character in the Narnia novels, the professor who has been to Narnia and who hosts the Pevensie children during the blitz, is a combination of Lewis's tutor, Kirkpatrick, and Lewis himself. Certainly much has been made of the parallel between Lewis and Kirke in their having had sick mothers and providing a safe house for children during the war.

The first Hogwarts champion chosen for the Triwizard Tournament is Hufflepuff House's Cedric Diggory. Harry and Cedric can't be said to be chums (they both have eyes for Cho Chang, for instance), but they help each other through the tournament and in the final trial agree to a tie. Unfortunately, this results in Cedric's death at Voldemort's command.

I believe Cedric Diggory and Digory Kirke are meant to be a match in assonance and meaning. No doubt Lewis would have been a Hufflepuff champion—and I believe Dumbledore's command in eulogy to "Remember Cedric Diggory!" is a celebration of the great Christian artist and apologist C. S. Lewis.

Sometimes a character's name tells us what animagus form he or she takes. Rita Skeeter, if not a mosquito, is an insect animagus. The late Sirius Black's first name is the word for the "dog star," and his surname points to his ability to change himself into a big black dog. That Sirius was given to depression and self-pity is also suggested; his name can be pronounced as "Serious Black."

Remus Lupin is not an animagus whose transfigurations are benign or self-chosen, but his name, too, tells us what he changes into at the full moon. Remus was one of the founders of Rome who was said to have been raised by a wolf, and *lupine* is the English word for "like a wolf." No surprise, then, when Lupin turns out to be a werewolf.

Albus Dumbledore's name may also fit into this category. We were not told even in the series finale what animagus form this former Master of Transfigurations takes, but there are several clues that he is the tawny owl at the opening of *Philosopher's Stone* and *Prisoner of Azkaban*. However, if his name is the indicator of his animal shape, then he must be a white or albino bumblebee because this is what *Albus Dumbledore* literally means.

In chapter 4 we discussed the names with alchemical significance. Sirius Black, Albus Dumbledore, and Rubeus Hagrid have names that correspond with the black, white, and red stages of the Great Work. Hermione's first and last names point to her as a budding alchemist; *Hermione* is the feminine form of "Hermes," not only Mercury on Mount Olympus but also the first great alchemist in Egypt, and *Granger* can mean "farmer." Farming and alchemy are linked because some think that *alchemy* comes from the Egyptian words for "black earth," referring to the floodplains of Egypt that could be tilled successfully. (Her initials, too, are the periodic table abbreviation for chemical mercury.)

James and Lily Potter, too, have names with alchemical meaning. Saint James is the traditional patron saint of alchemists, and both Lily and Luna Lovegood have first names that are used as symbols to represent the second, or white, stage of the transformation process.

Why bother studying the meanings of these names? Beyond just the fun of solving a puzzle, I think there are at least two reasons to play the name game: for insights into the character and for a deeper understanding of the story's meaning.

I enjoy playing with the names to see if I can tease out something about what sort of person would carry such a name. Here are a few of my reflections:

❖ SEVERUS SNAPE: I thought that Snape was a "cutting" personality because his first and last name both seem to be conjugate forms for severing or snipping. However, I read in the Rev. Francis Bridger's *A Charmed Life* that *snape* is "an English word meaning 'chide' or 'rebuke,' " and hence the whole name means "severe rebuke," an activity for

which Snape is well known.[3] Those who believe that Snape
is a half vampire, of course, think that the name should be
pronounced "sever his nape." But vampires bite the neck;
they don't cut it off. The name is a hint, it turns out, for
Severus's gruesome death in the Shrieking Shack in the
coils and teeth of Nagini.[4]

❖ PETER PETTIGREW: I have read the strangest interpretations
of what Peter's name may mean (many in my Barnes and
Noble University classroom in response to my own
thoughts). My favorite was from a young woman who
understood the name to mean "betrayer—pet who grew."
Peter, she explained, was the apostle who betrayed Christ,
just like Pettigrew betrayed the Potters. "Pet who grew" she
felt was an undeniable allusion to what Scabbers did in the
Shrieking Shack in *Prisoner of Azkaban.*

Neat thinking—but unlikely (although I enjoy "pet who
grew"). Judas, after all, betrayed Christ, not Peter. I think it is
more likely that with his name Rowling is pointing to
Peter's failings in masculine virtue because both his name
("Peter didn't grow very big") and nickname ("Wormtail")
suggest he lacks a full package. She has already made him
become a rat animagus; the name should suggest something nasty about this coward and turncoat who betrayed
his friends to Voldemort.

❖ THE WEASLEYS: Everyone loves the literally poor Weasleys.
Fred and George are a riot, Ron is the best friend you could
want, Ginny is fun, Arthur and Molly are believable and
endearing as the struggling parents of a big family with a
small income, Bill and Charlie have played their cameo
parts well, and Percy . . . well, every family has its black
sheep.

But what's with that last name? The first names are all
heroic and larger-than-life—kings, martial saints, and
renowned knights all—but "like a weasel"? What's the deal?

And it's not just the name. The Weasleys live at "The
Burrow," which is just outside the village of Ottery St.
Catchpole. It seems as if all indicators are pointing to their

being like weasels. A little reflection, I think, brings out an
important point.

Mr. Weasley, who works in the Misuse of Muggle Artifacts Office, is a notorious misuser of Muggle artifacts. As
Ron tells Harry in *Chamber of Secrets*, "If he raided *our* house,
he'd have to put himself under arrest."[5] Fred, George, Ron,
and Ginny have a remarkable ability to think rules are for
others—and even pompous Percy thinks that privilege of
place means being above the law (note his defenses of
Crouch in *Goblet of Fire*). The Weasleys *are* more than a little
weaselly, truth be told—and their sensitivity to any use of
the word "weasel" reflects this.

More sympathetically, the weasel is one of Rowling's
favorite animals. They're team players and are ferociously
loyal, according to legend. Of course, the weasel's taste for
rats and mice endears them to some, and they are famous
for fearlessly taking on animals several times their size.

One source I found even says that weasels are the
only animals that can kill the dreaded basilisk, though they
die sacrificially in this effort. Because of the link in the
popular mind of the basilisk/cockatrice with the devil, the
weasels' sacrifice to save others has made them a popular
symbol of Christ. A great name for these bold, redheaded
fighters![6]

❖ ARGUS FILCH: The Squib caretaker at Hogwarts is named
for the watchman in Greek mythology who watches the
gates of Hell. (That Argus had a thousand eyes is a nice
help for a watchman.) *Filch*, which means "to steal," suggests
both "filth" and "petty thievery."

So we're left with a contradiction, or at least an
unhealthy situation: "a thieving watchman" or "a caretaker
with sticky fingers." Filch is neither wizard nor Muggle and
is treated disdainfully by everyone except Dumbledore
(and Dolores Umbridge, whose sadism he shares).

Filch's name compelled many of us to watch him for all
seven books as a potential turncoat to Lord Voldemort and
the Death Eaters. Though they have no love for his kind,

my thought was that they would use the castoffs and neglected members of the magical world for their own ends (as they did Kreacher). I guess he was too happy in *Deathly Hallows* at the Death Eater–dominated Hogwarts to move on to serve the Dark Lord himself.

❖ NEVILLE LONGBOTTOM: Neville's name points both to his "nobody" status and to his eventual heroism. *Neville* breaks down to *ne,* meaning "no" or "not," and *ville,* "villa" or "village," for a sum of "noplace" or "nowhere." *Longbottom* gives us *long,* "big in size or duration in time," and *bottom,* "lowest place," for a composite of either "big buttocks" or "long time at bottom of heap." Every day Neville answers to a name meaning "nowhere-man big-bottom/ low-caste." How appropriate that Harry tells Stan Shunpike while hiding on the Knight Bus that his name is Neville Longbottom.[7] Besides pointing to Harry's shared destiny with Neville, it's a great name for an unassuming alias.

Neville, however, becomes a man to be dealt with in *Order of the Phoenix.* He works harder than anyone else in D.A. class and more than acquits himself in the battle with the Death Eaters under the Ministry of Magic at book's end. He saves Harry more than once, and if the prophecy was destroyed, it wasn't for lack of heroic effort and sacrifice on Neville's part. As we'll see in chapter 17, Neville becomes Rowling's model Christian who serves while waiting for the Lord's return.

How do we get that from "Nowhere Big-Butt"? Well, Neville's name also translates to "new city," as in the new Jerusalem Christians anticipate at the Second Coming. And *bottom* is an English euphemism for strength, endurance, and courage. Being "long bottom" means you will endure to the end in faith, which heroic Neville certainly does.

Remember that it is Neville's courage in *Philosopher's Stone* that defeats the Slytherins at book's end; this foreshadows the end of *Deathly Hallows,* in which "the last will be first." Mr. Nowhere-Man turns out to be a "true Gryffindor" in Harry's image, a hero equal to pulling the sword of Gryffindor from the Sorting Hat and destroying Voldemort's last Horcrux.

I could go on and on (what do you mean, I have already?). I'd love to tell you about Dolores Umbridge and what "grievous shadow" means as a name for the Hogwarts High Inquisitor. How about Mundungus Fletcher? ("World-filth Arrow-maker!") Pius Thicknesse?

Okay, enough fun for now. Let's get to the names of the major players and see what they tell us about this story and the Great Story.

Dumbledore/Voldemort

Albus Dumbledore, as noted above, has a name that means "white, glorious, resplendent" and "bee." The bee is a traditional symbol for the soul (bees move in clouds that struck many as a visible sign of how the Spirit "bloweth where it listeth" [John 3:8, KJV]). No surprise to find that the champion of all magical creatures, witches, wizards, and Muggles against the madness of the Death Eaters has a name pointing to his sanctity; "resplendent soul" recalls the light of Mt. Tabor (Matthew 17:1-9).

We've already examined Tom Marvolo Riddle. The birth name of the Dark Lord (whose letters can be rearranged to spell "I am Lord Voldemort") tells us his life is about his solving the "riddle" of his "twin" nature (*Thomas* is Aramaic for "twin"). Because he denies his being double-natured—a fallen human yet made in the image of God—he takes on the name Lord Voldemort, which can be interpreted as "willing death," "flight of death," or "flight *from* death." He imagines himself both as an angel of death and as an immortal who has escaped from death.

His exaggerated pride and the denial of both his humanity and access to divinity cause the birth of his vanquisher, who is his doppelgänger ("one in nature, two in essence"). But I'm getting

ahead of myself. The names confirm what we learned about Riddle/
Voldemort in chapter 5 on doppelgängers.

Potter/Malfoy

The wicked family in Harry Potter is the Malfoy clan. The father's
name is Lucius, and the mother is Narcissa. Their little boy, the dar-
ling of Slytherin House, is Draco—the Latin word for "dragon" or
"serpent." The serpent is a traditional Christian symbol for the devil,
because the Evil One takes the form of a snake in the Garden of
Eden. C. S. Lewis, in *The Voyage of the Dawn Treader*, depicts a really nasty
little boy (much like Draco) named Eustace Scrubb, who turns into
a dragon. Lucius, Draco's daddy, is perfectly wicked. He mistreats
his servants, patronizes everyone because of his "pure blood" and
wealth, and is rather impatient and nasty to his own boy. He gives
Riddle's diary to Ginny Weasley, which almost results in more than
a few deaths. In *Goblet of Fire* he reveals himself as a Death Eater
and a servant of Lord Voldemort, and in *Order of the Phoenix* he is the
leader of the bad guys in the battle for the prophecy.

That is no surprise if you look at his name. *Lucius* suggests "Lucifer," which means "light carrier" in Latin. The angel named Lucifer
turned on God and became the devil, or Satan ("the deceiver"). Like
his son, Lucius Malfoy has a satanic name.

Mom Malfoy's name is not another name for the devil, but it's
pretty bad. Narcissus is a young man in Greek mythology who was
very aware of his own good looks. He thought so much of himself
that he rejected the love of the nymph Echo. He spent so much
time admiring his reflection in a pond that some stories say he
drowned, and better ones say he became the beautiful narcissus
plant. A narcissist, consequently, is anyone of self-importance and
ego (usually a self-loving monster). *Narcissa* is not a nice name—and
it has enough sibilants in it that you sound like a snake saying it.
(In terms of the doppelgänger apposition of so many characters, it

is worth noting that the narcissus flower is of the same family as the lily.)

But the worst part of being a Malfoy is that last name. It is French for "bad faith" or "faith in evil." This can mean anything from "untrustworthy" to "Satan worshipper." I might move if the family next door was named "bad faith"! All the Malfoys are branded as black hats by their first and last names.

Let's look at the names for the good guys, by whom I mean the Potters. Harry Potter's late parents were named James and Lily. These have meanings over and above the few mentioned previously, as you've probably guessed—meanings quite different from the Malfoys' names. James, for instance, is the name of Christ's disciple who was also his brother. This brother was the only sibling to recognize Christ as the Messiah; he became (after the Resurrection, Ascension, and Pentecost) the first bishop of Jerusalem and the man in charge at the council recorded in Acts 15.

You may not be familiar with this connection between James and Christ, but be sure that the English are. Ambassadors from foreign countries to the British government are said to be going to the Court of Saint James; another name for the British royal court contains "Saint James." The name resonates with royalty, and through Saint James and the divine right of kings, with divinity.

Lily was the name of Harry's green-eyed mother. Lilies are magnificent, showy flowers of various colors and usually have a trumpet shape. They are symbolic of spring, though many people associate this flower with death; a white lily is often put in a corpse's hands before the funeral. This is done because the lily, as a symbol of spring, is also the flower of the Annunciation, the Resurrection, and the promise of Christ's return. Corpses are given a lily in hope of their resurrection with Christ at his second coming. Lily, then, like James, is a name with strong ties to Christianity.[8]

Which leaves us with *Harry Potter*. What does Harry's name mean?

Before beginning this discussion, it's best to acknowledge that Harry Potter, because of the worldwide success of this series, is a brand name in millions of people's minds, much like Mickey Mouse, Coca-Cola, or Apple computers. In this Potter-mania environment in which we live, it is difficult to assert that the names mean anything, because to most it has been a long time since the names were restricted to the boy wizard in these books rather than the social phenomenon his name also describes.

Also working against the assignment of any meaning to the name *Harry Potter* is that the name is not at all unusual. Unlike Severus Snape or Millicent Bulstrode, you may actually know a Harry Potter.[9]

I am frequently reminded, too, that Rowling has been asked where Harry's name came from and she has answered, "I got the name Potter from people who lived down the road from me in Winterbourne. . . . I liked the surname so I took it."[10] Please note, though, that this answer doesn't explain why she liked it more than the other names of the people on the street or why she thought it fit Harry. It's not a little bit like when she was asked about King's Cross and why Harry imagines himself there after his sacrifice in *Deathly Hallows*.

KATIE B.: Why was King's Cross the place Harry went to when he died?

J. K. ROWLING: For many reasons. The name works rather well, and it has been established in the books as the gateway between two worlds, and Harry would associate it with moving on between two worlds (don't forget that it is Harry's image we see, not necessarily what is really there.)[11]

The fact that "the name works rather well" doesn't spell out the obvious connection between Calvary and the action of the story at that point, and Rowling adds a distracting point to end the discussion. Are we supposed to think that because she chooses not to explain in detail what in other places she calls the "obvious" Christian content of her stories there is no greater meaning of King's Cross or Harry Potter than Rowling's fancy?[12]

Hardly. I think it's silly to believe that the principal player in the series, a series written by an author clearly fascinated with getting names just right on several levels of meaning, would have a meaningless name. Common sense seems to demand the name be picked over pretty closely by readers wanting to understand the meaning and consequent popularity of these best-selling books. Let's take a look.

Harry Potter: The Name

Harry can literally mean "to harass, annoy, or disturb." Usually someone described as "harried" is run down by too much work and too many distractions. I don't think that's what our Harry's name is meant to imply, even though he does lead an exciting life and, in *Order of the Phoenix*, several times seems on the edge of a breakdown.

Harry is also the familiar form of the names Henry and Harold. More than one Shakespeare play is about Henry IV—when he was the Prince of Wales, during his wild life with Falstaff before becoming king, and his heroic life thereafter. More than a few critics have suggested this is a pointer to Harry's destiny as Voldemort's vanquisher and the savior of the magical world.

As important is that Harold is consonant with the word *herald*. Harry may be the herald of something new and better. Put that thought on the shelf for a minute; it might be worth looking at again after this survey of all the possibilities.

There is something better though. As much as I like "herald," I believe that the Cockney and French pronunciations of Harry's name tell us what his first name means. These pronunciations are made without aspirating or breathing through the *h*. Instead of pronouncing the name as if you were saying he was covered with hair, say it as if you were calling him an airhead: "airy." 'Arry with a long *a* suggests the word *heir.*

The heir is the person who stands to get what someone—usually a parent—will leave behind at death. It is usually used to describe someone who will inherit a great deal of money or a position. A prince, for example, is heir to the king's throne. When the king dies, the prince gets the throne and becomes king.

If Harry means "heir-y," then what is our Harry "heir to" or "son of"? Perhaps this is another pointer to Harry's being Heir of Gryffindor. His name, after all, is not just Harry Potter but Harry *James* Potter. Certainly we are told again and again about Harry's likeness to his biological father.

This may very well be the case. A close look at the name *Potter,* though, points to a larger inheritance than just Harry's biological father's wealth and bloodline. For this job you might want to get a Bible concordance.

Looking up *potter* in the concordance, we find references to it in the prophets Isaiah, Jeremiah, and Zechariah, the book of Lamentations, Saint Paul's letter to the Romans, and in the book of Revelation.

Because Tupperware wasn't available in biblical times, it shouldn't be surprising to find mention of potters in Scripture. Pots held everything not kept in baskets. But to what are these Bible references alluding when they mention *potter*? Do they mean human potters?

When Bible scholars cite these "potter" passages, they often refer to God's creation of man as recorded by the prophet Moses. "And the LORD God formed man of the dust of the ground, and breathed into his nostrils the breath of life; and man became a living soul" (Genesis 2:7, KJV).

Other Scripture passages refer to human potters. But even then, they point to the potter's craft of shaping a vessel to indicate

God's activity in shaping us as creations in his image. Let's look at a couple of these "potter" references to see what I mean.

In Isaiah 64:8, the prophet says, "But now, O LORD, thou art our father; we are the clay, and thou our potter; and we all are the work of thy hand" (KJV).

Jeremiah says, "Then the word of the LORD came to me, saying, O house of Israel, cannot I do with you as this potter? saith the LORD. Behold, as the clay is in the potter's hand, so are ye in mine hand, O house of Israel" (Jeremiah 18:5-6, KJV).

Paul rebukes the stiff-necked Romans by writing, "Nay but, O man, who art thou that repliest against God? Shall the thing formed say to him that formed it, Why hast thou made me thus? Hath not the potter power over the clay, of the same lump to make one vessel unto honour, and another unto dishonour?" (Romans 9:20-21, KJV).

God is thought of as a *potter,* from the beginning of the Bible to the Epistles. Is there any reason to think this biblical usage survives to our times? Yes, there are abundant reasons to believe that.

Today, Orthodox Christians claim that they worship God in the same way the apostles did, keep the same feasts and fasts, and say prayers that have been said by holy men for centuries. During Great Lent, the time of special prayers and fasting to prepare for the celebration of Christ's Resurrection (they call it *Pascha* rather than the druid word *Easter*), the Great Canon of Saint Andrew is recited.

These prayers, said around the world by Orthodox Christians, call on God in repentance for their sins. One of these prayers says, "In molding my life into clay, O Potter, Thou didst put into me flesh and bones, flesh and vitality. But, O my Creator, my Redeemer and Judge, accept me who repent" (Canon of Saint Andrew 1:10). *Potter* is here the equivalent of Creator, Redeemer, and Judge in referring to God.

Remember that J. K. Rowling, besides being a member of the Scottish Episcopal Church, studied Latin from her earliest years and at the University of Exeter. As is evident in the books' spells, Latin is almost Rowling's second language. With this in mind, it is meaningful to see that the word *potter* is pronounced *exactly as is the Latin word for father (pater)*. This word, like the English word *father,* is used for both biological father and "Father which art in heaven" (Matthew 6:9, KJV). The most famous prayer in the Western Church is the "Our Father," which until the Second Vatican Council's liturgical reforms (not implemented until the late sixties) was said by the world's Roman Catholics as the "*Pater* Noster"—and of course many millions still do in private devotions. Harry's last name, deciphered, is both "God" from biblical usage and "Father" from the Latin.

Harry's name, then, taken altogether, means that he is an heir to God the Father (Pater/Potter) or a herald of the same. I rush to say this does not mean Rowling is necessarily offering Harry as a symbol of Christ, or as the Antichrist, or even as an allegorical Christ (which is how some people view C. S. Lewis's Aslan). Rowling has said that Harry is not even a saint, so we know he is not the Son of God as Christians believe Jesus Christ is, but in the manner that you and I and everybody are sons of God. Harry is the fallen man seeking to be both image and likeness of God. He is fallen, but he is a seeker (see Matthew 7:7).

Saint Athanasios the Great, a hero and confessor of the early Church, said that God became man that man might become God. Athanasios, who stood before the Aryan onslaught for the truth, believed that by means of his Incarnation, sinless life, and Resurrection from the dead, Christ made it possible for human beings to share in his Resurrection and become "little Christs within Christ" (a phrase attributed to Saint John Chrysostom). Man seeking God succeeds in Christ.

That Harry is given a name that means "heir," "herald," or even "son of God" points us to what the saints have taught for two thousand years. We are to love God, not in fear as slaves or in hollow obedience as servants, but as dutiful sons created in his image, who live in joyous expectation of our inheritance—at *our* death, if not before.[13] Harry Potter as "son of God" is not a symbol of Jesus Christ, but of humanity pursuing its spiritual perfection in Christ. Harry Potter is Everyman, hoping to live as God's image *and* likeness, now and in joy for eternity. Harry certainly rises from the dead at the end of *Deathly Hallows* as a symbol or type of Christ and his Resurrection, but the parallel readers are meant to draw is less about Harry being an allegorical Christ stand-in than an example of the power of faith and love in overcoming interior and real world evils (more on this in chapter 17).

The review of the Harry Potter books that we have made so far in these first ten chapters, looking at the structures, themes, predominant symbolism, even the names of the principal characters, indicates that they have a transcendent or spiritual meaning with strong Christian echoes throughout. In the second part of *How Harry Cast His Spell*, we'll take a quick look at each Harry Potter novel for its individual meaning. I doubt, after what you have read so far, that you will be surprised to learn they are profound, edifying morality tales that point to love and life in the Spirit as the answer to human mysteries.

11

THE PURIFICATION OF
THE SOUL

Spiritual keys to Harry Potter and the
Philosopher's Stone

The first ten chapters of this book include discussions of the elements that run through all the books with an eye toward the transcendent meaning of these themes, structures, and symbols. In the next nine chapters, we'll look at each book, not, I hope, to repeat what has already been said about love and death and specific symbols, but to reveal the several parts of these books that have "jumped off the page" in terms of their spiritual and specifically Christian meaning.

Much of the first book's meaning, not too surprisingly, is about alchemy. The original title, *Harry Potter and the Philosopher's Stone*, cues us to that. As we'd expect, knowing the alchemical formula, Harry moves through the black stage (the Dursleys, Snape), the white stage (Dumbledore), and the red stage (Rubeus, crisis event). The last is the red-hot crucible scene, in which Harry dies and rises from the dead in the presence of a symbol of Christ (here, the Philosopher's Stone he pulls from the Mirror of Erised).

In addition to alchemy, there are two other striking parallels with the Christian journey in *Philosopher's Stone*: the drinking of unicorn blood in the Forbidden Forest and the consequences for Quirrell when he tries to kill Harry.

Perhaps the scariest scene in the first book (and certainly the most misunderstood) is the detention in the Forbidden Forest where Harry and Draco see the Dark Lord drinking unicorn blood. "The cloaked figure reached the unicorn, lowered its head over the wound in the animal's side, and began to drink its blood."[1]

Harry is saved by Firenze the centaur, who explains to Harry why someone would drink unicorn's blood:

> "Harry Potter, do you know what unicorn blood is used for?"
>
> "No," said Harry, startled by the odd question. "We've only used the horn and tail hair in Potions."
>
> "That is because it is a monstrous thing, to slay a unicorn," said Firenze. "Only one who has nothing to lose, and everything to gain, would commit such a crime. The blood of a unicorn will keep you alive, even if you are an inch from death, but at a terrible price. You have slain something pure and defenseless to save yourself, and you will have but a half-life, a cursed life, from the moment the blood touches your lips."[2]

As we saw earlier, the centaur is a symbol of a perfect man and an imaginative icon of Christ riding into Jerusalem. Here, this centaur is talking about another symbol of Christ: the unicorn. That the blood of the unicorn will curse those who drink it unworthily, and that it has life-giving power, echoes Saint Paul's discourse on the unworthy reception of Communion, which is the blood of Christ:

> For I have received of the Lord that which also I delivered unto you, that the Lord Jesus the same night in which he was

betrayed took bread: And when he had given thanks, he brake it, and said, Take, eat: this is my body, which is broken for you: this do in remembrance of me. After the same manner also he took the cup, when he had supped, saying, this cup is the new testament in my blood: this do ye, as oft as ye drink it, in remembrance of me. For as often as ye eat this bread, and drink this cup, ye do shew the Lord's death till he come. *Wherefore whosoever shall eat this bread, and drink this cup of the Lord, unworthily, shall be guilty of the body and blood of the Lord.* But let a man examine himself, and so let him eat of that bread, and drink of that cup. *For he that eateth and drinketh unworthily, eateth and drinketh damnation to himself, not discerning the Lord's body.*
(1 CORINTHIANS 11:23-29, KJV, EMPHASIS ADDED)

Christians have disputed amongst themselves what eating and drinking the body and blood of Christ means, especially in regard to doing it "in remembrance." Men of good will, however, would be hard pressed to feign confusion about what Saint Paul says happens to Christians who do this "unworthily." They're damned, sure and simple.

Now, when Firenze the centaur explains to Harry that anyone who selfishly drinks the life-saving blood of the unicorn is "cursed" from the moment the blood touches his lips, he does everything but read from 1 Corinthians, chapter and verse.

Less explicit but just as important are the smuggled theological points in Harry's journey to the Mirror of Erised and Quirrell's fate in serving the Dark Lord and attacking Harry.

As we've already seen, alchemical work can be described as a salvation journey, using the terms *purification, dissolution,* and *recongealing.* The end result of alchemy is a soul that has turned or "transmuted" from lead to gold, from base desires and concerns for ego-focused individual advantage to Christlike love and freedom.

Harry Potter and the Philosopher's Stone is largely an exposition of the alchemical method shown through human character reagents. It is centered on Harry's spiritual purification so that he might be worthy of the Stone at the book's end; this requires his purification, dissolution by contraries, and philosophic congealment.

In chapter 8, we saw that change is a key theme in Harry Potter. In this first book, Harry changes from an orphan in a Muggle home into a wizard hero capable of saving the world from Voldemort's return. This happens in stages as the various character reactants distill the Muggle out of him. His final trials to get the Stone are symbols of his soul's journey to perfection.

Let's look at these trials. They begin with Fluffy, the giant three-headed dog that guards the trapdoor hiding the Stone. Hagrid purchased Fluffy from a "Greek chappie" in a bar—which makes sense, because the dog clearly refers to Cerberus, who played a role in several Greek myths as the monster guarding the gates of Hell. Orpheus got past Cerberus by lulling him to sleep with a lyre, and that is Fluffy's weak point as well. Quirrell uses a harp (much like a lyre), and Harry uses Hagrid's gift flute.

Cerberus, the otherworldly canine, is at the gates guarding the gauntlet of trials to the Stone (or spiritual perfection), because the first step in spiritual life and alchemical work is renunciation of the world. This is the first rung on the "ladder of divine ascent," and the most difficult.[3] The power-obsessed Quirrell/Voldemort struggles with the Fluffy obstacle above all others, which is why it takes him so long to enter through the trapdoor.

Renunciation is the better part of purification, and it is not until Harry throws off earthly concerns (the house cup, detentions, being expelled, life itself) that he is able at last to enter the trapdoor. In a heroic scene, he dismisses Ron and Hermione's concerns about school and family before the prospect of the return of Voldemort and takes the plunge.[4]

The trials the trio goes through to get to the Stone aren't arbitrarily assigned. We saw in chapter 9 how Hermione, Ron, and Harry are actually living symbols of the powers of the soul: Mind, Body, and Spirit (or Mind, Desire, and Heart). This Platonic doctrine of the soul (after its baptism and correction) became the teaching of the Christian Church. The trials, though, aren't from Plato but from Aristotle.

Each trial Harry faces in his race to get the Stone, believe it or not, reflects a faculty or kind of soul in the Aristotelian model. The path to the Stone is an obstacle course symbolizing the soul's qualities and powers as presented in Aristotle's *On the Soul* and adapted by medieval theologians. To reach perfection (the Philosopher's Stone), Harry must necessarily show himself to have surpassed each obstacle within himself.

The Scholastic model, following Aristotle and Aquinas, is that there are three kinds of soul: vegetative, sensitive, and intellective. The powers or faculties closely tied to each kind are: (1) nourishment and reproduction with the vegetative; (2) discrimination and will with sensitivity to data; and (3) the rational and spiritual with the intellective kind.[5] What do Harry, Ron, and Hermione find when they jump through the trapdoor? They descend "miles under the school" into a netherworld crucible where their worthiness will be tested. Then, in sequence from carnal to spiritual, this trio of the soul's powers pass through tests for their purification.

First is the test for the vegetative kind of soul, by means of the vicious plant "devil's snare." Then comes discrimination, or choice.[6] The team has to find the single winged key that fits the locked door at the opposite end of the Chamber, out of hundreds of flying keys. The right "key" here means both "answer unlocking a problem" and "musical note" perceived by the Heart. Desire or Mind cannot hear, find, or catch the right key except in obedience to Heart. Next test, please.

To pass the magical chessboard test, they must become players and win the game. Ron is in charge here, because this is the ultimate test of the willing, or desiring, faculty he embodies. Of course, Ron chooses the passionate, erratic knight and assigns the linear, analytical Hermione the rook (which only moves in straight lines). Harry, the Heart or spiritual center, becomes—what else?— a bishop.

Why is the chess game—what Americans think of as an egghead sport—the test for will and the last or highest test for Ron, our desiring part? Because to win this game, Ron must sacrifice himself. There is no greater challenge for the passionate faculty than to forgo its selfish interest and focus on the greater good. Ron transcends himself in selfless sacrifice, and the test is passed. On to the next test. (Don't forget to jump over the troll.)

"Pure logic!" Snape has left a word puzzle beside seven bottles of potions that will kill or liberate. This is Hermione's exam, of course, and Mind solves the puzzle without trouble. But this is the end of the road for Hermione; the last test is only for the highest faculty of soul, and she retires, deferring to Harry.

And this test? It's our old friend the Mirror of Erised. The Quirrell/Voldemort two-headed monster is standing in front of it, trying to find the Stone, and all Quirrell can see is himself giving it to Voldemort. Three days after Harry passes the test in front of the Mirror, Dumbledore tells Harry why this is: "You see, only one who wanted to *find* the Stone—find it, but not use it—would be able to get it, otherwise they'd just see themselves making gold or drinking Elixir of Life."[7]

Quirrell/Voldemort is clueless in front of the Mirror, but not Harry. Because of Dumbledore's coaching about the Mirror months before, and his understanding that the happiest man in the world would see only his reflection, Harry knows what he will see—it won't be his family. After the trials of purification he has just passed through, Harry knows he will see himself only wanting the Stone for itself.

What I want more than anything else in the world at the moment, he thought, is to find the Stone before Quirrell does.

So if I look in the Mirror, I should see myself finding it—which means I'll see where it's hidden! But how can I look without Quirrell realizing what I'm up to?[8]

The authentic and accomplished alchemist is able to produce the Stone because of his spiritual achievement. It is a *by-product* of that perfection, as are immortality and the riches of transcending the world, rather than the *end* or goal of it. We know Dumbledore and Flamel are of this perfected type because they willingly destroy the Stone at book's end.

Dumbledore has set up the final hurdle to getting the Stone in poetic fashion; the Mirror reflects the *spiritual* quality of whoever stands before it. To produce the Stone from the Mirror, the seeker must be passionless, which is to say, not desiring any private gain or advantage. One's worthiness to hold or find the Stone is a *reflection* of the quality of one's desires. Quirrell, consumed by Voldemort and his own lust for power, cannot get the Stone—but Harry, of course, being what Dumbledore later calls "pure in heart," sees himself put the Stone in his own pocket.

This is all very interesting, I hear you saying, but what do alchemy, Aristotle, and this Mirror/Stone puzzle have to do with spiritual accomplishment or Christian doctrine? Good question. The answer is "quite a bit," although it's not as obvious as the unicorn blood.

Alchemy was not its own religion or spiritual path—it only existed as a discipline within revealed traditions. To Christians, the alchemical process was symbolic of the way to spiritual perfection, and the Philosopher's Stone, as the end result of this process, was a symbol for Christ.

Having completed a trial by fire and spiritual purification, Harry is able to see and receive this symbol of Christ, because he has no desire to use it for his own advantage but seeks it in loving service to others. Only the pure in heart will see God (Matthew 5:8), and the Mirror reflects the heart's desire.

The purified Harry sees and receives the Stone (Christ), then flees from the two-faced evil of Quirrell/Voldemort—and something fascinating happens. The two-headed monster is unable to touch or have any contact with Harry without burning, quite literally. Dumbledore saves Harry in the end and (after Harry's three-day resurrection) explains what happened:

> "But why couldn't Quirrell touch me?"
>
> "Your mother died to save you. If there is one thing Voldemort cannot understand, it is love. He didn't realize that love as powerful as your mother's for you leaves its own mark. Not a scar, no visible sign . . . to have been loved so deeply, even though the person who loved us is gone, will give us some protection forever. It is in your very skin. Quirrell, full of hatred, greed, and ambition, sharing his soul with Voldemort, could not touch you for this reason. It was agony to touch a person marked by something so good."[9]

If there is a single meaning to the Potter books, as we saw in chapter 7 on love and death, it is that love conquers all. And of all loves, *sacrificial* love is the most important, because it has conquered death. Harry's protection against the assault of the Evil One is the love shown years ago by someone who made the greatest sacrifice for him. His bond with that sacrifice and the love it demonstrated permeates his person and repels all evil. Voldemort cannot touch him because of Harry's worthiness to receive the Stone (Christ), and because of the Christlike love and sacrifice of his mother, Lily, that shield him.

Let me take this a step further. Another echo of Christian teaching in the end of Quirrell/Voldemort is in the burning of Quirrell's hands and skin when they make contact with Harry; Quirrell burns and dies in agony. Rowling tells in graphic story form here the traditional Christian doctrine concerning God's judgment and the nature of Heaven and Hell. One Christian theologian explains it this way:

God is Truth and Light. God's judgment is nothing else than our coming into contact with truth and light. In the day of the Great Judgment all men will appear naked before this penetrating light of truth. The "books" will be opened. What are these "books"? They are our hearts. Our hearts will be opened by the penetrating light of God, and what is in these hearts will be revealed. If in those hearts there is love for God, those hearts will rejoice seeing God's light. If, on the contrary, there is hatred for God in those hearts, these men will suffer by receiving on their opened hearts this penetrating light of truth which they detested all their life.[10]

Another theologian explains:

God himself is both reward and punishment. All men have been created to see God unceasingly in his uncreated glory. Whether God will be for each man Heaven or Hell, reward or punishment, depends on man's response to God's love and on man's transformation from the state of selfish and self-centered love, to God-like love which does not seek its own ends. . . . The primary purpose of Orthodox Christianity, then, is to prepare its members for an experience which every human being will sooner or later have.[11]

Back to Harry and Quirrell. Professor Quirrell is possessed by the Evil One. He stands before the judging Mirror, looking at the quality of the desires reflected from his heart. It sees what possesses him: a selfish and self-centered love apart from God. He is unworthy of the Stone/Christ and the ensuing Elixir of Life, so these are kept from him. When he touches someone blanketed by the sacrificial love of a savior (here, of course, Harry's mother) and worthy of having Christ in him, the love of God therein burns Quirrell. His judgment reflects the judgment of Hell that rejecters of God will experience.

So what is *Harry Potter and the Philosopher's Stone* about? Written in the symbolism of alchemy and traditional Christian doctrine, it is an ode to the purification and perfection of the soul in Christ and his saving, sacrificial love. The perfected soul at death will experience the glory and love of God as joy; the soul that has not transcended, that has consumed itself with pursuit of power and love of self apart from God, will experience the same glory as agony and fire. Incredibly, Rowling has written an engaging and cogent parable about God's judgment on the spiritual qualities of our lives and about our capacity for (or our despising of) love—and this parable excites postmodern readers about becoming pure in heart and accepting the protection of sacrificial love. For generations immunized against any kind of fire-and-brimstone sermon or message, this is a borderline miraculous accomplishment.

Let me close here with a story. When I first read this book aloud to my children, my then eleven-year-old daughter Hannah (who had read the book with my permission already) was in the room. I asked her why she thought Quirrell couldn't hold on to Harry. She explained matter-of-factly that Harry was protected by his mother's love and that love burns people with hard hearts "just like heaven and hell being the same place." As much as we speak about such things in our family, I was still amazed that she'd made the connection on her own. I guess the world will always underestimate the wisdom and courage of its eleven-year-olds.

12

DANGEROUS BOOKS AND EDIFYING BOOKS

Spiritual keys to Harry Potter and the Chamber of Secrets

Rowling remarked at the release of *Goblet of Fire* that it and *Chamber of Secrets* were the hardest stories to write and her favorites among the books. She hasn't told us why, but I have a good guess.

Chamber of Secrets operates on several levels. As in all the books, it tells a rollickin' good yarn while advancing the larger story of Harry and his link to Voldemort. But *Chamber of Secrets* also provides an answer to her Christian critics of the time within its story and is a "book about books" to boot. Layered as it is as a story with a story-within-a-story, it couldn't have been easy to write, but I have to agree with her: *Chamber of Secrets* may be the best single volume of the series. It is simultaneously:

- ❖ A wonderful mystery/adventure story, tightly plotted
- ❖ A series of revelations about Riddle and other characters, which move along the larger story line

❖ A response to culture-war critics via a textbook demonstration of the meaning and power of edifying story

As a book about books, *Chamber of Secrets* discusses the quality, value,
and dangers of three separate books: Riddle's diary, Lockhart's oeu-
vre (lifework), and the very Harry Potter book the reader is holding
and experiencing. Let's look at each of these books in turn.

Chamber of Secrets turns on Tom Riddle's diary and what happens
when it returns to Hogwarts. When Harry and Ron discover the
diary in Moaning Myrtle's toilet, Ron warns Harry about the dangerous magic contained in books to keep him from looking at it.
Harry, after Ron's hysterical warnings and barely concealed predic-
tion of a fate worse than death, decides he'll have to read it to find
out. I don't doubt that this is a bit of advice for the sensible, sober
reader: In the matter of a controversial or supposedly dangerous
book, you should read it and decide for yourself what it is about.

However, we know we can't dismiss the possibility that books
can be dangerous—for Riddle's diary certainly is. Let's lay out what
we know about this evil book:

❖ It is the diary of Tom Riddle (aka Lord Voldemort)
❖ Delivered by Lucius Malfoy
❖ In a Transfiguration textbook
❖ To Ginny Weasley

Lucius Malfoy's intentions in planting the book in Ginny Weasley's textbook are not, as one might think, to restore Lord Voldemort. Malfoy could have done that on his own, in Quirrell fashion,
with any stooge. Dumbledore tells us that the book planting was a
"clever plan" to undermine Arthur Weasley's standing among wizards and to destroy the sponsors of the Muggle Protection Act.[1]
Mr. Malfoy is understandably nervous about this act and the consequent raids to round up "dangerous toys" from dark wizards.
Draco Malfoy also suggests that his father was trying to remove

the "Muggle-loving" Dumbledore from Hogwarts—which he succeeded in doing, at least for a while.

We can discern an important point about the effects of authentically dangerous books through the example of Riddle's diary:

- ❖ The innocent (Ginny can be read as "Virginia" or "virgin," though Rowling revealed after *Phoenix* was published that Ginny's given name is "Ginevra")
- ❖ Are transfigured (the diary is placed in the Transfiguration textbook)
- ❖ Into the wicked (the possessed Ginny is the one who opens the Chamber and releases the basilisk)
- ❖ By the author of a book of dark magic (Riddle/Voldemort is the bad guy)—
- ❖ A book that is hidden inside their textbooks and pretending to be what it is not.

The effect of the book on Ginny is that she turns into a rooster-murdering, basilisk-releasing servant of Riddle. She thinks she is losing her mind—and she is right. Her mind is now Voldemort's; in this is the death of her innocence and purity. The effect of the book on Harry, too, is remarkable. After his time inside the memory of Tom Riddle, he more than half-believes that Hagrid is the Heir of Slytherin. It is a pretty powerful drug or Confundus Charm—or evil magic—that could make Harry suspect his friend, the Dumbledore-adoring gamekeeper.

This isn't really a warning to beware of the sneaky diaries of dark wizards. *It's a warning about the dangers hiding in children's textbooks.* In this, Rowling follows C. S. Lewis's discussion of just this problem in his *The Abolition of Man*. The lead essay, "Men without Chests," exposes the harm done by the insidious and sentiment-destroying "moral philosophy" of textbook writers.

Lewis felt strongly that the hidden "dark wisdom" in our children's schoolbooks is what is transforming them from something human into people who are somehow less than human. Because they grew up "having read the wrong sort of books" (as with Eustace Scrubb in *The Voyage of the Dawn Treader* and Mark Studdock in *That Hideous Strength*), they are incapable of the sentiments and emotions that buttress and create moral excellences such as courage. We can see this real danger of the vacant naturalism and godlessness characteristic of textbooks through the mind of Tom Riddle hidden in Ginny's Transfiguration schoolbook.

I also think this is part of Rowling's intended response to the objections to magic in her books. Lewis's response to his own Christian critics was that literary magic can be a counterspell, and magic in edifying fiction is just that—a counterspell to the enchantments of modernity.

Let's move on to the most comic figure in the Potter series, Gilderoy Lockhart, and take a look at his books. Gilderoy Lockhart sure has written a bunch of books; he is the author of books ranging from how to deal with household pets, his (ahem) adventures around the world, and his favorite subject: himself. Here is what we know is true about each of these books:

- ❖ Their only purpose is to generate money and fame for Gilderoy.
- ❖ The adventure stories are all the accomplishments of other magical persons.
- ❖ Women (that is, witches) love them; wizards do not.

Beyond his being "Order of Merlin, Third Class, Honorary Member of the Dark Force Defense League, and five-time winner of *Witch Weekly*'s Most-Charming-Smile Award" (which he "won't talk about," but manages to mention four times in *Chamber of Secrets*), what we learn about Gilderoy himself is:

- ❖ He is despised by the teachers as an empty-headed braggart.
- ❖ He is adored by the girl students, but he sickens the boys.

- ❖ He lives for publicity, large photos of himself,
  and other people's admiration.
- ❖ He favors effeminate colors in robes (jade, lilac, midnight
  blue, etc.).
- ❖ He has one good trick (the Memory Charm).
- ❖ He is a coward ("Order of Scaredy Cat, First Class").

His cowardice is revealed in spades when Ginny Weasley is taken by Riddle into the Chamber of Secrets and the teachers tell Lockhart he has "free rein at last" to slay the monster. When Harry and Ron go to him to explain where they think the Chamber is, he tells them this sort of work wasn't in the job description. He reveals that he has done none of the heroic deeds recounted in his books—and tries to work a Memory Charm on the boys to protect his secret.

Harry and Ron disarm him, then force him to join in their pursuit of the Chamber. When he grabs Ron's broken wand while miles under the school, he causes a cave-in by trying another Memory Charm (the wand explodes). The backfiring charm "obliviates" his memory, which compels Dumbledore to say later, "Impaled upon your own sword, Gilderoy!" Most everyone cheers, professors and students alike, when it is announced at the Leaving Feast that Professor Lockhart "would be unable to return next year, owing to the fact that he needed to go away and get his memory back."[2]

In books promoting the virtues of bravery, selflessness, and loyalty, you're not supposed to like Gilderoy. We can laugh at him, but we're clearly not supposed to think of him as a role model. Gilderoy is a cartoon figure of everything self-important, self-promoting, superficial, effeminate, and emasculating—everything the Harry Potter books hope to overcome and replace with heroic, masculine virtues.

Even if we never met him, his name alone would tell us we weren't supposed to like him. *Gilderoy Lockhart* breaks down to *gilded,* or "given a deceptively attractive appearance," *roi*, which is French for "king," *lock*, "shut tight," *hart*, "heart." His name tells us he is a false, "pretty boy" prince with a closed heart, which is to say a "hard heart" that is spiritually dead. What more do we need to know?

The fact that his only magic (his "sword") is the Memory Charm reveals the real value of Gilderoy's books. They are lies, written only for the promotion of their author and, one has to guess, "not for guys." Their strength is that they help us forget; they're an escape wherein we can forget what we are about—and what the author really is about too.

I have to believe that Rowling hates Gilderoy's kind of fiction; it's everything her fiction is not. In this second "book within the book," I think she offers this character to her critics as a foil for her own work. Children's literature that does not come from true belief or genuine love and concern for young readers demeans them and distracts them from spiritual combat-readiness. There are no "stock responses" in Gilderoy's books, no right alignment of soul, and certainly no baptism of the imagination in traditional spiritual doctrines and symbols. Rather than Christ, the true king, all we find in Lockhart's books is himself: Gilderoy, the "false king."

The point of looking at Gilderoy and his books is to realize that this kind of book is as corrosive to right spiritual formation as the moral relativism and other poisons hiding in textbooks. Godless fiction is slow poison to the soul.[3]

But enough about Gilderoy. On to the third "book" inside *Chamber of Secrets*, which is the story line of *Chamber of Secrets* itself. In contrast with the Lockhart genre and Riddle's diary, the Harry Potter books don't demean or diminish readers by indoctrinating them with worldly philosophies. Here is a book to shape the hearts and minds in a different and much better mold!

This book ends with an answer for the Christian critics who criticized the magic of the first book: The best books for children are the ones that model for them a heroic life in battle with the Evil One, dependent on the spiritual graces only available in Christ. That "best book" model is evident in the battle scene at the end of *Chamber of Secrets*, a Christian morality play straight from the oldest English drama traditions for anyone with "eyes to see." I believe that the finish to *Chamber of Secrets* is the most transparent Christian allegory of salvation history since Lewis's *The Lion, the Witch and the Wardrobe*. Let's look at it in detail:

❖ Harry, our Everyman, enters the Chamber of Secrets to find and rescue Ginny Weasley. He finds her unconscious and cannot revive her. He meets Tom Riddle. Because he thinks Riddle is a friend, Harry asks for his help in restoring Ginny. No deal.

❖ He learns then that Tom Riddle is anything but his friend; Riddle is instead the young Lord Voldemort, Satan's stand-in throughout the Harry Potter books. Far from helping him revive Ginny, Riddle has been the cause of her near death. Harry boldly confesses to Riddle's face his loyalty to Albus Dumbledore and his belief that Dumbledore's power is greater than Lord Voldemort's.

❖ The Chamber is filled with the phoenix song at this confession, heralding the arrival of Fawkes (Dumbledore's phoenix), who brings Harry the Sorting Hat of Godric Gryffindor. The Dark Lord laughs at what Dumbledore sends his defender and offers to teach Harry a little lesson: Let's match the powers of Lord Voldemort, Heir of Salazar Slytherin, against famous Harry Potter and the best weapons Dumbledore can give him. He releases the giant basilisk from his reservoir, and the battle is joined.

❖ The look of the basilisk is death, so Harry runs from it with eyes closed. Fawkes the phoenix attacks the charging basilisk and punctures its deadly eyes. Harry cries for help to "someone—anyone" as the phoenix and the blind basilisk continue to battle, and he is given the Sorting Hat by a sweep of the basilisk's tail.

- ❖ Harry throws himself to the ground, rams the hat over his head, and begs for help again. A gleaming silver sword comes through the hat.

- ❖ Evil Tom Riddle directs the blind basilisk at this point to leave the phoenix and attack the boy. When it lunges for him, Harry drives the sword "to the hilt into the roof of the serpent's mouth"—but one poisonous fang enters Harry's arm as the basilisk falls to its death.[4]

- ❖ Harry, mortally wounded, falls beside it. The phoenix weeps into Harry's wound as Riddle laughs at Harry's death.

- ❖ Too late, Riddle remembers the healing powers of phoenix tears and chases away the phoenix. He then confronts the prostrate boy and raises Harry's wand to murder him. The phoenix gives Harry the diary, and Harry drives the splintered basilisk fang into it. Riddle dies and disappears, ink pours from the diary.

- ❖ Ginny revives, and the good guys (and Gilderoy) escape by holding the tail feathers of the phoenix, who flies from the cavern miles beneath Hogwarts to safety and freedom above. Harry celebrates with Dumbledore.

Now let's translate this morality play and allegory. First, we need to know the cast of characters and places and what reality each represents:

- ❖ Harry is Everyman
- ❖ Ginny is virgin innocence, purity
- ❖ Riddle/Voldemort is Satan, the deceiver
- ❖ The basilisk is sin
- ❖ Dumbledore is God the Father
- ❖ Fawkes the phoenix is Christ
- ❖ The phoenix song is the Holy Spirit
- ❖ Gryffindor's sword is the sword of the Spirit (Ephesians 6:17)
- ❖ The Chamber is the world
- ❖ Hogwarts is Heaven

The action of this salvation drama, then, goes like this:

❖ Man, alone and afraid in the world, loses his innocence. He tries to regain it but is prevented by Satan, who feeds on his fallen, lost innocence. Man confesses and calls on God the Father while facing Satan, and is graced immediately by the Holy Spirit and the protective presence of Christ.

❖ Satan confronts man with the greatness of his sins, but Christ battles on man's side for man's salvation from his sins. God sends man the sword of the Spirit, which he uses to slay his Christ-weakened enemy. His sins are absolved, but the weight of them still means man's death. Satan rejoices.

❖ But the voluntary suffering of Christ heals man! Man rises from the dead, and with Christ's help, man destroys Satan. Man's innocence is restored, and he leaves the world for Heaven by means of the Ascension of Christ. Man, risen with Christ, lives with God the Father in joyful thanksgiving.

I can imagine where different types of Christians could disagree with this thumbnail sketch of Everyman's salvation drama, in terms of emphasis and specific doctrines. However, we can all understand the basic structure of the story and admire the artistry of the allegory. Using only traditional symbols, from the Ancient of Days figure as God the Father to the satanic serpent versus the Christlike phoenix (the "Resurrection Bird"), the drama takes us from the fall in the Garden to eternal life without a hitch. There's nothing philosophical or esoteric here. (Can you say, "No alchemy"?)

This is why I believe that these books are spiritual textbooks written in Christian language and in bold opposition to the spiritually dangerous books our children are often given at home and in schools. *Chamber of Secrets* is an unequaled example in the fantasy literature genre that provides an engaging, enlightening, and edifying reading experience for children—as well as a powerful rebuke and wake-up call to Christian critics who cannot see the spiritual forest for the magical trees.

What is *Chamber of Secrets* about? These stories are edifying fiction, written in such a way that they prepare children and older readers for the challenges of authentic spiritual life and for combat with evil.

It's clear from this book, too, that our real enemy is not the magic of Harry Potter, but both the dark magic hidden in our children's textbooks and the "good children's books" written by atheists and the worldly minded.

Chamber of Secrets is a tour de force operating on at least three levels of meaning simultaneously. I can understand Rowling's struggle in writing it, and I agree with her early estimation that it was the best single volume of the series. As a nod to its movie adaptation, I give *Chamber of Secrets* five stars and two thumbs up.

13

DESPAIR AND DELIVERY

Spiritual keys to Harry Potter and the
Prisoner of Azkaban

Prisoner of Azkaban is a much different book from *Chamber of Secrets*. In fact, though I have learned that *Prisoner* is far and away the "best book" according to many Harry Potter fans, many others do not care for it at all. Please note that the books in the series alternate in their emphasis and mood. The first, third, and fifth books are relatively "interior" or psychological novels, and the second, fourth, and sixth are "exterior" or social novels. My unprofessional surveys among serious readers and fans of the books confirm this in that folks who describe themselves as extroverts prefer *Chamber of Secrets*, *Goblet of Fire*, and *Half-Blood Prince*, and self-proclaimed introverts like *Prisoner of Azkaban* and *Order of the Phoenix*.

Prisoner of Azkaban is really a book about escapes and revealed secrets. Who escapes? Who is revealed?

❖ *Sirius Black* escapes from Azkaban and is revealed to be, not the murderer of Harry's parents and servant of Lord Voldemort (as everyone assumes), but Harry's long-suffering protector and authentic godfather.

❖ *Buckbeak the hippogriff* escapes execution and is revealed to be, not the dangerous bird the Ministry thinks he is, but the means of Sirius's salvation.

❖ *Peter Pettigrew,* we learn, escaped Sirius and a death sentence years ago (by feigning his own murder at Black's hands), and he is revealed to be the real Judas. He is a secret-keeper, servant, and spy for Voldemort—as well as the betrayer of James and Lily Potter.

❖ *Pettigrew* also escapes execution in the present (because of Harry's mercy) along with capture, and is revealed to be an animagus—a rat, literally and figuratively.

❖ *Remus Lupin's* werewolf status is revealed at last, but he "escapes" from his own mistaken beliefs both about his friends Black and Pettigrew and about the limits of Dumbledore's ability to understand and forgive.

The most important escapes, changes, and revelations in *Prisoner of Azkaban*, though, revolve around Harry Potter himself.

❖ He escapes from Privet Drive and the badgering of Aunt Marge at the beginning of the book, revealing himself to be an angry young man with a host of unresolved issues about his parents and his own identity.

❖ He escapes from these passions via dissolution of his confusion (and revelation of his past) in the alchemical crucible of the Shrieking Shack, revealing himself by his protection of Pettigrew to be the merciful son of his father.

❖ He escapes his fears and depression that crystallize in the presence of the Dementors, revealing himself by his conjuring of the Patronus at book's end and by his defeat of the Dementor host to be an advanced magician of heretofore unsuspected power.

We've already discussed the first two of these escapes and revelations at some length in previous chapters on choice and change. But Harry's battle to overcome the Dementors is the larger part of

the plot in *Prisoner of Azkaban,* so it warrants a closer look and interpretation.

It's important to remember that the Dementors are incarnations
of depression and despair. Their name reflects this meaning: besides
being a demonlike prefix, *de* is Latin for "from" or "out of," while *ment*
comes from the Latin word *mens* meaning "mind." The Dementors
are literally the demonic "drive-you-out-of-your-minders." Lupin
gives us some details about these guardians of Azkaban:

> Dementors are among the foulest creatures that walk this
> earth. They infest the darkest, filthiest places, they glory in
> decay and despair, they drain peace, hope, and happiness out
> of the air around them. Even Muggles feel their presence,
> though they can't see them. Get too near a Dementor and
> every good feeling, every happy memory will be sucked out of
> you. If it can, the Dementor will feed on you long enough to
> reduce you to something like itself . . . soulless and evil. You'll
> be left with nothing but the worst experiences of your life.[1]

Dementors, then, crush their victims' humanity by feeding on their
hope, happiness, and desire to survive. Lupin reports that "they
don't need walls and water to keep the [Azkaban island] prisoners
in, not when they're all trapped inside their own heads, incapable
of a single cheerful thought. Most of them go mad within weeks."
But they have a "last and worst weapon . . . the Dementor's Kiss"
by which they "suck out [the victim's] soul." So what? Well, if it happens to you, Lupin explains, "There's no chance at all of recovery.
You'll just—exist. As an empty shell. And your soul is gone forever
. . . lost."[2]

The kiss is a poetic expression of the human "consolation"
found in despair: a living death, worse than physical death—soulless existence. The Dementor's effect on Harry even without this
kiss is remarkable enough. Just being near one, Harry experiences
the live replay of his parents' murders by Lord Voldemort over his

crib. Needless to say, this knocks him out and off his feet—and at the climax of one Quidditch match, off his broomstick. The fall nearly kills him, and Gryffindor loses the match.

This won't do. Harry needs a defense against these Dementors and goes to the Defense Against the Dark Arts teacher, Remus Lupin. Though Lupin protests that he is not "an expert at fighting Dementors . . . quite the contrary,"[3] he agrees to give Harry tutorials in how to dispel a Dementor.

In *Prisoner of Azkaban*, Lupin acts as Harry's tutor and de facto Jungian analyst. He is not only coaching Harry in Dementor defense, but in his repeated exposure to his parents' dramatic demise, Harry is also overcoming this trauma. This is an echo of Dumbledore's psychological mentoring in *Philosopher's Stone*, when he taught Harry that it wouldn't do to stand before the Mirror of Erised and long for his dead parents. Harry relearns this critical lesson with Lupin. After one especially traumatic session, Harry reflects:

> He felt drained and strangely empty, even though he was so full of chocolate. Terrible though it was to hear his parents' last moments replayed inside his head, these were the only times Harry had heard their voices since he was a very small child. But he'd never be able to produce a proper Patronus if he half wanted to hear his parents again. . . .
>
> "They're dead," he told himself sternly. "They're dead and listening to echoes of them won't bring them back. You'd better get a grip on yourself if you want that Quidditch Cup."[4]

Chocolate, the ultimate comfort food, helps speed recovery from exposure to a Dementor, but defense from these soul-sucking nasties involves what Lupin and Hermione both classify as "extremely advanced magic." What Lupin tries to teach Harry is how to conjure a Patronus using the Patronus Charm.

This is no easy feat, and Lupin is pained by the experience as well. When Harry says he heard his father speaking, Lupin almost loses it. No doubt the analyst is experiencing some catharsis of the unresolved issues surrounding James Potter's death, namely, Lupin's still being Black's Secret-Keeper. He almost bites Harry's head off when he is asked in all innocence if he knew Sirius Black.

The Patronus Charm requires the wizard to say the words *"Expecto Patronum"* and to concentrate as hard as possible on a happy memory to fill the heart with joy. At first, Harry is only able to conjure a thin, wispy Patronus when he practices with the Boggart. The problem is he "half wants" to hear his parents even in their death throes. After he gives himself a stern talking-to, he finds he can do it. He conjures a magnificent Patronus while chasing the Snitch at his next Quidditch match and dispels the Dementor impersonators from Slytherin.

However, Harry struggles in later attempts to conjure the Patronus, and is only able to do it in the presence of the real thing after his remarkable experience in the Shrieking Shack. A closer look at the words of the charm reveals why—and reveals the larger meaning of *Prisoner of Azkaban* as well.

David Colbert has written a charming companion book for the Harry Potter books called *The Magical Worlds of Harry Potter.* It's a hoot! But in one section called "Latin for Wizards," there's a mistake. Mr. Colbert's Latin is probably in better shape than my own, but he blows the translation of the Patronus Charm. He says *Expecto Patronum* comes "from *expecto,* to throw out; and *Patronus,* guardian."[5] It makes sense as a charm—"I throw forth a guardian"—but it's not what the Latin says.

Expecto is an elision of *ek* or *e* ("out from, out for") and *specto* ("look, watch"). *Expecto,* consequently, doesn't mean "to throw out" (that would have been *expello*—as in "I punched the teacher so they expello-ed me from school"). What it does mean is "to look out for, await, long for expectantly." In the Latin version of the Nicene Creed, the "await, look for" conclusion (*"I look for* the resurrection of the dead and the life of the world to come"*) begins with the word *expecto* ("Et expecto resurrectionem mortuorum, et vitam venturi saeculi").

Patronus can mean "guardian." But in the context of *Prisoner of Azkaban*, it's good to realize the word comes from the root *pater*, which, as we learned in the discussion of Harry's name in chapter 10, means "father." *Patronus* means "little father" or "second father," which is obvious in the English word that derives from it: *patron*, the person—like Dad—who pays the bills. The word can be used as "godfather" (especially as in the movie with Marlon Brando), "guardian," or "deliverer" (as in "from danger"). In this last sense, "savior" is not a bad or infrequent translation.

Expecto Patronum, consequently, can be interpreted a couple of ways. Because Harry's Patronus comes in the shape of his dad as animagus, you could say it means "I look for the figure of my father."

The way Rowling uses this phrase, however, echoes its use from the Nicene Creed—"I long for my savior and deliverer." The charm is said in joyful expectation and in faith that deliverance is coming. I have three reasons for thinking this explicitly Christian meaning is the correct interpretation:

1. Lupin isn't very good at this charm. His haunting problem is not his trouble with lunar cycles, but his lack of faith in Dumbledore's love. Dumbledore has been his "second father" and "patron," but Lupin cannot sincerely say *"Expecto Patronum"* with joy and faith because he doesn't trust that Dumbledore would love him if he knew the truth about him.

2. Harry's Patronus takes the shape of a stag that shines "as bright as a unicorn."[6] Both the stag and the unicorn are traditional symbols of Christ.

3. Harry is able to conjure his Patronus only after the Shrieking Shack experience and after seeing what he thinks is the ghost

of his father conjuring a Patronus to save him from the Dementor's Kiss.

What is it about these experiences that creates the breakthrough for Harry? The Shrieking Shack is an alchemical crucible with character catalysts for Harry's purification, dissolution, and perfection (as in *Philosopher's Stone*'s finish). At the side of the lake, he realizes his identity with his father, on earth as in Heaven. That may seem like a reach, so let's walk through it.

In the Shrieking Shack, Harry is surrounded by the alchemical catalysts and colors we learned in chapter 4 and reviewed in the discussion of *Philosopher's Stone*. Ron is still "red," passionate sulfur; Hermione is still "mercury" or "quicksilver." The black and white elements, however, are different (though Snape makes an appearance when Sirius is revealed to be not so "black"). Sirius Black, of course, takes the "black" part of being unclean: "guilt, original sin, hidden forces." As Dumbledore did with the Mirror in *Philosopher's Stone*, Lupin this time performs the "white" initial or minor work, clearing away Harry's paralyzing longing for his parents. He has "flecks of gray" in his brown hair; my mental picture of a werewolf (unconfirmed by the text) is of a silver-gray, giant wolf. Close enough to "white."

Under these contrary influences, Harry's anger, misconceptions, and passion dissolve. He learns the identities of Moony, Wormtail, Padfoot, and Prongs, along with the remarkable story of betrayal and escape surrounding the Fidelius Charm that was supposed to protect Harry's family in Godric's Hollow. He is transformed by these revelations, so he is no longer the out-of-control, angry boy who blew up Maggie Thatcher—I mean, Aunt Marge—on Privet Drive for carelessly insulting his parents. Harry has become a young man capable of forgiving both Black for making Pettigrew the Potters' Secret-Keeper and Pettigrew for betraying his family to Voldemort.

This last act is one of superhuman mercy, which no one else in the Shack is capable of. The "gold" purified soul does this in imitation

of his father. As Harry says, "I'm not doing this [preventing your exe-
cution] for you [Pettigrew]. I'm doing it because—I don't reckon my
dad would've wanted them to become killers—just for you."[7] This
humility, compassion, and mercy are evidence that he has indeed
achieved a degree of spiritual perfection; his will and his father's will
are one and the same, just as we can read about in John 17:21 and
Matthew 6:10; 26:39.

But Harry is just beginning to realize the connection between
himself and his father. They leave the shack, and Lupin transforms
into a werewolf in the light of the full moon. Black, too, converts
to his animal form to protect everyone from the werewolf, and in
the confusion Wormtail escapes. The children hear Black screaming
and run to his aid at the side of the lake. Dementors! Harry struggles to conjure a Patronus but fails. He is saved from the Dementor's kiss, however, by a spectacular unicornlike Patronus, conjured
from across the water by a figure he thinks is his father.

Dumbledore sends Harry and Hermione back in time to rescue
Buckbeak and Black. On this trip, Harry cannot help himself; he has
to see if it was his father who saved him. He realizes at last he had
not seen his father conjuring the Patronus—he had seen himself.
He conjures the spectacular stag Patronus, the image of his father
as Prongs (and Christ; see chapter 9) that saves Hermione, Sirius,
and himself from the Dementors. Hermione is stunned that Harry
is capable of this sort of advanced magic:

> "Harry, I can't believe it. . . . You conjured up a Patronus that
> drove away all those Dementors! That's very, very advanced
> magic. . . . "
>
> "I knew I could do it this time," said Harry, "because I'd
> already done it. . . . Does that make sense?"[8]

It makes sense, Harry, but perhaps only if you look at this as a Christian who is familiar with the Gospel according to Saint John.

Saint John's Gospel tells us that the Son's relationship with the Father, and ours to the Father through the Son and his Spirit, are the essential relationships of Christian salvation. That Harry's father appears in the form of a Christ symbol (the stag), and that Harry's deliverance (as son) comes at his realization that he is his father (in appearance and will), are poetic expressions of the essential union of Father and Son (in Christian language) for our spiritual perfection.

In *Prisoner of Azkaban*, Harry at last comprehends his likeness with his father. By this knowledge he is able to summon a Christ figure as his salvation, in hopeful, almost certain, and joyous expectation of deliverance. He yells "EXPECTO PATRONUM" without having to think a happy thought because his expectation itself is one pure, happy thought.

Sirius Black tells Harry in his last words before flying away from Hogwarts on the wings of a happy hippogriff: "You are—truly your father's son, Harry."[9] Dumbledore tells him during their end-of-book consultation, "I expect you'll tire of hearing it, but you do look *extraordinarily* like James." Harry at the end of *Prisoner of Azkaban* has realized his identity with his father.

The Lessons of Azkaban

I said at the beginning of this chapter that *Prisoner of Azkaban* isn't an easy book. It is a difficult read, and because of its subject matter, many people have told me they find it depressing—which I think is an understandable reaction. *Prisoner of Azkaban* is about how to combat some of the demons characteristic of the modern world: the depression and despair consequent to lack of faith or conscious spiritual life.

Harry Potter's answer for this problem, though, is anything but depressing. Implicitly, and almost explicitly at times, we see that the answer is our ability to call on a spiritual savior or protector in faith. We need to escape our ego attachments and identify instead, using the Christian tradition's terminology, with our heavenly Father as his children in the Spirit. Following Harry's path, we can find these steps for success in combating despair:

1. Understand yourself as a child of God in need of both patronage and a Savior. Harry is a troubled young man when he arrives at Hogwarts this year. He enters counseling for tutorial help in understanding his problems. His enlightened counselor steers him toward the advanced magic of selfless and joyous expectation of a deliverer.

2. Understand that without humility, there can be no grace. Harry is not equal to this magic until his ego concerns have been purified and dissolved. Only when his family history is clear to him is he capable of the humility necessary to forgive and have mercy. It is a formula that goes back to the desert fathers of the first centuries in the Christian era—"No humility, no grace"—that explains Harry's new abilities to see and act after the Shrieking Shack.

3. In humility and in joy, cry out in faithful expectation. Consequent to his forgiveness and mercy in the Shack (in imitation of his father), Harry is able to see his likeness with his father and to cry out in confident (literally "with faith") expectation of his savior. This achievement in vision and faith is the cure for depression and despair.

4. Look for your Patronus to expel despair. Harry is saved by the stag Patronus that he conjures, and Sirius is saved by the hippogriff Harry and Hermione ride to his tower window. In our contact with the salutary spiritual reality we call into our lives, we too are delivered from death and from the shadows cast by death in this life: depression and soulless despair.

This may not be as straightforward a tit-for-tat Christian morality play as the one acted out in *Chamber of Secrets*. But it reflects the edifying themes, Christian symbolism, and doctrine that we have seen in all the Potter books. That *Prisoner of Azkaban*, despite its complexity and profundity, did not derail or even slow the Potter-mania juggernaut, speaks to both the hunger for this barely concealed spiritual message and the traditional Christian art with which Rowling delivers it. Although I prefer *Chamber of Secrets* to all the other Harry Potter books as a stand-alone novel, it is *Prisoner of Azkaban* that I reread most often. As a son, man, and daddy, I find the transcendent Christian meaning especially helpful.

Muggles, we read in Harry Potter, cannot see Dementors but they can feel them. Certainly I have felt frightened and alone, Muggle that I am, and my only escape from such fears and isolation is my traditional faith in God. Harry Potter, and especially the *Prisoner of Azkaban* installment of his annual adventures, is support and encouragement in the faith and in battling the demons of our culture and times.

14

GIRDED WITH VIRTUE

Spiritual keys to Harry Potter and the
Goblet of Fire

As we've already discussed, the Harry Potter books alternate in emphasis and focus. *Philosopher's Stone, Prisoner of Azkaban,* and *Order of the Phoenix*—the first, third, and fifth novels—are psychological or inward experiences for Harry. *Chamber of Secrets, Goblet of Fire,* and *Half-Blood Prince,* in contrast—the second, fourth, and sixth novels—are less about what Harry learns about himself (his interior life) than what he learns about his world (his exterior life). This alternating of emphasis conforms to the principle of alchemy in which contraction follows expansion (and vice versa) as night follows day and odd numbers follow even.

Goblet of Fire is a big book (certainly the longest single book I had read out loud to my children—until *Phoenix* was published!), and it doesn't lack for events and meaning. Here's a quick summary:

❖ There are important changes in Harry from the beginning to the end of *Goblet of Fire.* He moves from being a spectator at the World Cup and an unhappy school champion to shouldering a grown wizard's burden against the Dark Lord. He matures from a teenager concerned about the opinions of others to a young man of integrity and self-confidence.

❖ There is an expansion of the story line and focus from Hogwarts and Harry's internal and school-yard struggles to the world stage and the social drama of good versus evil. Rowling skewers more than a few sacred cows in her satirical portraits of everything authoritative and institutional, from the courts and prisons to schools, the media, government, and sports.

❖ There is a continuation of the alchemy theme of purification and perfection by trial, both in the crucible of the phoenix song cage with Voldemort and in the four tasks of the Triwizard Tournament. These tasks echo the steps of purification before Harry gets to the Mirror in *Philosopher's Stone*. The Tournament tasks are keyed to the four elements of alchemy: air, earth, fire, and water. Each suggests classical or medieval tournament sport:

AIR: fighting dragons (reference to knights' warfare)
WATER: rescuing hostages (again, knights' work)
EARTH: finding the center of a maze despite obstacles
    (Theseus's hero journey)
FIRE: combat of the champion with the Evil One in a grave-
    yard (morality play)

As we mentioned in chapter 4's discussion of alchemy, the sequence of *Goblet of Fire*'s Triwizard tasks (dragon to egg to bath to submersion to maze to graveyard) follows the images used to describe the alchemical Great Work. As in *Philosopher's Stone*, Harry is being prepared for his confrontation with Voldemort at book's end by the obstacles and tasks he must overcome to get there.

In this book, we can see that sport and combat are a metaphor for the spiritual life. Harry and Hermione admire Viktor Krum's decision to grab the Golden Snitch in the World Cup Final—though it meant his team would lose—because it reflected Krum's doing the right thing even if it meant losing. Honor, bravery, sacrifice—this is what we learn in sports if our focus isn't only on winning and losing. We see it again and again in Harry's choices at the Triwizard Tournament:

❖ Task 1: Harry clues in Cedric that it's about dragons.
❖ Task 2: Harry saves more than just his hostage.
❖ Task 3: Harry saves Cedric twice in the maze.

It has to be noted here that Harry is an *unwilling* champion who *never* prepares properly for his event except in an ad hoc mad frenzy in the days immediately before the event—and that it is always the intervention of outside forces or information that get him through. In the end, Harry has to be ordered by Cedric to share the victory with him. Winning is obviously not the only thing to Harry Potter. In fact, in the Triwizard Tournament it as often as not seems to mean barely *anything* to him.

I would go so far as to say that Harry's indifference and his consequent charity and nobility in life-and-death contests are really the reason he is able to escape Voldemort in their graveyard battle. If that seems far-fetched, it's important to note that Harry does well in the tournament only because of "charity" he receives (from those who want him dead—Moody/Crouch Jr. and Bagman), and only escapes Voldemort because of charity (from Voldemort's victims—those who are already dead). Although he's been tempted to take the low road of advantage in the tournament tasks rather than fighting the other champions, Harry refuses every time, and therefore he is equal to Voldemort's wiles because of his virtue.

The Rebirthing Party: Lessons in Spiritual Combat

Goblet of Fire has its crucible scene in a graveyard, where Voldemort is reborn in a mockery of everything sacred to Christians. A close look at what the Dark Lord calls his "Rebirthing Party" shows it to be a Black Mass.

A Black Mass is the demonic mockery of traditional Christian liturgy and sacramental worship. A Black Mass inverts everything that is sacred; death and darkness trump life and light. In the magic potion and ceremony that Voldemort orchestrates as black magician-priest, all the Christian sacraments are turned on their head with demonic consequences:

- ❖ The Eucharist, or life-giving body and blood of God, are mocked in the potion's requirements of the blood of an enemy, flesh of the servant, and bone of the father (inverting blood of the Savior, flesh of the Master, and Spirit of the Father).

- ❖ The baptismal font and immersion in the name of Father, Son, and Holy Spirit are turned qualitatively inside out in the Voldemort baby's immersion in the cauldron with three magical, physical ingredients (and the "old man" rather than the "new man" or "babe in Christ" rising from the font).

- ❖ Confession, or the sacrament of reconciliation, occurs after (instead of before) this Black Mass and "old man" baptism — and the black arts priest neither forgives nor absolves the Death Eaters' sins and unworthiness but demands eye-for-an-eye service.

- ❖ Consecration of priests and disciples has its carnival mirror image in the blessing of Wormtail and the promised ordination and reward of Voldemort's true servants (and excommunication or murder of those who have broken faith with him).

- ❖ The Liturgy of the Word, or sermon, is mocked in Voldemort's edifying lesson and instruction to his disciples concerning his passion and resurrection.

- ❖ The mystery of Christian burial is turned on its head by the graveyard of a church becoming a birthplace of devils rather than a resting place for those hopeful of an authentic resurrection from the dead.

Harry not only witnesses the death of his friend and this series of demonic desecrations of holy things, he is part of it because his blood, made magically powerful by the sacrificial death and love of his mother, is necessary to the potion (another inversion of the Eucharist). And yet Harry decides to stand and fight as the image of his father. This steadfastness in faith, despite the darkness and perversion surrounding him, recalls his victory in the Chamber of Secrets and is the cause of Harry's consequent epiphany (realization of truth) and theophany (realization of God) in battle.[1]

This courage in making a choice, wrapped up with the love of the father, invites the golden light and inspires the phoenix song that envelops him when he locks wands with Voldemort. We find in *Fantastic Beasts* that the phoenix song is "reputed to increase the courage of the pure in heart and to strike fear into the hearts of the impure."[2] We've already noted that in *Chamber of Secrets* this song is a symbol of the Holy Spirit, and the Trinity is again evident in the Light cage: The association with Dumbledore and the voice from the phoenix song suggest the words from the Father at Jesus' baptism (see Matthew 3:13-17), the phoenix feathers in the wand as a phoenix represent Christ, and the song with its effects points to the Holy Spirit.

Harry only experiences this symbolic epiphany of the Trinity because he is pure of heart. Again, in every task of the tournament, in every difficulty with close friends and media, he has stood courageously on the side of the truth rather than going for the easy win, quick fix, or safe path. As modern day Aesop's fables, the Harry Potter books seem to be telling us that it is not study, your special external preparations, or even your piety that save you in the end. Rather, it is your internal quality—the courage, love, and virtue within—that determines your receptivity to the graces that will save you in spiritual warfare.

If you think I overstate the case, please note that Harry's one-on-one combat with Voldemort in the graveyard (as in the earlier books) is a textbook illustration of what Christians believe works in the battle to overcome the three enemies of ennobling faith: the world, the flesh, and the devil. Here's a closer look at the steps to face these enemies, with examples especially drawn from *Chamber of Secrets* and Harry's battle at the Rebirthing Party in *Goblet of Fire:*

- ❖ Recognize and name the enemy.
- ❖ Recognize your helplessness to combat this spiritual foe on your own.
- ❖ Confess your loyalty to the good.
- ❖ Look for the graces of the Trinity in the Holy Spirit.
- ❖ And finally, work these providential graces as best you can to overcome the enemy.

Throughout the Harry Potter series, combat and sports are used as metaphors for spiritual warfare. Through this, we learn the martial virtues of selfless sacrifice, bravery, and courageous combat—the three virtues Voldemort tells Harry his parents displayed at their deaths.[3] I believe the author has chosen to connect sports to the spiritual because she is aware that sports and warfare have supplanted the Western Church in the hearts and minds of many as places for masculine initiation and heroic virtue. Nonetheless, through these play and mortal battles, we can see the truths of the revealed religious traditions and the greater battle against a very real demonic foe who wants our spiritual death as much as our physical death.

In this, *Goblet of Fire* is no different from the other books of the series; where it differs is in the breadth of the effect that Harry's purity of heart has. We have seen in each book how our preparations and personal choices shape the outcome of our personal struggles with evil; in *Goblet of Fire*, we can see the larger consequences of this personal struggle for our friends and the world. Harry has not only survived, but his victory in escape has mobilized and inspired all the white hats to take on Voldemort. So, too, our pursuit of spiritual perfection, however private and personal, ennobles and enlightens the world.

The Goblet of Fire

> Dumbledore now took out his wand and tapped three times upon the top of the casket. The lid creaked slowly open. Dumbledore reached inside it and pulled out a large, roughly hewn wooden cup. It would have been entirely unremarkable had it not been full to the brim with dancing blue-white flames.[4]

Dumbledore tells us that "the champions will be chosen by an impartial selector: the Goblet of Fire" (chapter 16). Moody later describes it as "a very powerful magic object" (chapter 17). Is this a clever invention of Rowling's?

Well, yes and no. No, it has a referent in medieval legend, but yes, Rowling has changed it a bit to suggest a specific meaning to that legendary piece. In Arthurian legend, the magical object that selected those champions worthy to behold it was the Holy Grail.

The Holy Grail, however, isn't just a magical object like a Sneak-o-scope or Foe glass that detects defects in people. It has its power because it is the Communion cup of Christ's Last Supper; others say it caught the blood of Christ as he was crucified. Legend has it that it was brought by Joseph of Arimathea to England, at that time the most distant outpost of the Roman Empire. Readers of the Arthurian tales know that it could be found only by the most pure of heart (notably, Sirs Perceval and Galahad).

Rowling has made some interesting changes. The Grail of legend is silver, and it is sometimes represented more as a platter than what we would call a goblet. Her large, roughly hewn wooden cup is a Grail suggested by *Indiana Jones and the Last Crusade.* (Do you remember how Harrison Ford picks up a simple cup in a room full

of ornate chalices, pointing to the link between the plain, earthen-
ware cup and the Nazarene *carpenter*?)

But the more interesting changes are the casket and the flames.
The flames might be a touch to satirize the Olympic torch, but the
casket makes me think she is referring to what is inside a Communion cup: the body and blood of Christ. Traditional Christians say
pre-Communion prayers that refer to their Savior's life-giving body
and blood as fire:

> If thou wishest, O man, to eat the Body of the Master,
> approach in fear, lest thou be scorched, for it is fire.
> (DIDACTIC VERSES)

> Let the live coal of Thy Most Holy Body and Blood be for
> the sanctification and enlightenment and strengthening
> of my humble soul and body. (FIRST PRAYER OF SAINT JOHN
> CHRYSOSTOMOS)

> And rejoicing and trembling at once, I who am straw partake
> of fire; and strange wonder! I am ineffably bedewed, like the
> bush of old. (PRAYER OF SAINT SYMEON THE NEW THEOLOGIAN)

> Behold I approach for Divine Communion. O Creator, let
> me not be burnt by communicating, for Thou art fire which
> burneth the unworthy; but purify me from every stain. (SAINT
> SYMEON METAPHRASTES)

> Thou hast ravished me with longing, O Christ, and with Thy
> divine love Thou hast changed me. But burn up with spiritual
> fire my sins and make me worthy to be filled with delight in
> Thee. (COMMUNION TROPARION)

The Goblet of Fire in the fourth book title is a fictional Holy
Grail. However, Rowling's working title until shortly before the book
went to press was *Harry Potter and the Doomspell Tournament*. I think the
title was changed so the tournament would have a more Trinitarian

feel (the Triwizard Tournament)—and so the title would point to the overarching meaning of the book.

The strangest characteristic of the fire in this Goblet is that it is a nonconsuming fire (the cup, remember, is made of wood, not clay). Applicants throw pieces of parchment into these flames, and the fire does not burn them. Though it may seem a stretch to modern Americans, most Christians can't help but note its parallels with the nonconsuming fire of the burning bush on Mount Sinai, the purifying flames of what Catholic believers call purgatory, and the glory or love of God, represented in the iconographic halo or nimbus in sacred art. All these are signatures or correspondences in the Christian literary tradition within which Rowling is writing with God's Word, or *Logos,* which became man as Christ.

Goblet of Fire is named for an object that appears in only one of its thirty-seven chapters and plays a small, mechanical part in the drama of the story, as compared to, say, the Triwizard Tournament or Voldemort's return. Its remarkable Christian meaning, however, makes it an apt title, and we will see its meaning and appropriateness echoed in the title of the fifth book in the series, *Harry Potter and the Order of the Phoenix.*

15

DARK NIGHT OF
THE SOUL

Spiritual keys to Harry Potter and the
Order of the Phoenix

I thought the release of *Goblet of Fire* had been a big deal. Compared to the release of *Harry Potter and the Order of the Phoenix, Goblet of Fire's* publication was a nonevent. Five million copies of *Order of the Phoenix* were sold in the first twenty-four hours of its availability. No one in the publishing industry expected this record to be broken— until the sixth book, *Half-Blood Prince,* was released, and incredibly, the record was shattered.

Order of the Phoenix, though, as popular as it is, disappointed millions of fans who wanted another *Chamber of Secrets* or *Goblet of Fire*. Sixty-five percent of fans who registered their opinion on a MuggleNet.com poll that first weekend said they did not like the book. I suspect the disappointed percentage was higher among younger fans and adult readers who were hoping for a light read at the beach.

They were disappointed because, frankly, *Order of the Phoenix* is a heavy read from beginning to end—what my Latin students called a "real downer." Harry is anything but lovable; he opens the book by bullying Dudley and screaming at Ron and Hermione. By book's end he has raised the stakes by tearing apart Dumbledore's office and shouting rude remarks at the headmaster. I was buried in electronic owls (e-mails) from fans and reporters within thirty-six hours of the book's release, asking me to explain what the "new Harry" was about.

What I told them was essentially this: The clue to understanding the "new Harry" in *Order of the Phoenix* is first to understand how *consistent* the fifth book is with the first four books, despite the seeming changes in tone and direction.

Note, for example, that this book keeps to the pattern of alternating extrovert books with introvert books. The themes of *Order of the Phoenix*, too, are the themes developed in the first four books. Pride and Prejudice—as embodied in the nightmarish High Inquisitor Dolores Umbridge—takes a front place in the book's meaning. Choice, change, and destiny continue on as themes as well. Harry learns at long last of his destiny as the prophesied vanquisher (or victim) of the Dark Lord, although he learns too late to avert an unnecessary tragedy. The theme of love over death, as detailed in chapters 5 and 7, also takes on new depth in *Order of the Phoenix*. Dumbledore tells Harry that his ability to vanquish the Dark Lord—the incarnation of the absence of life and love (and therefore, of death)—is in his tremendous capacity for love.

The structures of the first four books also return in *Order of the Phoenix*. All the elements we are accustomed to find in Harry's annual trip to Hogwarts continue according to formula despite the many changes at the school. And again we have an alchemical Great Work where the beginning reflects the end and the end is the inversion of the beginning.

But there is change beginning to end, too, and quite a remarkable change at that. On Privet Drive at the beginning of the book,

Harry is hot and dry (or choleric, angry) as is the whole world he experiences, where there is a drought and heat wave. At book's end, however, after Harry's tantrum and his lesson about the prophecy, he is changed. Here Harry is described as cold and moist: "The sun had fallen before Harry realized that he was cold. He got up and returned to the castle, wiping his face on his sleeve as he went."[1]

His face is wet from tears, and we soon learn in his exchange with Luna that he is capable of more than anger and self-piteous grief. "An odd feeling rose in Harry—an emotion quite different from the anger and grief that had filled him since Sirius's death. It was a few moments before he realized that he was feeling sorry for Luna."[2] The transformation of Harry in *Order of the Phoenix* from hot, dry, and angry to cold, wet, pitying, and even compassionate signals the most important change in him since his discovery that he was a wizard in *Philosopher's Stone.*

I think it is the agony of this chrysalis that creates the most discomfort and disappointment for readers of *Order of the Phoenix*. As we touched on in chapter 4, *Order of the Phoenix* includes the three stages of the alchemical Great Work but focuses on the black stage, or nigredo, and as one might expect from these colorings, it is a dark business.

Lyndy Abraham's *Dictionary of Alchemical Imagery* describes the nigredo as:

> The initial black stage of the opus alchymicum in which the body of the impure metal, the matter for the Stone, or the old outmoded state of being is killed, putrefied, and dissolved into the original substance of creation, the prima materia, in order that it may be renovated and reborn in a new form.[3]

Citing the alchemists' dependence on Christ's teaching—"Verily, verily, I say unto you, Except a corn of wheat fall into the ground and die, it abideth alone: but if it die, it bringeth forth much fruit" (John 12:24, KJV)—Abraham concludes:

The beginning of spiritual realization is always accompanied by some kind of sacrifice or death, a dying to the old state of things, in order to make way for the new insight and creation. Burckhardt observed that the turning away of the outer world to the inner to face the shadow of the psyche is frequently experienced as a nox profunda, before the dawning of the new light of illumination. The nigredo is a difficult phase, but only through experiencing it can the adept gain the wisdom and humility necessary for illumination.[4]

Order of the Phoenix is Harry's dark night of the soul, or nigredo, in which everything in his world is either turned on its head or taken from him. What is left of Harry by book's end? He is not a Quidditch player, he is not enamored of Cho Chang, he is not distinct from Voldemort (the man he must kill or be killed by), he is no longer the son of a hero and of a "match made in Heaven," he no longer over-shadows Ron and Hermione in all things outside the classroom, he can no longer think of Privet Drive and his life at Hogwarts as separate realms without overlap or confusion (Hogwarts has been revealed as a paradise that can become a hell almost overnight), and he is no longer a hero in the public mind or able to play the hero in crisis without self-doubts. After Sirius's death—the climax of the nigredo being poetically expressed as the "death of Black" after a year in the House of Black—Harry is a shattered person. He knows the prophecy that set the events of his life in motion and that will shape his end, but the process of his breakdown in the grievous shadow (the meaning of the name *Dolores Umbridge*) of his fifth year leaves him unable to know who he is or what he wants.

Harry could not stand this, he could not stand being Harry anymore. . . . He had never felt more trapped inside his own head and body, never wished so intensely that he could be somebody—anybody—else. . . .

Whenever he was in company, he wanted to get away,

and whenever he was alone he wanted company. . . . Perhaps the reason he wanted to be alone was because he had felt isolated from everybody since his talk with Dumbledore. An invisible barrier separated him from the rest of the world. He was—he had always been—a marked man. It was just that he had never really understood what that meant. . . .[5]

Harry has been broken down to a formless condition akin to the prime matter of the alchemists in order to be able to understand himself exclusively in the light of the prophecy. He struggles at water's edge in the sunshine to come to grips with the fact that his life must include, or end in, murder. Everything in his life will come down to his ability to vanquish Voldemort—his "old man"—or his failure to meet this destiny.

Why does this put so many readers off? Because in living through the nigredo with Harry, as closely as we all identify with him, *we are stripped down ourselves.* With Harry, we are reduced to our fundamental decision in life: Do I live a life of love for the "new man" and for my spiritual development, or do I appease the "old man" and live with death and my individual ego priorities until my biological death seals my choice? This is a decision few readers are delighted to be confronted with in any circumstance—and certainly not when reading a diversionary, supposedly children's novel!

If the language of alchemy and Christianity makes your eyes go glossy, look at *Order of the Phoenix* as a psychology course. We can understand the "old man" as "dad," the way we use the phrase in common speech. *Order of the Phoenix* is, in large part, about Harry's coming to terms with his being the heir of his biological father, James. He is, it seems, living both *in* James's shadow and *as* James's shadow; note that at the beginning of the book Harry's behavior toward Dudley is not much different from James's bullying of Snape, which we learn about in the Pensieve via Severus's memory. Harry confronts this image of what he is becoming, rejects it, and then experiences the consequences of this rejection—the death of his father-shadow in the death of his godfather Sirius.

Neville in many ways is Harry's twin. Both were born at the same time, have similarly heroic parents, were effectively orphaned by Voldemort, and are linked in the prophecy. Neville goes through a similar break with his past when, in combat with the Death Eaters, he breaks his father's wand. Neville's grandmother has always told Neville he doesn't measure up to his father; by breaking his dad's wand, Neville is free to be his own man with his own wand. Sometimes a wand is just a wand, but here we are certainly meant to reflect on the wand as a Freudian image.

Likewise, at the end of *Order of the Phoenix* Harry has been stripped of his ideas of himself and has further rid himself of his obligation to live as the image of his father. The only thing he is given to replace this no-longer-living psychological matrix is his revealed destiny as Voldemort's vanquisher or victim. Dumbledore explains that his identity as vanquisher lies in his capacity for love. Harry must decide between his old identity, the "old man" and image of James, or this "new man" of love, a power that is not his own and that he does not understand, appreciate, or embrace.

Order of the Phoenix ends with this question unresolved, although it seems unlikely that Harry will be able to deny his prophesied destiny now that it has been revealed to him. The book is a difficult experience for the reader because we identify with Harry as his old self-understanding is being stripped from him and as he is angry at the process (and at it taking so long!). The ending, in which he is shown his new identity (one he has already taken on at least in part as leader of Dumbledore's army), is stunning to us, even though we can see that the nigredo has prepared him for it.

Why are we stunned and uncomfortable with what Harry has experienced in *Order of the Phoenix*? I believe it's because we live in a culture without rites of transition from childhood to adulthood (unless taking the SAT or a driver's license test qualifies as a harrowing rite of passage). The United States is largely a commercial, desire-driven country in which children become independent children rather than autonomous adults. *Order of the Phoenix* is the story of a boy who is burnt to a crisp and then rises from the ashes as a new man, conscious of his prophesied destiny beyond his birthright to conquer death by love. Though all human beings are called to this destiny and to a decision to make this destiny the focus of our lives, few do so because of the demeaning distractions and diversions of our time.

This is suggested by the Disillusionment Charm used by Moody. By "disillusioning" the boy, the Auror makes Harry essentially invisible before their long flight to London from Privet Drive. The charm makes Harry a "human chameleon" indistinguishable from his surroundings. We would probably have called this an Illusionment Charm rather than a Disillusionment Charm, but the spell is well named. Being able to see through ourselves and see only those things external to us that shape us is disillusionment or enlightenment of a kind, because the forms we take on as our identity *are* delusion or illusion; we are, objectively speaking, really only transparencies of our environment, our heritage, and the accumulation of such influences over time. *Order of the Phoenix* is a book-length disillusionment for Harry to rid himself of his self-illusions and to prepare him for the revelation of who he *really* is at bottom: the destined vanquisher or victim of the Dark Lord, *as are we all.*[6]

Harry Potter and the Order of the Phoenix is a disturbing book for this and other reasons. The most important of these is the primary place love is given. This book nearly beats its readers over the head with love, and since few of us are as loving as we'd like to hope we are becoming, this disturbs us.

Some notable "love moments" in *Order of the Phoenix* include:

❖ Dumbledore tells Harry that his grief is a reflection of his love.

❖ Dumbledore clarifies for Harry that the prophesied power of Voldemort's vanquisher—"the power the Dark Lord knows not"—is love.

❖ Harry learns that the sacrificial love of his mother lives on in the "bond of blood" he has with her via Aunt Petunia.

❖ Hagrid models sacrificial love in his care for Grawp, his half brother.

❖ Harry is victorious over Voldemort during the Dark Lord's takeover of his body via his love for Sirius.

❖ Harry is unable to use an Unforgivable Curse effectively.

We learned in *Goblet of Fire* from Moody/Crouch Jr. that there are three Unforgivable Curses, the use of which means an automatic life sentence in Azkaban. These three curses call to mind the unforgivable sin in the Christian tradition of speaking against the Holy Spirit (see Matthew 12:32; Mark 3:29; Luke 12:10). Let's look at how each of these curses is "speaking against the Holy Spirit":

Avada Kedavra: The Killing Curse, a combination of the commonplace "abracadabra" and "I have a cadaver," takes a life. The wizard who uses it supplants God as the giver and taker of life.

Crucio: The Cruciatus Curse tortures its object with excruciating pain until the curse is lifted. The curse itself means literally, "I crucify (you)." This points to the fact that cruel treatment of our fellow human beings translates to cruel treatment of God and a forsaking of the spiritual life (see Matthew 25:40).

Imperio: The Imperius Curse is Latin for "by command" or a variant of *impero,* which means "I give orders (to you)." This curse supplants the principal gift of God to man, his free will, by the will of the wizard performing the curse. Though not as damaging to the physical person as the other two curses, the Imperius Curse is the greater sin against the Holy Spirit.

The reason these curses are unforgivable is not so much in the nature of the curses themselves as it is in the *spiritual condition* the witch or wizard must be in to perform them correctly: one of willful separation from God and the good. The righteous can say the words, but the curses will lack the power they have when they are performed by the unrestrainedly wicked. Even in righteous anger, Harry, as a vehicle of love in the world, cannot yet sin against the Holy Spirit in this way. His connection with the good prohibits him from using weapons of darkness to defeat Voldemort or his Death Eaters, as we see in the battles at the end of *Order of the Phoenix* and *Half-blood Prince*.[7] (Harry's successful use of the Cruciatus Curse on Amycus Carrow in *Deathly Hallows*[8] deserves special mention in chapter 17.)

All these instances of the power and qualities of love remind us that we as individuals are not as loving as we are designed to be (John 15:12), but that we embrace advantage and death to greater or lesser degrees. Harry's struggle to embrace his prophesied destiny as the Dark Lord's vanquisher through love and light is the *human* struggle to do the same with the darkness in our spiritually opaque, hardened hearts.

Our discomfort with *Order of the Phoenix* might be summarized as our resistance to the demands of spiritual life in general and the "Christian walk" in particular. As we watch Harry's childish ideas of himself dissolve in the nigredo during his fifth year at Hogwarts, we are confronted by our own need to renounce the world and its claims on us in order to transcend ego and follow Christ. In Harry's struggles with obedience in learning Occlumency, we experience our own resistance to watch over our hearts, minds, and tongues, although we know it's necessary in order to cleanse them of carnalmindedness, temptation, and sin. Reading about the bond of blood that protects Harry, *homo religiosus* beings that we are living in a post-Christian world, it would be strange if we didn't even think of the bond of blood Christians believe they have in Christ by his sacrifice and the Eucharist he left to preserve the faithful in that bond. And in the death of Sirius Black and Harry's agony over his part in it, Rowling points again to the importance of choices in realizing human destiny, not the least of which is our spiritual destination.

Order of the Phoenix contains the most explicitly Christian references of the series so far in the battle at the Ministry of Magic, where Sirius is killed. Harry gets a glimpse beyond the veil—a reference both to the veil of the Temple and the shack in Lewis's *Last Battle*—to an afterlife where the righteous will meet again. We also see the mysterious power behind the door, which is both "more wonderful and more terrible than death, than human intelligence, than forces of nature."[9] This power burns the unworthy and protects the beloved (see the end of *Philosopher's Stone*): a reflection of God's love, also known as his judgment, mercy, and glory. And Dumbledore tells Harry—and us—that we can find the answer to the riddle of death and our fallen nature and bad choices only in Love, the power that the Dark Lord "knows not" and that will mean his defeat. "God is love" (1 John 4:8), and our spiritual faculties, the eyes of our heart, resonate with the message.

Even the title of the book, *Harry Potter and the Order of the Phoenix*, confirms a transcendent meaning of this book. The Order of the Phoenix is the band of magical folk allied to combat Voldemort's Death Eaters. As we've already seen, the term *Death Eaters* points to antagonism toward Christians, who are commanded by God, who is Life, to be "Life Eaters" in remembrance of him. But the Order of the Phoenix points specifically to the Christian life and to spirituality in general in more ways than just its opposition to Voldemort's Death Eaters.

The word *order* is a religious term, referring to a group with a specific vocation (until modern times almost always primarily contemplative) within the Church. That this order is "of the Phoenix," a traditional symbol both of the end of alchemy and of Christ himself, highlights this otherworldly meaning.

And what does the phoenix do? As we see Fawkes do in spectacular fashion at the end of *Order of the Phoenix*, the living story-symbol of Christ swallows the Death Curse of the enemy, dies in flames (the nigredo), renouncing the world and life itself in sacrificial love for its brother—and in the hope of being "born again," as Christians would say, in the image of a savior rising from the dead. We are designed for a life greater than ourselves and to perceive and pursue the sacred; we respond to the celebration of this beginning and end of human existence even in the darkest of the Harry Potter books.

Fortunately, *Phoenix* was the nigredo and Harry's nadir, or dark night of the soul. The war with the Dark Lord opens up in *Half-Blood Prince*, but Harry's life brightens quite a bit during his illumination and purification in the penultimate novel of the series. Turn the page to learn what it is about.

16

BAPTISM INTO A
SACRIFICIAL DEATH

Spiritual keys to Harry Potter and the
Half-Blood Prince

Potter-mania was by no means exhausted after the release of the fifth book and third movie of this popular series; if anything, the book and movie only created a greater interest in the young wizard from the UK. The sixth book, *Harry Potter and the Half-Blood Prince*, when released in July 2005, had a first-run printing of more than 10 million hardcover copies in the United States alone—7 million copies more in a first run than any previous book in publishing history that was not by J. K. Rowling.

Fortunately, *Half-Blood Prince* disappointed very few fans and only confirmed Rowling's place in the hearts of children and adult readers. Unlike the reception for *Order of the Phoenix*, which was "mixed" to "poor" at first but which was eventually embraced by fandom as perhaps the best of the series (in part because it is the longest!), *Half-Blood Prince* has been a fan favorite since it came out of the gates. Why? Well, for starters, it is a lot less painful to read!

Black to White—Phew!

As we have already seen, *Phoenix* is the alchemical reduction by fire of Harry from all his ego concerns. The alchemical nigredo, or "black work," however, ended with the death of Sirius Black and the closing of *Phoenix*. The opening of *Prince* had to be in a cold rain as the books entered the albedo, or alchemical "white work." *Half-Blood Prince* is the Potter novel in which Harry is purified for the final work of spiritual transformation by the immersion in cleansing waters and the dissolution of contraries in the story. This part of Harry's journey, compared with his dark night of the soul in *Phoenix*, at least, is a lot of fun!

SNOW, BOOZE, AND TEARS IN THE WHITE WORK

If you have a *Dictionary of Literary Alchemy* on hand, look up *white, ablution,* or *albedo.* What you'll find is a host of specific things to look for, including *luna,* the nighttime stars, the white lily, a swan, water, cold, and whiteness—anything pale, silvery, or white.

We learn in the opening pages of *Prince* that an unseasonable "chilly mist" pervades Britain this July, and cold, wet weather is the backdrop of the entire story. Rain, sleet, snow, and banks of mist are the rule for *Prince*. When Ron waves his wand "vaguely in the direction of the ceiling" near the book's end, it begins to snow.[1] This Harry Potter adventure, for the most part, takes place in the fog, near a body of water, or stepping in from wet weather.

The fluid in every scene isn't restricted to what's in the atmosphere. Almost every chapter in *Half-Blood Prince* includes a drinking scene. From the two large glasses of whiskey that Cornelius Fudge conjures "out of thin air" for the Muggle Prime Minister in the opening chapter, the "bloodred wine" Snape pours for his guests in Spinner's End, and the glasses of "Madam Rosemerta's finest oak-matured mead" Dumbledore serves the Dursleys on his visit to Privet Drive, to the poisoned mead that almost kills Ron on his birthday, the cooking sherry that Professor Trelawney drowns her professional sorrows in, and the bottles of elf-made wine that Professor Slughorn drinks with Hagrid after Aragog's funeral, it's a rare chapter in which Muggles and wizards aren't drinking strong spirits.

All this imbibing stops, however, with the twelve crystal goblets of emerald phosphorescent potion that Dumbledore drinks on the island in the cavern lake, which begins the climax of the alchemical drama.

In a book about purification and fluid, of course, everyone cries real tears (or at least has moistened eyes) somewhere in this drama. Some characters are crying because their love is unrequited, others weep because of fear or joy, and Dumbledore himself gets teary because he is touched by Harry's loyalty.[2] Even the hard-hearted characters cry openly at Dumbledore's death and funeral. The "white work" of alchemy is about purification by washing, and Rowling obliges the formula by immersing us in drinks, tears, and wet weather.

A TEEN ROMANCE WITH SPIRITUAL MEANING?

Rowling's books are all detective fiction: largely about solving a mystery. This year's mystery is Draco's secret suicide mission from Lord Voldemort. In between this action, however, we are buried in teenage romance.

This is not any less appropriate to the subtext of the alchemical white stage than rain, booze, and tears. Ron and Hermione, alchemical sulphur and quicksilver, respectively, have in previous books been the "quarreling couple" of alchemy, whose differences and agreements have been the refining work of Harry's purification in drama. In *Prince*, after a comedy of misunderstandings and attempts to show up the other, these two at last recognize their destiny together.

In fact, the book ends very much like a Shakespeare comedy or Austen novel, with every couple coming together at long last for a happy ending of sorts. Bill and Fleur's union is finally blessed by

Mrs. Weasley's tears, Tonks and Lupin hold hands at the funeral in anticipation of their nuptials, Harry and Ginny become the long foreshadowed King Arthur and Queen Guinevere, and Ron and Hermione are the crowned red king and white queen of Harry's alchemical dreams.

The action of the book, then, is ablution, and the scrubbing is the attraction and repulsion of contraries that are finally resolved. This is not a painless process, as those who have been scrubbed clean by their mother remember. But it sure beats being reduced to a cinder from merciless heat, as we as readers were in the fifth Harry Potter book.

WASHING IS ABOUT PURIFICATION

When you bleach, wash, and scrub your favorite white dress shirt, it comes out brilliantly white, doesn't it? And we have white images galore in this white stage book: Slughorn's magnificent mustache; the snow that falls indoors and out for months at a time; the beautiful, blonde Luna in "spangled silver robes" at the Christmas party; the dreadful Inferi living in the cavern lake; the white flame, white smoke, silver Phoenix Patronus, and white tomb at Dumbledore's funeral. This book needed a white cover, no?

And few people blush in this book. Everyone turns white, pale, or gray at one point or another. Tonks goes colorless; Draco is white or gray; everyone who is startled, angry, tired, or otherwise emotionally elevated is "white."

But the whitest part of the book is the reappearance of Albus Dumbledore, whose first name in Latin means "white" or "resplendent." Largely absent in *Phoenix*, the headmaster is never very far from Harry's mind in the sixth book. In *Prince*, Dumbledore gives five tutorials, all of which are instructions in the life and ways of Lord Voldemort. After he reveals the ways of the Evil One and what must be done to defeat him, Dumbledore the alchemist marvels at the love within Harry and at his purity:

"You are protected, in short, by your ability to love!" said Dumbledore loudly. "The only protection that can possibly work against the lure of power like Voldemort's! In spite of all the temptation you have endured, all the suffering, you remain pure of heart, just as pure as you were at the age of eleven, when you stared into a mirror that reflected your heart's desire, and it showed you only the way to thwart Lord Voldemort, and not immortality or riches. Harry, have you any idea how few wizards could have seen what you saw in that mirror? Voldemort should have known then what he was dealing with, but he did not!

"But he knows it now. You have flitted into Lord Voldemort's mind without damage to yourself, but he cannot possess you without enduring mortal agony, as he discovered in the Ministry. I do not think he understands why, Harry, but then, he was in such a hurry to mutilate his own soul, he never paused to understand the incomparable power of a soul that is untarnished and whole."[3]

Proclaiming Harry's purity and love as his best weapons against the Dark Lord, the White Wizard then takes Harry on a trip to destroy a Horcrux of Lord Voldemort—Harry's baptism by water and fire.

A Story like All Other Stories

But I'm well ahead of myself. *Half-Blood Prince* is very different from the previous books in this series because of the alchemical step it represents in Harry's "Everyman" journey to spiritual perfection. These differences, though, should not obscure the fact that this is, indeed, a Harry Potter book, in every way like every other Harry Potter book.

By this I don't just mean we have the same characters at the same school with the same likes and dislikes, however true this is.

Prince also has all the themes, formula structures, and traditional spiritual meaning and Christian symbolism that mark Harry Potter as surely as his lightning bolt–shaped scar.

THE HARRY POTTER FORMULA CHECKLIST

Let's run through our Harry Potter checklist. Mystery? As we've already seen, our mystery is in trying to figure out what terrible secret mission Draco has been assigned by the angry Lord Voldemort. Check this off the list.

Narrative traction? Quarreling Ron and Hermione, Lord Voldemort's life story in tutorial flashbacks with Dumbledore. Two checks.

Hero's journey from Privet Drive to King's Cross? With the exception of the ending that seems to have *multiple* symbols of Christ, all saving Harry from death again and again but without a trip to King's Cross, everything is in place here, too.

Is the magical world still divided neatly along the Gryffindor/Slytherin axis? This remains the conflict at the heart of the books—it's still either Voldemort's way or the selfless way of moral courage, but the world isn't neatly divided (outside of Hogwarts, anyway) between white hats and Death Eaters. We meet even more politicos and worldly types among the witches and wizards who are nominally opposed to Voldemort but who resist him with the methods of a Death Eater or not at all.

And the four themes that define this seven-book series—change, choice, prejudice, and love's victory over death—are all here too.

Death: Horror of Horcrux. The question that hangs over the Harry Potter novels until the final chapters of *Deathly Hallows*, the series finale, is, "What is the link between Harry and Lord Voldemort?" The mystery of both Harry's survival of the dreaded *Avada Kedavra* curse as an infant and Voldemort's survival of the rebounded curse is the key. We take a big step forward in understanding this mystery in *Half-Blood Prince*, in which we learn of the existence of Voldemort's Horcruxes. These Horcruxes also play a key role in developing the theme of death, as well as love's victory over death—a large part of the series' meaning.

The Horcrux is "'the word used for an object in which a person has concealed part of their soul. . . . You split your soul, you see,' said Slughorn, 'and hide part of it in an object outside the body. Then, even if one's body is attacked or destroyed, one cannot die, for part of the soul remains earthbound and undamaged.'"[4] The "horror" in Horcrux is that splitting the soul is only possible "by an act of evil—the supreme act of evil. By committing murder. Killing rips the soul apart. The wizard intent upon creating a Horcrux would use the damage to his advantage. He would encase the torn portion" by a spell into an object.[5]

The nightmare of Voldemort's immortality experiments is that he has six Horcruxes outside of his body for a total of at least seven soul fragments that must be destroyed.

The word *Horcrux* is an interesting combination of Latin and French derivations. *Hor-crux* from the Latin would be "frightening or horrible" (*horreo*) and "cross" (*crux*); rather than finding the way to immortality in the lifesaving sacrifice of Christ on the Cross, the Horcrux accomplishes the task through murder.

Although the word *Horcrux* is probably a Rowling invention, the idea of encasing part of the soul into a physical object apart from the body is not an innovation in literature, folk tales, or myths. It even reflects obliquely the Christian teaching on the nature of a saint's incorruptible body at death (i.e., the grace-filled power of relics).

Rowling's brilliant spin on this literary cliché, however, is to say the soul is "rent" by sin and "split" by the greatest of sins against love for others (their murder, physically or spiritually). Lord Voldemort, the arch villain, pursues immortality apart from God and the Cross by pouring his soul into physical objects apart from his body. In this, Voldemort is simultaneously a materialist and a dualist—and no longer human, as Dumbledore says, because he fails to understand the power of a human being who is whole, an integer of body and soul, and pure, which is to say "not rent or split."[6]

To destroy Voldemort, then, Harry must find and destroy four or more remaining Horcruxes and Lord Voldemort *while at the same time* being careful to remain "pure of heart." Dumbledore warns Harry that, even after the Horcruxes are destroyed, "while his soul may be damaged beyond repair, his brain and his magical powers [will] remain intact. It will take uncommon skill and power to kill a wizard like Voldemort even without his Horcruxes."[7] This power, Dumbledore tells Harry, is Harry's love.

Two things are especially worthy of note here. First, Voldemort's path to escape death (his name meaning, literally, "flight from death") is clearly the wrong one—the path that the reader is taught to see as an atrocity. This way to immortality is the way of ego preservation, identification with material things, disregard for the body as an integral aspect of the human person, and quite literally the rendering of the soul for power and personal advantage. Looking at the monster that the soul-twisted and torn Voldemort has become, we see in story form the answer to Christ's rhetorical question: "What shall it profit a man, if he shall gain the whole world, and lose his own soul?" (Mark 8:36, KJV).

In contrast, Harry the hero does not fear physical death. If anything, he seems more than a bit reckless with his life when he gets caught up in what Hermione calls his "saving-people-thing."[8] His close attachment to his ego concerns was largely broken in his fifth year at Hogwarts, when almost every activity he loved and the ideas he identified with were taken from him or spoiled. He is a young man who loves his friends, loves the good, and loves romantically as well. More than anything else, he is determined to do the right thing, whatever it costs him personally.

This contrast brings me to my second point about the Horcrux. What does the reader of this Harry Potter novel come away with as the meaning of death in these books?

Soon after *Prince* was published, a Catholic friend in Canada and a young student in a Louisiana seminary both wrote me to say that Dumbledore's death on the Astronomy Tower "sends a disturbing, confusing moral message" to children about mercy killing and euthanasia (they believed, correctly, that Dumbledore had planned his own death). My earnest friends have missed entirely the point Rowling has delivered to her readers' hearts. It's not about death being acceptable only on the dying person's terms or pain free; it's close to the opposite of Dr. Kevorkian's message.

"You have a soul. The purity of your soul and its capacity for love are your greatest strengths. Sin and evil rend your soul and diminish your whole person, body and soul, toes to nose. Invest your soul in the good and in those you love, not material objects. Love as sacrificially and as selflessly as you can," Rowling seems to say, "and an untarnished and whole soul will defeat death and his minions."

Rowling does not argue for the soul's existence, and she does not didactically offer Harry's way as superior to Lord Voldemort's twisted path. Her story, however, makes care for the soul and love of the good, true, and beautiful all things readers recognize as the best and most desirable things.

What we have learned about death in *Half-Blood Prince* is that the death we must fear is a spiritual one. If we care for our souls and work to be as loving as we can, we may cheat death and those who fear and serve the Dark Lord.

Formula Ending: Who or What Is the Christ Symbol in *Half-Blood Prince*?

The four principal themes—change, choice, prejudice, and death—then, can all be checked off our Rowling formula master list. We know too that she is still using the alchemical formula in making *Half-Blood Prince* the "white stage" novel. What remains? Her hero journey formula ends every year with Harry's resurrection from the dead in the presence of a traditional symbol of Christ and with the revelation of a bad guy who seemed good (or vice versa).

This year we have both, in spades. In fact, Harry seems to be saved from death by *three* different Christ figures, and we seem to have learned at last the real master and consequent allegiance of Severus Snape. Let's look first at the end of Harry's journey, his near death, and his being saved again.

Every year after the mystery has come to a crisis, Harry and his friends confront the bad guys underground, Harry dies a figurative death, and he survives because of love in the presence of a symbol of Christ. He comes to terms with the battle's meaning, a good guy is revealed as a bad guy (or vice versa), and everyone travels home on the Hogwarts Express to King's Cross station. In *Half-Blood Prince*, we have all these elements except the train ride home (canceled because of the funeral), as well as a plurality of lifesaving events and symbols of Christ.

The symbol most like previous symbols is Buckbeak the hippogriff, who saves Harry from a seemingly murderous and unhinged Severus Snape. After a long chase from the top of the Astronomy Tower to the Hogwarts grounds (this year's descent underground), Harry lies helpless before Snape's wrath when the hippogriff swoops in with his razor-like claws to drive the former Potions Master out the gate.

Snape, too, hard as it may be for some to believe, must also be considered one of Harry's saviors in *Half-Blood Prince*. He saves Harry from the other Death Eaters, right after Harry makes his formulaic speech about, *This must be it, the pain is too great, I must be dying.*

Snape, an unlikely Christ symbol I'll admit, qualifies as such because of this rescue, his being in fact the "Half-Blood Prince" of the title—a pointer to the "Double Natured King," certainly—and because of his being the "great physician" in this year's adventure. He not only "stoppers Dumbledore's death" by sealing the arm wound Dumbledore received when destroying the Slytherin ring Horcrux, but he also saves Draco Malfoy's life (and Harry from a trip to Azkaban) by sewing up the Sectumsempra Curse slash by singing the healing charm (shades of Aslan).

As interesting as Buckbeak and Snape are, however, I doubt they are really the saviors of this year's adventure. Albus Dumbledore rescues Harry in the cave of the Inferi, and his actions there and on the Astronomy Tower mark him as a powerful image of the Man-God beyond any concern about literary formula requirements and checklists.

DUMBLEDORE AT *HALF-BLOOD PRINCE'S* STYGIAN LAKE

At the crisis of this year's mystery, Harry learns simultaneously that Draco Malfoy has succeeded in whatever project he has been working on all year in the Room of Requirement, that Dumbledore is ready to leave Hogwarts on a Horcrux search-and-destroy mission, and that it was Severus Snape who overheard the prophecy years before and told Voldemort about it. Pulled in three different directions by these revelations, Harry leaves the castle with Dumbledore on the mission of two minds about Snape—only after sending his friends on a mission to prevent Snape and Malfoy from carrying out an attack on Hogwarts in their absence.

Harry and the headmaster apparate from Hogsmeade to a seaside cave. Once inside the cave, and after Dumbledore performs a necessary "crude" blood sacrifice, they gain entrance to a much larger cave that holds a vast lake of glass-smooth black water. They travel by magic boat to an island at the center of this Stygian lake, in which lives an army of magically animated corpses called *Inferi*.

At the center of this small island is a stone basin filled with a phosphorescent emerald-colored fluid that proves impenetrable to magic. Dumbledore is confident that the Horcrux they are seeking is at the bottom of this basin and decides he must drink the fluid to reveal the Horcrux. After extracting Harry's promise to force him to drink it all, he forces down twelve chalices of the green fluid, screaming for mercy and death, and then collapses with a death rattle. Harry revives him and is unable to give him the water he requests until he dips the chalice into the lake, which brings the Inferi to the island to protect the Horcrux.

Harry, after some struggle with these living dead, resigns himself to death in the lake they are carrying him into. But Dumbledore rises from the ground and from his seeming death, and drives the Inferi away with a ring of fire. He grabs the locket in the basin, and they escape the island and the cavern lake, and apparate back to Hogsmeade. The headmaster, near collapse, is more than half carried by Harry from the cave but reassures Harry by telling him that he is not worried: "I am with you."

Let's review what happens in the cave.

* ❖ Dumbledore offers his blood sacrificially at the cave entrance.
* ❖ He drinks twelve cups of a green fluid and suffers horribly.
* ❖ He rises from death to turn back with warmth and light the Inferi who have captured Harry.
* ❖ He reassures Harry by expressing confidence in him with the magisterial, "I am with you."

The blood sacrifice Dumbledore himself calls "crude" and is an obvious cue that this is Dumbledore's walk to Calvary. His drinking the twelve cups on the island, the center of darkness and death, represents his taking upon himself the totality (twelve being the number of a complete cycle) of sins and evil in the world. (Green, with few exceptions in these stories, is the color of Slytherin and the Dark Lord.) He suffers horribly and dies in his voluntary acceptance of the bitter cup (compare to Christ in the Garden of Gethsemane, Matthew 26:39). The headmaster rises from the dead and harrows the denizens of hell with light to save his disciple (compare to John 1:4 and Matthew 17:2). He reverses and echoes his early pronouncement of Harry being safe because "you are with me" when he first meets Harry with his "I am with you" (compare to Matthew 28:20 and John 17:21).

But though near death, Dumbledore flies from Hogsmeade on a rescue mission to Hogwarts, which he and Harry see upon their return is under the Dark Mark, the sign of death. On his arrival at the Astronomy Tower, which has been foretold will be his doom, he is disarmed and attacked by a student who has betrayed him to his enemies. He is merciful to the student, who mistakenly believes that he has the greatest wizard who ever lived at bay because he is wandless, and Dumbledore offers him forgiveness, sanctuary, and the freedom to choose to turn from evil and death of his own volition, uncoerced. Dumbledore is surrounded by tormentors before the boy can accept his love, and then Dumbledore is seemingly murdered by a friend and blasted from the Tower.

This morality play is not given with scriptural references within the story. I have to think, nonetheless, that few serious readers who have made their way through the New Testament even once struggle to see the parallels with Christ's loving, sacrificial death on Calvary.

- ❖ Dumbledore comes to Hogwarts to die and to save its occupants from the rule of death that hovers over the castle.
- ❖ He is tormented by those he could destroy even without a wand or escape by transfiguration, even though he is weakened from his suffering in the cave (Plato's allegory of the world).
- ❖ He is merciful, loving, and respectful of man's free will to accept or deny this mercy and love.
- ❖ He is betrayed by a disciple and murdered by those he has come to save.
- ❖ His death is, on the surface, ignominious, brutal, and senseless.

At Dumbledore's funeral, too, Rowling repeats the theme of Harry's safety being linked to Dumbledore's presence. Harry explains to the Minister of Magic that Dumbledore may be dead but he is not gone and that Harry's loyalties remain with the headmaster. But as we have seen, Harry may be Dumbledore's man by public confession, but he is not yet a Dumbledore man through and through, because of his prejudices and anger. As we learn in the last year of his Hogwarts adventures, Harry has another year to struggle from just being Dumbledore's image to being his likeness. This is possible if Harry continues to imitate Dumbledore in his choices, and specifically his choice to believe in Dumbledore despite his doubts.

Dumbledore has revealed to Harry that freedom exists primarily in our freewill efforts to realize our destiny. Dumbledore's choices in his death are Christlike, and if Harry is to defeat Lord Voldemort with love, he has to follow in his headmaster's footsteps.

Harry has been ascending the ladder of love that Plato described in *The Symposium*. The four Greek words for love are *storge* (familial affection), *philia* (friendship), *eros* (sexual or romantic love), and *agape* (selfless love). Harry has managed to climb from the family love he never knew at the Dursleys (but found at Hogwarts) to a romantic love with Ginny at the end of *Half-Blood Prince*. What is left for him to master is the selfless or sacrificial love that his mother showed in her choices while battling Voldemort and that Dumbledore showed in the cave and on the Tower.

Conclusion: Meaning of *Half-Blood Prince*

Every Harry Potter novel prior to this book has been an obvious or opaque allusion to Christ, and *Half-Blood Prince* is no exception. You do not need to be a theologian or even a Sunday-only Christian to make the leap from "Half-Blood Prince" to the "Double-Natured King."

Half-Blood Prince, as the "white work" in the alchemical drama, is largely the story of Harry's immersion in water, purification of heart, and ultimately baptism into the sacrificial suffering and death of Albus Dumbledore—Rowling's story symbol of the God-Man. Harry has, if you will, "put on Christ" (see Romans 6:3-12 and Galatians 3:27) but is not yet the "through and through" man of faith that he thinks he is. As he gathers and destroys the remaining Horcruxes in his seventh year, the test of *Deathly Hallows* is about whether he has realized and taken to heart the power of love that can defeat death.

The first six books of the Harry Potter series reveal, in large part, the centrality and the power of faith in story form, and the series ending in *Deathly Hallows* turns on a loving sacrifice of self. Before discussing the remarkable seventh book, it's appropriate to marvel at the great gift these novels are to the world and the countercultural phenomenon they represent. Readers around the world for more than ten years have been fully engaged and shaped by images of love, by transcendent messages of sacrifice resonant of Christ, and by a plotline based on the virtues of courage, loyalty, and purity. In a world seemingly enamored of death, violence, and pornographic images, who could have guessed that the first decade of the twenty-first century would be dominated by an edifying spiritual tale by a writer in the best traditions of English literature?

Because every trip is more about the journey than the destination, I could not be more grateful for my time (and my children's time) with Harry and friends, even if the ending had not been as great as it turned out to be. Harry's remarkable popularity in my home and his unrivaled success in homes around the world speaks to the human heart, however many dragons may guard it, still having a God-shaped hole we long to fill.

Harry Potter, of course, is not the plug for this hole. In the best tradition of English culture and letters, however, reading Harry's adventures points us to and prepares us for the journey to the cure for our heart disease in the "real world." We can ask for no greater gift from our reading than the imaginative baptism we enjoy in *Half-Blood Prince*. The spiritually lame may not walk after finishing the Harry Potter novels, but every reader on any kind of spiritual journey is engaged, encouraged, and edified by his adventures. As the lyrics of a popular song have it, "Who could ask for anything more?"

17

CHOOSING TO
BELIEVE

Harry Potter and the Deathly Hallows
as the struggle with faith in story form

There is something silly about the argument that Harry Potter fascinates readers around the world because of the symbolism, doppelgängers, and alchemy of the stories, most of which artistry these readers miss. Even if, as C. S. Lewis wrote, "an influence which cannot evade our consciousness will not go very deep,"[1] we have to assume there is something much more relevant and current in Rowling's artistry that hooks her readers. If it were just the Christian symbolism and hermetic flourishes that drive Potter-mania, *The Pilgrim's Progress, The Faerie Queen,* and *Orlando Furioso* would be fighting with Harry Potter for the top of the best sellers list.

A big part of Harry's relevance to his postmodern audience is the message in the books about prejudice. As a rule to which there are very few exceptions, we think the great triumph and continuing battle of our historical period is our engagement against racial, sexual, and just about any other kind of intolerance and discrimination.

To call someone racist, sexist, elitist, or a religious bigot is to tar that person with a heavy brush. The crime of prejudice is considered so great in this age that the accusation of guilt is often a conviction that can never be wiped clean from the public mind. Harry's war with the Death Eaters, who are obsessed with "purity of blood," and his victory over Voldemort (with his shades of Nazism) are in many ways the epic narrative of the twentieth and twenty-first centuries' attempt to shatter all restrictive or prejudicial metanarratives (see chapter 6).

In *Deathly Hallows* though, Harry's story gets another hook that makes a deep connection with almost every reader of the last two or three generations. We live in a time of great skepticism about religious belief, and some would say, as a result, that our age also has the qualities of moral disarray and confusion. Our epoch-defining struggle with belief results from the intersection of this skepticism and our innate spiritual capacity; as Abraham Maslow wrote, "a capacity is a need," and our need for spiritual growth and experience is blocked in large part by our doubts about any revealed religion's ability to deliver on its promises of grace and transformation or salvation.

Harry Potter and the Deathly Hallows is about just this struggle to believe in our secular culture—a struggle we all make or resist to some degree. The message *Deathly Hallows* delivers is a profound affirmation of not only the importance of belief but also the difficulty and effect of choosing to believe despite our doubts. The series finale also points the way to both what we should avoid believing and the benefits we should expect consequent to this difficult choice, namely, our spiritual transformation and victory over interior and exterior evils.

This "struggle to believe" story line is told as Harry's agony about how to remember and whether he should trust or believe in the late Hogwarts headmaster Albus Dumbledore. Harry is "Dumbledore's man through and through" at the end of *Half-Blood Prince*. After the first chapters of *Deathly Hallows*, however, in the face of contradictory evidence, his faith in his mentor, in Dumbledore's virtue, and in his mission for Harry to defeat Voldemort are broken. I'll assume for the sake of this discussion that Dumbledore, inasmuch as he stands for anything allegorical, represents "the object of religious belief," be it God, the Church, or a specific spiritual guide or confessor. Harry is an Everyman figure in a heroic, comic morality play. Call him "the Seeker" like his angry Gryffindor Quidditch teammates did in *Philosopher's Stone*.

Deathly Hallows, looked at as an exercise or struggle to believe, has three parts that parallel the alchemical black, white, and red stages of the Great Work. Harry begins the book convinced that he will never see Dumbledore again, abandons his faith more and more through the first eighteen chapters (culminating in "The Life and Lies of Albus Dumbledore"), chooses to believe in Dumbledore though he lacks sure knowledge to substantiate this faith and trust, and then overcomes his internal demon and external foes because of this choice.

Curious as it might seem, Harry's thoughts in the book's second chapter suggest that he doesn't believe in an afterlife. Luna believes the voices she heard beyond the veil confirmed that she would see her dead loved ones again. Harry, though speaking about the impossibility of seeing Dumbledore again on this side of the veil, clearly does not think the way Luna thinks about death:

> A flash of brightest blue. Harry froze, his cut finger slipping on the jagged edge of the mirror again. . . . . He had imagined it, there was no other explanation; imagined it, because he had been thinking of his dead headmaster. If anything was certain, it was that the bright blue eyes of Albus Dumbledore would never pierce him again.[2]

Dumbledore is dead, Harry thinks, *and that's that*. By story's end, of course, Harry has seen Dumbledore again "face-to-face," and the transformation of his beliefs from beginning to end is largely forgotten.

But it is quite a trip. Harry moves from beliefs that protect him from his grief for the headmaster he cannot contact to doubting in his mentor's goodness and a denial that Dumbledore loved him, before Harry reconsiders what he believes. Rowling uses two characters to represent "unexamined belief" and "unexamined disbelief," both of whom undermine Harry's faith in Dumbledore because Harry wants his belief to be based on the truth, not reflex opinion.

The two characters are Elphias Doge and Rita Skeeter. Their contradictory testimony is the focus of chapter 2, "In Memoriam," in which we read Doge's eulogy for his friend Albus and an interview with Rita Skeeter about her new book, *The Life and Lies of Albus Dumbledore*. We see the pair again at the wedding (chapter 8), where Harry listens to an argument between Doge and a Skeeter advocate, Auntie Muriel. Ron's aunt pretty much wipes the floor with Dogbreath, to whose every objection she has a pointed answer, often with damning testimony from witnesses. As the nigredo begins in chapter 9, Harry's childlike faith in the headmaster, his surety that "help will always come to those who ask for it," is on the rocks.

What is most interesting in the Doge/Muriel exchange is the way Rowling frames Harry's struggle. She makes his struggle to believe not about personal doubts and surety but a function of choice, a theme running through the whole series, with an emphatic statement of its importance in Dumbledore's explicit teaching on this subject in *Chamber of Secrets*.

> "Don't believe a word of it!" said Doge at once. "Not a word, Harry! Let nothing tarnish your memories of Albus Dumbledore!"
>
> Harry looked into Doge's earnest, pained face and felt, not reassured, but frustrated. Did Doge really think it was that easy, that Harry could simply *choose* not to believe? Didn't Doge understand Harry's need to be sure, to know *everything*?"[3]

Rowling draws our attention to choice and belief again in chapter 10, "Kreacher's Tale," when Harry and Hermione go at it about whether to believe like Doge or to join the Skeeter skeptics like Auntie Muriel:

> "Harry, do you really think you'll get the truth from a malicious old woman like Muriel, or from Rita Skeeter? How can you believe them? You knew Dumbledore!"
>
> "I thought I did," he muttered.
>
> "But you know how much truth there was in everything Rita wrote about you! Doge is right, how can you let these people tarnish your memories of Dumbledore?"
>
> He looked away, trying not to betray the resentment he felt. There it was again: Choose what to believe. He wanted the truth. Why was everybody so determined that he should not get it?"[4]

In his meeting with Doge, Harry asks himself how Doge could think Harry could "choose not to believe" Auntie Muriel's nastiness about Dumbledore. With Hermione, he reframes the question into a choice whether to believe the for- or against-Dumbledore advocates without demonstrative proof or sure evidence from either side. He has his positive experience, and he is learning what Dumbledore never shared with him; if the two contradict as obviously as his experience and these reports do, how is the seeker to choose to believe one way or the other and maintain his sanity? In Harry's mind, choosing your beliefs is a little like choosing what you see and hear, namely, the mark of an idiot. You believe what is true, not what you want to believe.

Dumbledore may have left him clueless about important things, but he didn't leave him without an important teaching about choice. "It is our choices, Harry, that show what we truly are, far more than our abilities." Rowling has said this scene at the end of *Chamber* is a critical point in the books.[5] I think we all understood it in the context of what she was saying about prejudice and choice trumping birth-right. If what we believe about what we cannot know for sure, how-ever, comes down to personal choice, as Harry says, Dumbledore's teaching about choice is resoundingly relevant. It is what we choose in those subjects that are not certain or empirically studied that most tell us what we are (i.e., our beliefs about our end as human beings, the existence of God, worship, etc.).

Before Harry makes his conscious choice one way or the other, he throws off his "acquired, not chosen" Dumbledore man beliefs:

> His fury at Dumbledore broke over him now like lava, scorch-ing him inside, wiping out every other feeling. Out of sheer desperation they had talked themselves into believing . . . that it was all part of some secret path laid out for them by Dumbledore; but there was no map, no plan. Dumble-dore had left them to grope in the darkness, to wrestle with unknown and undreamed-of terrors, alone and unaided: Nothing was explained, nothing was given freely.[6]

After reading "The Greater Good" chapter in Skeeter's *Life and Lies* book, he reaches bottom:

> "Look what he asked from me, Hermione! Risk your life, Harry! And again! And again! And don't expect me to explain everything, just trust me blindly, trust that I know what I'm doing, trust me even though I don't trust you! Never the whole truth! Never!" . . .
>
> "I don't know who he loved, Hermione, but it was never me. This isn't love, the mess he's left me in. . . ."
>
> He closed his eyes at her touch, and hated himself for wishing that what she said was true: that Dumbledore had really cared.[7]

No longer a Dumbledore man, Harry apparates with Hermi-one undercover to the Forest of Dean. Harry feels "as though he was recuperating from some brief but severe illness."[8] And then the light begins to shine in the darkness:

> A bright silver light appeared right ahead of him, moving through the trees. Whatever the source, it was moving soundlessly. The light seemed simply to drift toward him.
>
> He jumped to his feet, his voice frozen in his throat, and raised Hermione's wand. He screwed up his eyes as the light became blinding, the trees in front of it pitch-black in silhouette, and still the thing came closer. . . .
>
> And then the source of the light stepped out from behind an oak. It was a silver-white doe, moon-bright and dazzling, picking her way over the ground, still silent, and leaving no hoofprints in the fine powdering of snow. She stepped toward him, her beautiful head with its wide, long-lashed eyes held high.
>
> Harry stared at the creature, filled with wonder, not at her strangeness, but at her inexplicable familiarity. He felt that he had been waiting for her to come, but that he had forgotten, until this moment, that they had arranged to meet. His impulse to shout for Hermione, which had been so strong a moment ago, had gone. He knew, he would have staked his life on it, that she had come for him, and him alone.[9]

Is this Goudge's *Little White Horse*? Sort of. It is certainly the Cervus Fugitivus of literary alchemy. In *The Dictionary of Alchemical Imagery*, Abraham explains that "the fleeing deer or hart symbolizes Mercurius in his role as the intermediary soul which unites the body and spirit of the Stone."[10] In what I think is the most successful sewing of a tapestry of alchemical, Arthurian, and Christian threads in Rowling's seven books, Harry and Ron pull the sword from the baptismal pool, and Ron is purified and rejoined to the triptych of mind, body, and spirit because he and Harry followed the silver doe.

The critical thing to grasp here, beyond the alchemical symbolism, is that Harry, without beliefs or pronounced disbelief but with broken faith and wand secure near his heart, knows the silver doe is there for him. "Caution murmured it could be a trick, a lure, a trap. But instinct, overwhelming instinct, told him that this was not Dark Magic. He set off in pursuit."[11]

We know from Snape's memory that this is his Patronus, the Patronus of Lily Evans Potter. Harry's immediate, intuitive identification with this icon without the need of proof and his instinctive decision making throughout the chapter (going into the pool after the sword of Gryffindor, having Ron destroy the Horcrux, etc.) speaks to a cardiac rather than a cranial intelligence guiding Harry. Lupin understands Harry as well as any man but Dumbledore:

> "And what would you say to Harry if you knew he was listening, Romulus?"
>
> "I'd tell him we're all with him in spirit," said Lupin, then hesitated slightly. "And I'd tell him to follow his instincts, which are good and nearly always right."[12]

Dumbledore called this cardiac intelligence, not "instincts" or "intuition," but "love." Harry's heart, though, was darkened by his confusion of Dumbledore-man beliefs and thinking-person disbelief. Having passed through the nigredo and having been stripped of this muddle, he begins to see with the eye of the heart. And he makes the choice to believe.

It isn't an easy thing, and it is only in the context of the temptation of the Deathly Hallows and Dobby's heroic death that Harry makes this choice. Xenophilius Lovegood has told them the story of the three brothers from Beadle the Bard, and Harry has figured out what the three Hallows are—and that he has two of them and Voldemort is after the third. It is in his excitement about this last point that he breaks the name taboo and is taken to Malfoy

Manor. Harry asks Aberforth for help, and Harry's disciple, Dobby the house-elf, arrives.

Dobby's heroic efforts save the trio (Harry, Ron, and Hermione), as well as Griphook, Dean Thomas, Luna, and Ollivander. But it is his death that saves Harry. Dobby's life and death, along with Neville's heroic resistance while waiting for Harry's return, are the two examples of Christian discipleship in *Deathly Hallows*.[13]

Dobby? The Vladimir Putin look-alike comic-effect figure of the stories? Yep.

Dobby is a slave in the "House of Bad Faith" (Mal-foy). He hears about "the Boy Who Lived" who was a savior who had delivered his people from the Dark Lord. When he learns that the Malfoys are plotting against Harry Potter in *Chamber of Secrets*, Dobby resolves against all convention and house-elf obedience to serve his true master. This sacrificial, loving, and often funny service results in Harry freeing Dobby from his Malfoy masters and Dobby's greater love for Harry Potter.

In *Deathly Hallows*, Dobby is called on to save Harry and his friends. He returns to the place of his worst nightmares, the house of Malfoy, to demonstrate his freedom and fidelity to his savior. Not very surprisingly, this exercise results in Dobby's dying for his friends and, most especially, to save Harry. He dies in Harry's arms near Shell Cottage with his beloved Harry Potter's name as his last words.

Allegorical? I think so. Just plug in "Christ" for "Harry Potter" in the above story and you have a story-form version of the Christian Everyman, slave to passions and misconceptions, liberated by a child's belief in the Messiah, and a growth in love that imitates at life's end the sacrificial and unrestricted love of his Savior. Certainly Dobby's faith in and sacrifice for him knocks Harry off his feet.

Harry's intelligence is arational for the most part, which serves him well in the Cloud of Unknowing. To his credit, he gets the meaning of Dobby's Christian example in choice, belief, obedience, and sacrifice. Malfoy Manor, the place of his servitude and the place from which his faith in Harry Potter freed him, had to be the last place Dobby wanted to go, but go he did. Dobby is comic relief for much of the books, but it is his death and his example that cause something of a faith chrysalis in Harry.

He goes underground. He experiences a revelation. And he makes a choice. Believe in Dumbledore; forsake the Deathly Hallows temptation and get the Horcruxes as instructed.

> Grief, it seemed, drove Voldemort out . . . though Dumbledore, of course, would have said that it was love. . . .
>
> In the darkness, with nothing but the sound of his own breath and the rushing sea to keep him company, the things that had happened at the Malfoys' returned to him, the things he had heard came back to him, and understanding blossomed in the darkness. . . .
>
> Dobby would never be able to tell them who had sent him to the cellar, but Harry knew what he had seen. A piercing blue eye had looked out of the mirror fragment, and then help had come. *Help will always be given at Hogwarts to those who ask for it.*
>
> Harry dried his hands, impervious to the beauty of the scene outside the window and to the murmuring of the others in the sitting room. He looked out over the ocean and felt closer, this dawn, than ever before, closer to the heart of it all.
>
> And still his scar prickled, and he knew that Voldemort was getting there too. Harry understood and yet did not understand. His instinct was telling him one thing, his brain quite another. The Dumbledore in Harry's head smiled, surveying Harry over the tips of his fingers, pressed together as if in prayer.

You gave Ron the Deluminator. . . . You understood him. . . . You gave him a way back. . . .

And you understood Wormtail too. . . . You knew there was a bit of regret there, somewhere. . . .

And if you knew them. . . . What did you know about me, Dumbledore?

Am I meant to know but not to seek? Did you know how hard I'd find that? Is that why you made it this difficult? So I'd have time to work that out?

Harry stood quite still, eyes glazed, watching the place where a bright gold rim of dazzling sun was rising over the horizon.[14]

And then in the golden pink (yes, white to red, like the stones on the grave, the transition to rubedo) of dawn, Harry makes his decision. He knows, but he doesn't seek the Deathly Hallows. He chooses to believe in Dumbledore and in the mission he was assigned:

Harry hesitated. He knew what hung on his decision. There was hardly any time left; now was the moment to decide: Horcruxes or Hallows?

"Griphook," Harry said. "I'll speak to Griphook first."

His heart was racing as if he had been sprinting and had just cleared an enormous obstacle.[15]

Harry has made the leap of faith, not in ignorance but with knowledge of his choices and how he might proceed to defeat Lord Voldemort. He chooses Dumbledore's designated path, and the story is over in large part. With this choice, Harry "has shown what he truly is," to paraphrase the headmaster, and the victory over Voldemort, if not a done deal, is before us.

That Harry has made a choice and is committed to it consciously is revisited in his conversation with Albus's shadow, his

brother Aberforth, who, unlike Rita Skeeter, knows the headmaster's faults as intimately as a second self. But even Aberforth
does not sway Harry from the choice he made underground by
the sea:

> Harry kept quiet. He did not want to express the doubts and
> uncertainties about Dumbledore that had riddled him for
> months now. He had made his choice as he dug Dobby's
> grave, he had decided to continue along the winding, danger-
> ous path indicated for him by Albus Dumbledore, to accept
> that he had not been told everything that he wanted to know,
> but simply to trust. He had no desire to doubt again; he did
> not want to hear anything that would deflect him from his
> purpose.[16]

Rowling has told her readers that her "struggling with religious
beliefs and so on" are "quite evident" in *Deathly Hallows*. And they are.
But this is not the struggle of a skeptic or of a schoolchild who is
beginning to reexamine mechanically held beliefs. This is the struggle of one who knows that there is no knowing for certain rationally
but that not believing has consequences and belief in many ways is
always a choice. Seeing what happens to those who choose not to
believe or, to use another word Rowling contrasts Harry and Voldemort with, those who choose not to *trust*, Harry chooses to believe
and to trust.

And it is this choice that makes all the difference.

So if Harry is Everyman and a seeker after truth, the moral of
the story, if you will, is to believe. But what is Dumbledore representing in this morality play? God? The Church?

Listen to Dumbledore in King's Cross:

> "Can you forgive me," he said. "Can you forgive me for not
> trusting you? For not telling you? Harry, I only feared that you
> would fail as I had failed. I only dreaded that you would make

my mistakes. I crave your pardon, Harry. I have known, for some time now, that you are the better man."[17]

That's a pretty rough speech for God or the Church to make. I'd almost prefer a Freudian psychological interpretation with the headmaster "old man" representing the superego. But I think "loving authority" or "spiritual director," even "father," is as good.

We see in the story of Harry's transformation from Dumbledore man to Dumbledore denier to Dumbledore's better—even his confessor—the trials and consequences of the struggle to believe. Religious belief is a struggle and a choice, we learn in story form, and it is essential to believe in order to overcome both internal failings and external enemies.

Without Harry's decision in the grave, Voldemort's soul piece wins the battle for Harry, and Voldemort wins the world as well. And perhaps as important, in hearing Dumbledore's confession and request for forgiveness and redemption, we see that spiritual authorities are fallen people with tragedies and failings of their own. Their failings are not reason to choose disbelief or the temptations of worldly power.

In *Deathly Hallows*, a seeker's religious beliefs are hard won, a day-to-day choice, and this choice is critical in understanding the sort of person Harry is and the person he is becoming. In *Deathly Hallows*, Harry's decision to believe in Dumbledore—in the face of all the reasons and evidence fostering his doubts and disbelief—is what makes him successful in cleansing himself of the Voldemort Horcrux and defeating the Dark Lord despite the Elder Wand. Rowling elegantly and seamlessly ties together in *Deathly Hallows* what we have learned about choice in the previous six books with Harry's struggle to believe.

Deathly Hallows, then, is an argument *for* the choice of religious belief. Harry recognizes in Dobby's example that those who believe are different—and better—than those who do not (think Auntie

Muriel, Rita Skeeter, and Lord Voldemort). But if Rowling in *Deathly Hallows* is making an argument for religious belief, however difficult the struggle to choose to believe, what *specific* recommendations does she make about this belief, if any? Does *Deathly Hallows* answer Christian critics who have been concerned about Harry Potter as a gateway to the occult?

What Are We to Struggle to Believe?

The story line of *Deathly Hallows* gives particularly strong rebukes to beliefs that are "spiritual," not "religious," about power and individual gain rather than transformation, and to beliefs that are just "knowing better." Rowling's critics who claim her books are soft on the occult and who assert that Harry Potter is an invitation to New Age and amorphous, insubstantial beliefs have not read or understood *Deathly Hallows*.

The Muggles featured in the stories are Harry's aunt, uncle, and cousin, all of whom are concerned only about their material wealth, the perception of others about their status and "normalcy," and their comfort. In *Deathly Hallows*, Rowling gives a spectrum of possibilities about the redeemability of such people. Uncle Vernon, the businessman? Totally lost and unable to see beyond the restricted area of vision defined by his prejudices and ignorance. Aunt Petunia? She wants to say a kind word at Harry's farewell but finds herself unequal to even right sentiment.

Only Dudley, who has faced Dementors with Harry (and seen himself as he is under their influence), is able to escape the meanness and spiritual barrenness of his upbringing. He startles Harry at their farewell by his earnest if awkward expression of goodwill. The only hope is with the children, it seems—the intended audience of Harry's magical story.

What does the story share with these children? What should they struggle to believe in if more toys and computer games aren't the *summum bonum* of human existence? Well, witchcraft and New Age beliefs aren't what the story promotes. *Deathly Hallows* is a textbook about what is wrong with the occult and New Age, as we see in the story's treatment of Horcruxes and the three Deathly Hallows.

Horcruxes and Deathly Hallows: Occult Magic, Idolatry, and the Vanity of the New Age

Lord Voldemort's pursuit of individual immortality through murder and dark magic is certainly a pointer to "secret knowledge" or gnostic spirituality. As much as occultists claim a secret way, an esoteric wisdom that elevates them above the empty exoterism of the common herd, the depiction of the astrologer centaurs in *Deathly Hallows'* Forbidden Forest and in the Dark Lord's means of salvation is equating their path as mistaken, even evil and inhuman. "Occult" comes from the Latin word *occultus*, meaning "secret" or "hidden." Harry Potter does not make an argument for private spirituality or secret wisdom.

The Horcruxes, too, are in a sense worse than "occult objects." As discussed in chapter 7, the act of creating a Horcrux—the murder of a person and the deposition of a soul into a physical object—is also an act of idolatry and self-love much like materialists make. Most of us do not fall into the temptations of occult practice or worship more seriously than looking up our birthdays in newspaper astrology columns. I suspect, however, that we all have invested soul fragments in things we own or ideas of ourselves that we secretly hope will make us live forever in one form or another. Rowling, in making the Horcrux the focus of her Evil One stand-in and Harry's shadow self, is pointing to this idolatry and private means to immortality as the conceptual failing and ego-driven spirituality we need to understand as a greater danger to us than occult groups.

Harry's big temptation was never to learn how to make a Horcrux and ensure his personal immortality. The decision that is the turning point of the whole book, as discussed above, is Harry's choice not to pursue the Elder Wand and complete the set of Deathly Hallows but to destroy Voldemort's Horcruxes in obedience to Dumbledore's instructions. Dumbledore tells Harry in King's Cross after his sacrificial death that in being equal to the temptation of the Hallows he was a "much better man" than the headmaster.

We can tell Dumbledore is not kidding because he *wasn't* equal to the temptation of the Hallows. The three greatest wizards of the seven-book series, in fact—Gellert Grindelwald, Albus Dumbledore, and Lord Voldemort—each fall consequent to their fascination with the power of the three magical objects the legendary Peverell brothers received from death: the Elder Wand, the Resurrection Stone, and the Invisibility Cloak. The tales about the Hallows concluded that the witch or wizard who possessed all three would be the "master of death" and undefeatable.

The great wizards, consequently, pursue other Hallows and especially the Wand of Destiny as Hitler pursued the Spear of Destiny: for occult power and individual gain in the name of the "greater good." Fascination with the Hallows was what brought Dumbledore and Grindelwald together—and what led to Ariana's accidental death and Dumbledore's decision to never pursue personal or political power. His death, however, despite this resolution, was largely a consequence of his excitement and momentary regression to his childish error on discovering the Resurrection Stone in one of Lord Voldemort's Horcruxes. The Peverell ring had been cursed, and only Severus's genius with the Stoppered Death potion prevents the headmaster's immediate demise.

The moral of the story isn't obscure. The way of the occult in this story is the path to spiritual and physical death. Even the relatively comic treatment of New Age seekers in these books also makes their private preoccupation and parlor-game spirituality seem a dead end.

Sibyll Trelawney, the teacher of divinations at Hogwarts, is always presented as a self-important and more than a little pathetic loony tune. Dumbledore suggests that she is kept on at Hogwarts only as an act of charity—and to protect her from Lord Voldemort and his search for the exact wording of the original prophecy. She has her student admirers (all as goofy as their mentor), but the disdain with which she is treated by Umbridge, McGonagall, and Hermione Granger marks her as a New Age nut.

Professor Trelawney barely enters into the story of the Deathly Hallows. It is from Xenophilius Lovegood, on the other hand, that Harry, Hermione, and Ron learn the story of the Deathly Hallows—and to him the children's fairy tale as recorded by Beadle the Bard is history, not fantasy. Xenophilius, it turns out, seeks the Hallows as a New Age believer practices numerology, astrology, and tarot card reading, which is to say, as a path to his individual enlightenment.

Lovegood, though a comic figure like Professor Trelawney, is anything but "hallowed" by his beliefs and pretense. Super-seeker that he pretends to be and champion of the absurd and countercultural, when push comes to shove, his principles are revealed to be empty posturing. Sibyll at least fights for the right in the Battle of Hogwarts. Xenophilius ("friend of the strange," by the way) delays Harry, Ron, and Hermione when they come to his ziggurat tower; he hopes he will be able to trade them for his daughter, whom the Death Eaters have taken prisoner to ensure his silence and obedience.

His New Age foppery give him the principles and package of Peter Pettigrew.

The struggle to believe and the importance of the choice to believe are the central messages of *Deathly Hallows*. Readers aren't to believe just anything "spiritual," however, or ideological. Secularism, occultism, and New Age beliefs as "spiritual paths" darken the hearts and diminish the characters of the people who choose to follow them. A large part of Harry's achievement in *Deathly Hallows* is in his choosing the path of trust and obedience rather than the way of personal power and occult enlightenment. But in what exactly is he trusting and believing?

18

CHRISTIAN BIRTH AND BAPTISM

Harry Potter and the Deathly Hallows
as the alchemical adventures of a
Christian Everyman

Harry's spiritual life, to speak frankly, is presented in the closing chapters of *Deathly Hallows* and the 4,100-page Harry Potter epics as the path of a disciple of Christ. This last novel is certainly not an in-your-face altar call; it is, nonetheless, a story so saturated in specifically Christian points of reference and meaning that to deny them is to miss a large, perhaps even the greater, part of the transcendent meaning of the books.

Most notably, the book's three alchemical parts, its black, white, and red sequencing, in which Harry is broken down, illumined, and triumphant, are told in the sequence of the three principal Christian feasts that parallel these three stages in chronological sequence. When we examine the chapters of *Deathly Hallows* in which Harry celebrates the holy days and meanings of Christmas, Theophany, and Easter, his final spiritual chrysalis and transformation into a "little Christ" is, as Ms. Rowling has said herself of the stories' Christian content, "obvious."[1]

Christmas Eve at Godric's Hollow

Harry and Hermione resolve in chapter 16 to go to Godric's Hollow to see if Dumbledore had hidden the sword of Godric Gryffindor there with the aged Bathilda Bagshot. They arrive in the small village as Polyjuiced, middle-aged Muggles and discover that the village is largely a magical memorial to the Potters, whose deaths to save the "Boy Who Lived" also saved the wizarding world from Voldemort. The war memorial changes into a statue of the family as Harry and Hermione pass by, and their home is marked with a sign saying it has been left unchanged "as a monument to the Potters and as a reminder of the violence that tore apart their family."[2] The sign is covered with graffiti from magical tourists expressing their love for and faith in Harry.

This last really lifts Harry's spirits because the adventure in Godric's Hollow is undertaken almost in desperation and certainly in the depths of Harry's spiritual winter and doubt. The trio had been broken in the previous chapter when Ron Weasley departed in anger and disgust over their inability to eat as much as he'd like or find and destroy Horcruxes. Harry's camping trip with Hermione alone thereafter is miserable, at least until they agree to venture to Godric's Hollow, because they have no plan beyond evading capture.

The villagers carrying presents on the way to the Godric's Hollow church reveal to the Polyjuiced couple that it is Christmas Eve. They decide to go to the church as well when Hermione sees a graveyard behind it in the light from the windows. "They'll be in there, won't they? Your mum and dad?"[3]

The first gravestone Harry stumbles upon is the Dumbledore family marker over the graves of Kendra and Ariana, Aberforth and Albus's mother and little sister. "Upon the frozen, lichen spotted granite" are carved the words: "Where your treasure is, there will your heart be also" without the notation that this is from the Sermon on the Mount (Matthew 6:21, KJV).[4] Harry is convinced that Albus must have chosen these words, but their meaning escapes him and he feels only bitterness about all the things the headmaster never told him.

They find the grave of Ignotus Peverell with the Deathly Hallows symbol before Hermione stumbles on the Potter tombstone. Its inscription, "The last enemy that shall be destroyed is death" (from 1 Corinthians 15:26, KJV), also leaves Harry frustrated and angry.

> "'The last enemy that shall be destroyed is death' . . ." A horrible thought came to him, and with it a kind of panic. "Isn't that a Death Eater idea? Why is that there?"
>
> "It doesn't mean defeating death in the way the Death Eaters mean it, Harry," said Hermione, her voice gentle. It means . . . you know . . . living beyond death. Living after death."
>
> But they were not living, thought Harry: They were gone. The empty words could not disguise the fact that his parents' moldering remains lay beneath snow and stone, indifferent, unknowing.[5]

Hermione leaves a wreath of Christmas roses at the grave as Harry weeps in denial of the scriptural message he has read. The lights in the church have gone out, as they seem to have in Harry's heart as well.

And then things go horribly dark. Harry and Hermione meet who they believe is Bathilda Bagshot, and she takes Hansel and Gretel to her home. But this is only the snake-animated corpse of the author of *A History of Magic*; it is a Voldemort trap and a nightmare of Gothic horror. Voldemort's snake, Nagini, bursts from Bathilda's body and attacks! Harry and Hermione barely disapparate in time before the Dark Lord arrives. He isn't happy as Christmas Day arrives: "Voldemort . . . screamed with rage, a scream that mingled with the girl's, that echoed across the dark gardens over the church bells ringing in Christmas Day."[6]

Harry's Christmas gift from Lord Thingy? A trip down memory lane that Harry shares through their Horcrux mind link. Voldemort remembers the Potter murders on Halloween 1981, and Harry learns at last the grisly details of his parents' execution and sacrifice. As bad, when he revives in the tent, he learns his holly and phoenix-feather wand was irreparably broken in the fight with Nagini. After reading the Skeeter book they had picked up at Bathilda Bagshot's home, *The Life and Lies of Albus Dumbledore*, Harry tells Hermione that he believes the headmaster never loved him and is responsible because of his secretiveness for the mess they are in.

Christian Undertones in the *Deathly Hallows* Christmas Chapters

This is without doubt the lowest of the several nadirs and nigredos in all the Potter novels. What do these trials and feelings of despair and abandonment have to do with the Nativity of Christ with which they coincide? Why does the darkest of Harry's dark nights of the soul take place on Christmas Eve, of all times, when the Light came into the world that darkness has never comprehended (John 1:5)?

First, we have to see that Harry and Hermione's adventure is supposed to remind the reader of the Christmas story. A couple in disguise travel to the man's ancestral home. They have no place to stay, and they have a great secret they cannot share with anyone. In case you miss the parallel with Mary and Joseph coming to Bethlehem, Joseph's family origin, and the location of taxation, there is a holy family crèche of sorts in the village center, with baby Harry sans scar and his loving mother and father. That it is actually Christmas Eve and the action of the first half of their visit takes place in the light shining through stained-glass windows in a church graveyard while carolers sing inside just drives the obvious home.

But Christmas is a time of great cheer and hope; why the darkness of Harry's Christmas Eve with the despair he feels at his parents' grave, the desperation of his struggle with Nagini, and the doubts he has about Dumbledore's love and care for him? Rowling uses Nativity and, specifically, the night before Nativity as the occasion of Harry's nigredo because of the darkness of the world before the advent of Jesus of Nazareth, the Light of the World.

Nagini's Gothic nightmare attack on Harry and Hermione from within the Bagshot corpse, then, represents—as does the whole Godric's Hollow story—the reason for the Incarnation of Christ, namely, the Evil One's dominance in the world before Nativity. Nagini's failed attack parallels the plotting of the serpent-Devil to destroy the Christ child through Herod. The retelling of the story of the "Boy Who Lived" as the bells of the church toll in Christmas Day with Voldemort's screams are retellings of Nativity and the holy family's escape into Egypt despite the slaughter of the innocents.

It isn't a tit-for-tat allegory, of course, but the parallels are strong enough that we have some experience of the darkness of the world before Christ in Harry's doubts about the love and covenant with his mentor (here, I think, along with Dumbledore meant to be understood as God). We also get the hope of Christians in the dead of winter and the depth of darkness in the coming of their Savior as a child who will escape and eventually be victorious over the prince of the world. Harry's holly wand with its Christmas association is broken and held together only by the feather of the Resurrection Bird, but however much he disavows God/Dumbledore, he keeps the remnants of his faith in the bag next to his heart. He clings to his broken faith through the nigredo.

THEOPHANY IN THE FOREST OF DEAN: "THE SILVER DOE"

Fortunately, we don't have to wait long for some light to shine in our favorite boy wizard's darkness. In the very next chapter, "The Silver Doe," Ron returns, they find the sword of Gryffindor, Ron destroys the Horcux necklace, and the trio is reunited, even if Hermione doesn't do backflips when she learns Ron is back.

We discussed Harry's encounter with and trust in Severus's doe Patronus as an act of faith. Let's look at where the *Cervus Fugitivus* takes him in the details of this chapter. It is evidently one of Rowling's favorite chapters because she chose to read it to her Carnegie Hall audience on the Open Book Tour she made through the United States and Canada after the publication of *Deathly Hallows*. Its seamless combination of alchemical symbols, Arthurian legend, and traditional Christian content makes "The Silver Doe" perhaps the finest single chapter in the seven novels and the best example of Rowling's peculiar genius and artistry.

In a nutshell, the doe Patronus leads Harry to a frozen pool in the Forest of Dean. Harry sees that the sword of Gryffindor is in the pool and resolves to do the heroic Gryffindor thing and go get it. Stripping himself of all clothing except his underwear and the Horcrux necklace, he breaks the ice and enters the freezing waters of the pool. Incredibly, the Horcrux attacks him: "The chain of the Horcrux had tightened and was slowly constricting his windpipe."[7]

Ron, *deus/amicus ex machina*, appears out of nowhere and rescues Harry from the pool and the attack necklace. He also retrieves the sword from the icy pool. After a brief catch-up, Harry tells Ron that Ron must be the one to destroy the Horcrux; Ron, well aware that the Horcrux affects him more strongly and perversely than the others, reluctantly agrees.

Ron was right to hesitate. He destroys the locket Horcrux with the sword but only after the soul fragment of the Dark Lord reveals all Ron's poisonous doubts about the love of his mother, Hermione, and even Harry, his best mate, in odious fashion. Harry embraces and encourages him after this victory and before they return to the tent. Ron explains to Harry and the hysterically angry Hermione where he has been and his Deluminator-driven return.

CHRISTIAN UNDERTONES IN "THE SILVER DOE"

I don't think many readers struggle with understanding the Christmas Eve scenes in Godric's Hollow as Harry's nigredo and a snapshot of the world before Christ's nativity. We all know the story well, and the Harry Potter version is fairly explicit in its Christmas references. The Christian content of "The Silver Doe," however, is relatively opaque because we are not as familiar with the event from the life of Christ that is being depicted. Let's start, then, with the alchemical and Arthurian meanings to get at the spiritual heart of this especially rich chapter.

Alchemically, the albedo, or white and cleansing (ablutionary), stage follows the nigredo, or black, breakdown phase. Except for the ending in the warmth of the tent, "The Silver Doe" takes place completely out-of-doors in the white snow of day and features a frozen pool into which both Harry and Ron enter against all common sense and self-preservation. The doe as alchemical *cervus* represents the joining of body and spirit, and in this chapter that turns on ritual cleansing with water and confrontation of one's darkest doubts, we see Ron and Harry reconciled.

The central Arthurian element is the drawing of the sword, both from stone at the pool's bottom and from the water itself. In this, of course, we have echoes of Arthur's demonstrating his linage with Uther Pendragon by pulling the sword from the stone and his receiving Excalibur from the Lady of the Lake after Arthur's sword is broken in battle with King Pellinor. Harry remembers the meaning of the sword of Gryffindor when he sees the sword at the bottom of the pool:

> What was it, Harry asked himself . . . that Dumbledore had told him the last time he had retrieved the sword? *Only a true Gryffindor could have pulled* that *out of the hat.* And what were the qualities that defined a Gryffindor? A small voice inside Harry's head answered him: *Their daring, nerve, and chivalry set Gryffindors apart.*[8]

The little voice is the voice of the Sorting Hat, which sang about the four houses and their peculiar qualities in *Philosopher's Stone*.[9] We learned in *Goblet of Fire*[10] that the Sorting Hat was Godric Gryffindor's hat, enchanted with "some brains" by the four founders. *Gryffindor*, you'll recall, means "golden griffin" and is a pointer to Christ. By pulling the sword from the pool with selfless and sacrificial acts, Ron and Harry demonstrate that they are both "mental," as Ron puts it, and also "true Gryffindors." Ron saves Harry's life much like symbols of Christ do at the end of the first six books, a salvific event Harry notes five times before the end of this chapter.

Which leads us to the spiritual meaning and specifically Christian content of the chapter. It is a retelling of Christ's baptism in the Jordan River, with Ron's enlightenment experiences illustrating what this means for the Christian believer.

The baptism of Christ, Theophany in the Eastern Orthodox tradition (meaning "the appearance of God"), is not celebrated with school closings, trees in homes, or sales in stores, so few people know much about it. It should be noted that in the ranking of holy days, however, Theophany is considered to be the most important feast celebrated on the Christian calendar with the exceptions of Easter and Pentecost.

What was the big deal? Christ submitted to baptism by John the Baptist (though the Baptist felt he needed to be baptized by Christ; see Matthew 3:14) to "fulfill all righteousness" (Matthew 3:15, KJV). And when John baptized Jesus, "the heavens were opened unto him, and he saw the Spirit of God descending like a dove, and lighting upon him: And lo a voice from heaven, saying, This is my beloved Son, in whom I am well pleased" (Matthew 3:16-17, KJV; see also Luke 3:21-22). God revealed himself at the baptism of Christ in the Jordan as the Holy Trinity: Christ as Son, the Father in the voice from Heaven proclaiming his pleasure, and the Holy Spirit in the form of a dove. Theophany is the feast above all others except the Resurrection of Christ and the "birthday" of the Church at Pentecost because it is the revelation of God as he is, that is to say, in his three *hypostases*, or "persons."

Harry's immersion and Ron's enlightenment do not include a trinitarian moment, but they do show what baptism means in a Christian's life while closely paralleling the Gospel accounts. Let's take another look.

First, Harry, the Chosen One, is the Christ figure of the piece. He has already demonstrated he is a true Gryffindor in the *Chamber of Secrets* and has little to prove here. Like Jesus, he only enters the pool to "fulfill all righteousness," that is, to do what a Gryffindor must do. James Thomas, an English professor at Pepperdine, has said we know this is the case because we have "Ron the Baptist" there to do the deed.[11] It is Ron who pulls Harry from the water and retrieves the sword from the pool's bottom.

At this point, though, it is Harry who takes charge and tells Ron he must be the one to use the sword to destroy the Horcrux. It is Harry who opens the Horcrux, who stands by shouting encouragement and instruction during Ron's psychological scourging, and who embraces and lifts Ron up after this shattering victory over his inner demons. Ron plays the part of John the Baptist, certainly, in the pool, and of his savior in taking the Horcrux that was strangling Harry from his neck. Harry, though, is Ron's master through his illumination.

Baptism comes from the Greek word meaning "immersion," and there is some dispute among Christian groups about whether a "baptism" must be a complete dunking. In some cases the word is used to describe a washing or ritual ablution (see Luke 11:38). Saint Paul's understanding seems to leave little doubt that the mystery of baptism involves a burial of sorts (see, Romans 6:2-13; Colossians 2:12-13). In "The Silver Doe," Ron and Harry are fully immersed and ritually cleansed by their sacrificial time in the pool.

Ron's experience is the most important because his symbolic baptism and liberation from the demons darkening his heart afterward is an enlightenment or illumination. Traditional Christians use the word *photismos,* or "illumination," for baptism.[12]

> The sanctification that comes with the Spirit's descent in baptism bestows illumination and perfection, making illumination the immediate effect of baptism, which leads in turn to adoption, perfection, and ultimately, immortality. Indeed, [to Clement] baptism is the "one grace" of illumination and the illumination we receive is knowledge (*gnosis*). Clement comes close here to suggesting that a virtual infusion of knowledge accompanies baptism.[13]

Ron explains to Harry and Hermione in the tent that he was only able to find them when he regretted his departure because of Dumbledore's gift to him, the Deluminator. He describes his experience with its light after he clicked it in response to hearing Hermione use his name Christmas morning:

> Ron raised his empty hand and pointed in front of him, his eyes focused on something neither Harry nor Hermione could see.
>
>   "It was a ball of light, kind of pulsing, and bluish, like that light you get around a portkey, you know? . . . I knew this was it," said Ron. "I grabbed my stuff and packed it, then I put on my rucksack and went out into the garden.
>
>   "The little ball of light was hovering there, waiting for me, and when I came out it bobbed along a bit and I followed it behind the shed and then it . . . well, it went inside me."
>
>   "Sorry?" said Harry, sure he had not heard correctly.
>
>   "It sort of floated toward me," said Ron, illustrating the movement with his free index finger, "right to my chest, and then—it just went straight through. It was here," he touched a point close to his heart, "I could feel it, it was hot. And once it was inside me I knew what I was supposed to do. I knew it

would take me where I needed to go. So I Disapparated and
came out on the side of a hill. There was snow everywhere." [14]

Now the sequence here is not exactly like a Christian baptism experience, but all the elements of illumination or *photismos* in
Christ via the Holy Spirit are here. Step by step:

Ron departs from the fellowship of his vocation—and immediately repents and feels remorse about his betrayal. He is ensnared
(by Snatchers) and finds himself unable to find his way back on
his own. He waits and listens for his name to be called. On the day
Christ first came into the world, Ron hears his name and follows
the light that has appeared to him. This light enters his heart and
illumines him; he knows what he "was supposed to do." He finds
Harry at the pool of icy water and enters it to save the life of his
betrayed friend. Consequent to this willing, sacrificial immersion
or baptism, Ron is guided by Harry, who recognizes him as a true
Gryffindor, to complete his purification by using the power of the
golden griffin to reveal, confront, and slay his personal demons.
This exorcism post illumination completes Ron's initiation and
purification, and he reenters the fellowship provisionally, a soul
triptych which once again is a trinity.

The sequence of the path to baptism in Orthodox Church traditions, dating from the first centuries of the Christian era, is repentance, acceptance of Christ as Savior, instruction as a catechumen,
tonsuring, exorcism, threefold immersion in the name of the Trinity, which leads to illumination of the darkened intellect or *nous*, the
eye of the heart. Rowling jumbles this order, of course, in the process of weaving her alchemical, Arthurian, and Christian tapestry
that illustrates the event of Theophany and the meaning of baptism or initiation in the life of a believer.

I cannot remember, however, any artist ever attempting anything as grand as this in English literature and pulling it off without waking the sleeping dragons of skepticism and resistance to

religious dogma. "The Silver Doe" as a piece of literary baptism initiates the readers into a universal path to illumination using the symbols and rites specific to faith and literary traditions. It is simultaneously engaging, challenging, even inspiring—and, I would argue, her finest and most effective chapter in the series.

Incredibly, the rubedo chapters, in which Harry's experiences parallel the Passion narratives of the Christian Gospels, are as profound and important as his Christmas Eve and Theophany adventures. Just go to the next page to begin unwrapping Harry's cross and his victory in self-sacrifice over death.

19

VICTORY
OVER DEATH

Harry Potter and the Deathly Hallows
as the Passion gospel of a Christian Everyman

The fruits of Harry's choice to believe (discussed in chapter 17) begin to show themselves in "The Forest Again." The author has admitted repeatedly that writing this chapter caused her no little cathartic pain.[1]

As we did with Harry's Christmas and Theophany adventures, then, let's review this chapter's events in sequence before unpacking the spiritual freight. In brief, Harry's decisions before entering and while in the Forbidden Forest make this the story of his Good Friday and death to ego and self.

The chapter begins as Harry wakes up on the floor of Dumbledore's office after his trip through Severus Snape's memories in "The Prince's Tale." Harry has learned that he has a Horcrux and that the headmaster's Machiavellian plan all along was for him to destroy Horcruxes and then sacrifice himself to Voldemort. Harry, though dizzy with the revelations of Snape's memories, accepts his destiny as a Horcrux and the need to sacrifice himself to defeat Voldemort.

Under the Invisibility Cloak, Harry makes his way to the Forest and his fate. He reveals himself only once, to his faithful disciple Neville, the only friend who never doubted Harry would return. After giving Neville instructions to kill Nagini if he has the chance, Harry returns to the concealment of his Cloak and reaches the edge of the Forest.

Harry opens the "I open at the close" Snitch with the words "I am about to die." The Resurrection Stone brings Lily, James, Remus, and Sirius—"less substantial than living bodies, but much more than ghosts"—something like "memory made nearly solid."[2] His parents, his godfather, and his favorite teacher accompany him through the Forest, acting "like Patronuses to him."[3]

Harry meets the Death Eaters Dolohov and Yaxley, who are searching for him. He follows them into Voldemort's camp, where he takes off his Cloak, stuffs it and his wand into his robes, and deliberately drops the Resurrection Stone. His ghostly family vanishes. He draws the Dark Lord's attention and is killed without making a move of resistance. As Sirius had told him at the edge of the Forest, dying was "quicker and easier than falling asleep."[4]

Spiritual Freight and Christian Content of "The Forest Again"

"The Forest Again" is simultaneously a retelling of the Crucifixion and a story of the death of a Christian Everyman. Harry's choices and his successful struggle to believe have transformed him into a transparency of the God-Man. The Passion narrative here first, and then Harry as Everyman.

Harry has Garden of Gethsemane desires and chooses to act in obedience as savior. The night before his death on the Cross, Christ didn't sleep like a babe. He sweat blood and prayed, "O my Father, if it be possible, let this cup pass from me: nevertheless not as I will, but as thou wilt"

(Matthew 26:39, KJV). He embraced the necessity of conforming to the divine will, but it was no party cup he would be drinking from. Similarly, Harry hesitates at the abyss when he reaches the Forest:

> A swarm of Dementors was gliding amongst the trees; he could feel their chill, and he was not sure he would be able to pass safely through it. He had no strength left for a Patronus. He could no longer control his own trembling. It was not, after all, so easy to die. Every second he breathed, the smell of the grass, the cool air on his face, was so precious: To think that people had years and years, time to waste, so much time it dragged, and he was clinging to each second. At the same time he thought that he would not be able to go on, and knew that he must. The long game was ended, the Snitch had been caught, it was time to leave the air.[5]

Harry walks the Via Dolorosa, stumbles, and is helped by Lily, his mother. The Via Dolorosa, "Street of Sorrows," is an actual avenue in Jerusalem along which Christians believe their Savior carried his Cross to Golgotha, or Calvary. According to tradition, Christ fell under the weight of the Cross as many as three times in different places along the Via Dolorosa after being tortured the previous night. He was comforted by his mother, by Veronica, and by the grieving women (see Luke 23:27); his Cross was borne at least part of the way by Simon the Cyrenian (see Luke 23:26).

Harry's mother, who appears with James, Remus, and Sirius when Harry opens the Snitch and turns the Resurrection Stone "over in his hand three times,"[6] is also a great comfort to Harry on his walk to his own "Place of the Skull."

> Harry looked at his mother.
>
> "Stay close to me," he said quietly.
>
> And he set off. The Dementors' chill did not overcome him; he passed through it with his companions, and they

acted like Patronuses to him. . . . He stumbled and slipped toward the end of his life, toward Voldemort."[7]

Harry dies sacrificially and without resistance to defeat the Dark Lord, as Christus Victor died on the Cross. When Christ was betrayed and his disciples began to fight, he rebuked them, saying:

> Put up again thy sword into his place: for all they that take the sword shall perish with the sword. Thinkest thou that I cannot now pray to my Father, and he shall presently give me more than twelve legions of angels? But how then shall the scriptures be fulfilled, that thus it must be? (MATTHEW 26:52-54, KJV)

Christ went to his Crucifixion in this same spirit, as a lamb to the slaughter. Harry learns via Severus's memories in the Pensieve that Dumbledore believed he must die and "Voldemort himself must do it, Severus. That is essential."[8] Harry does not make any attempt to defend himself; consequently, when he reveals himself to the Dark Lord in the Forest clearing, "his hands were sweating as he pulled off the Invisibility Cloak and stuffed it beneath his robes, with his wand. He did not want to be tempted to fight."[9] Harry dies as a sacrifice.

One Jewish reader told me she said a prayer when she bought *Deathly Hallows* that "if nothing else, the story not become some kind of Christian allegory with Harry as Jesus." You may be surprised to hear she thought *Deathly Hallows* was undeniably Christian yet sufficiently universal that she found it to be spiritually satisfying.

This is a critical point in understanding the popularity of Harry Potter. It is undeniably Christian, that is, loaded with specific Christian symbolism and meaning from the author's literary traditions, yet sufficiently universal to be spiritually satisfying to anyone. This last explains both the popularity of the Harry Potter novels and, at least as important, the tenacity and pervasiveness of Christianity despite millennia of persecution and attacks. Truth is not something one can modify with adjectives or ideological tag; when truth is prefixed by "blue," "Marine," "feminist," or even "Christian," truth then means "opinion," because in the restriction of the modifier, truth loses its universality. There are truths that are revealed exclusively in the revelations of Christ, but these are universal human truths, not Christian opinions. But when readers who are not believers encounter explicitly Christian content, their thought is often, Oh, no! I'm about to be confronted by Christian propaganda, rather than, Hey, these Christians know something true that will make my life more human and more conformed to reality.

Christians survived the Soviet holocaust—despite the loss of 60 million believers to the Communists—by clinging to this sustaining truth. They endured five centuries of Muslim occupation and dhimmitude in the Balkans for the same reason; apostatizing from their faith would have meant denying the answers to human questions—answers they had empirical evidence were true and worked.

Of course, not everyone embraces these truths; the specific forms in which they come wrapped may not match the psychological locks they have been fit into by their culture. In Christian or post-Christian cultures, just the power of the spiritual immunizations many people have received are sufficient for them to reject anything labeled "Christian." The popularity of Harry Potter, despite its "obvious" Christian content and pervasive Christian symbolism, however, indicates that if it comes without the Christian label or, better, comes with the label "rejected by Christians everywhere," the truth within the Christian tradition is spiritually satisfying to everyone. *It answers universal questions about what it means to be human.* It works.

I confess to wondering what non-Christians make of scenes like the one in which Harry puts the Golden Snitch/Resurrection Stone to his lips and opens it with the words, "I am about to die."[10] This is essentially a picture of Harry's communing—that is, receiving the body and blood in hope of his resurrection—and drawing strength from this sacrament to carry on into the Forest and face his death.

I doubt these non-Christian readers can see the specifically Christian content, buried as it is in the alchemical symbolism of the Snitch and because of the obscurity of the Communion reference to nonsacramental readers, Christian or not. And Harry's sacrifice, with its clear echoes of Christ's march to Calvary? Just as Christ's sacrifice is an example to all people of what a human life is all about, so is Harry's. Consider the Gospel passage in which Christ tells his disciples:

> Whosoever will come after me, let him deny himself, and take up his cross, and follow me. For whosoever will save his life shall lose it; but whosoever shall lose his life for my sake and the gospel's, the same shall save it. *For what shall it profit a man, if he shall gain the whole world, and lose his own soul?* (MARK 8:34-36, KJV, EMPHASIS MINE)

Nonbelievers may gag on the exclusive claim that only people dying "for my sake" are saved, but who can deny the universal truth evident in the balance measuring the whole world and a man's soul? Not Harry Potter readers, it seems. They identify and cheer Harry's decision to die in order to save his friends. Like the alchemists, they see in this story a restatement of the truths revealed in Scripture, too:

> Verily, verily, I say unto you, except a corn of wheat fall into the ground and die, it abideth alone: but if it die, it bringeth forth much fruit. (JOHN 12:24, KJV)

> Thou fool, that which thou sowest is not quickened, except it die. (1 CORINTHIANS 15:36, KJV)

> Greater love hath no man than this, that a man lay down his life for his friends. (JOHN 15:13, KJV)

And Harry's trip into the Forest in the company of Lily, James, Sirius, and Remus? Yes, it is a parallel story of the Stations of the Cross. It is also a restatement of the universal hope we have, in Saint Paul's words, in being "compassed about with so great a cloud of witnesses," those who have successfully completed the spiritual test set before us:

> Wherefore seeing we also are compassed about with so great a cloud of witnesses, let us lay aside every weight, and the sin which doth so easily beset us, and let us run with patience the race that is set before us, looking unto Jesus the author and finisher of our faith; who for the joy that was set before him endured the cross, despising the shame, and is set down at the right hand of the throne of God. (HEBREWS 12:1-2, KJV)

J. K. Rowling tells Harry's story in language resonant with the Passion accounts in the Gospels. As those narratives reflect transcendent reality and human truths, they touch the hearts of all human beings without hardened hearts and Christ-o-phobia.

From Calvary, then, to King's Cross!

"King's Cross"

Rowling has been asked about Harry's afterlife experience at King's Cross:

> KATIE B.: Why was King's Cross the place Harry went to when he died?
>
> J. K. ROWLING: For many reasons. The name works rather well, and it has been established in the books as the gateway between two worlds, and Harry would associate it with moving on between two worlds (don't forget that it is Harry's image we see, not necessarily what is really there).[11]

"The name works rather well. . . ." After a chapter on Harry's sacrificial death paralleling the death of the King of Heaven and earth on the Cross, yes, the name does "work rather well." I have to admire Rowling's reticence in spelling it out for Katie B.

But what do we learn at Harry's mystical King's Cross station, and what does it mean?

EVENTS OF KING'S CROSS

Harry wakes up naked in the misty train station with a suffering Voldemort soul fragment squealing nearby. Harry thinks he wants some clothes, and his desire is instantly satisfied. He meets Dumbledore—just as the proven Dumbledore denouement formula says we should at this point—and Harry learns from the departed headmaster that he is *not* dead yet but sustained in the world by means of his connection with his mother's sacrifice and blood that are the substance of Lord Voldemort's new body.

Dumbledore has become positively voluble in death; Harry learns Hallows lore and the headmaster's story, from Grindelwald and Ariana to his incapacity to wield power and what he and Voldemort have in common (the desire to be "masters of death"). Dumbledore apologizes to Harry for his secretiveness and foolishness; he confesses that Harry is the better man and that he has known this for some time.

He explains, too, that Harry is the "worthy possessor of the Hallows" and "the true master of death, because the true master does not seek to run away from Death. He accepts that he must die, and understands that there are far, far worse things in the living world than dying."[12] Harry decides to return after Dumbledore tells him that "by returning, you may ensure that fewer souls are maimed, fewer families are torn apart."[13] Harry seeks some assurance that his conversation has been real and not just in his head; Dumbledore departs while saying, "Of course it is happening inside your head, Harry, but why on earth should that mean that it is not real?"[14]

CHRISTIAN ECHOES AND SPIRITUAL MEANING OF KING'S CROSS

The action in King's Cross is all consequent to Harry's sacrifice and seeming death in "The Forest Again," but the title "works well," as has been noted, because it points to Christ's sacrifice on the Cross as "King of the Jews" (Mark 15:26). The meaning of King's Cross is not allegorical or two dimensional. We learn from Dumbledore that because Harry died willingly and without resistance, Voldemort's curse has killed only that soul fragment Harry had been carrying in his forehead since he became the Chosen One.

Consequently, Harry is not a fictional messiah or a Jesus-double as much as he is an Everyman figure. He has died to the evil within him, and freed from this very real burden, he can (to risk using Christian language) be "born again." Not unlike Ron's confrontation with the necklace Horcrux in "The Silver Doe," Harry has had to stare down and die to the worst part of himself—and choose this death even though he could not know that it wouldn't mean the death of his own soul as well. Again, Mark 8:35 (KJV): "Whosoever will save his life shall lose it; but whosoever shall lose his life for my sake and the gospel's, the same shall save it."

Harry survives, but only because of the bond of blood he has with the person whose sacrificial death long ago saved him from the Dark Lord. The Christian echo here rings out; Harry's choice to die only works out with his victory over death (here, as "master of death") because of his communion and shared life with a savior via that savior's blood. This is, to risk stating the obvious, the "bond of blood" that scandalized Jesus' followers in his time and even some today:

> Jesus said unto them, Verily, verily, I say unto you, except ye eat the flesh of the Son of man, and drink his blood, ye have no life in you. Whoso eateth my flesh, and drinketh my blood, hath eternal life; and I will raise him up at the last day. For my flesh is meat indeed, and my blood is drink indeed. He that eateth my flesh, and drinketh my blood, dwelleth in me, and

I in him. As the living Father hath sent me, and I live by the
Father: so he that eateth me, even he shall live by me. (JOHN
6:53-57, KJV)

Harry is saved by sacrificial death and blood just as Christians
are saved by Christ's sacrifice and blood. This doesn't offend readers,
I think, because Harry is not drinking blood of any kind (as Voldemort drinks the unicorn's blood unworthily and unto damnation in
Philosopher's Stone; see chapter 11) and the focus of the story is Harry's
willingness to die that brings the salvific power of Lily's sacrifice into
play. All of us wanting to change "the man in the mirror" recognize
this difficult first step—choosing to change, even to let part of one's
identity die—as the foundation of spiritual transformation. Whatever
graces are available to us in our spiritual traditions, we have to prepare the ground for them or they will fall and not take root. Consider the parable of the sower in Matthew 13:3-23; the sower does
not plow or prepare the path he walks and over which he casts seed.
That preparation for the sower is the responsibility of the "workers
in the field," i.e., individual believers and their pastors.

Harry's time in the netherworld has its Christian equivalent or
parallel in Christ's breaking the gates and "harrowing" of Hell between
his Crucifixion and Resurrection. Harry's perfected body in his limbo
afterlife? The perfection of the saints after judgment. And Harry's
decision to return reflects Christ's decision to drink the bitter cup,
to die, and to rise again. The victory over the Evil One, the Prince of
the World, was not complete at Christ's death on the Cross; that
was won at his Resurrection and his preparing his disciples for the
advent of the Holy Spirit at Pentecost.

Harry is not especially excited about leaving the "warm and light
and peaceful" way station: "He knew that he was heading back to
pain and the fear of more loss." Dumbledore assures him, though,
that "I know this, Harry, that you have less to fear from returning
here than [Voldemort] does."[15]

Voldemort's agony is vividly shown as a "small, naked child, curled on the ground, its skin raw and rough, flayed looking, and it lay shuddering under a seat where it had been left, unwanted, stuffed out of sight, struggling for breath."[16] Harry thinks he ought to help the child but cannot get over his revulsion. Dumbledore assures him, "You cannot help" and directs him to seats well away from the suffering, whimpering, and trembling soul fragment.

This is perhaps the most difficult part of Rowling's picture of the afterlife and perhaps her greatest accomplishment. The righteous who have tried to embody love and die to themselves are in something like paradise, where their slightest wish is granted, with one notable exception. They are unable to help those who chose the path of ego, personal advantage, and self-advancement. These misshapen souls are judged by their own deeds and take the form of their soul's capacity for love at their death. In Voldemort's soul fragment we see the irreparable condition of souls unprepared for eternal life.

Christ told the same story in the parable of Lazarus and the rich man in Hell. The rich man begs Abraham for help only to learn from him that "between us and you there is a great gulf fixed: so that they which would pass from hence to you cannot; neither can they pass to us, that would come from thence" (Luke 16:26, KJV). The rich man asks that a messenger be sent from the dead to tell his brothers what to do to avoid the torments awaiting them. Abraham says quite simply that this will not help: "If they hear not Moses and the prophets, neither will they be persuaded, though one rose from the dead" (Luke 16:31, KJV).

I maintain that Rowling's retelling of this parable with the suffering and inconsolable soul fragment is perhaps her greatest accomplishment because if there is one message postmodern readers do not, perhaps cannot, hear, it is that they will be judged in an afterlife for their thoughts, words, and deeds. In "King's Cross," Rowling presents this judgment in such a way that it seems anything but the work of an angry judge; our condition in eternity will be the consequence of our choices and our capacity for love—and there will be no helping those who enter God's glory with atrophied spirits and darkened hearts (see the end of chapter 11). She portrays transcendent justice without a juridical, anthropomorphic "heavy" who is only the servant of the greater god, necessity.

In the last chapter, Harry tries to help Lord Voldemort and learns that Abraham was right: "Neither will they be persuaded, though one rose from the dead."

"The Flaw in the Plan"

Rowling does not want her readers to think of Harry as an Aslan or a "cardboard Jesus":

> Harry is not, and never has been, a saint. Like Snape, he is flawed and mortal. Harry's faults are primarily anger and occasional arrogance.[17]

It is inevitable, though, because—as Rowling says—the Christian symbolism of the books is "obvious" that Harry will be remembered largely as a Christ symbol. I think this is an unfortunate simplification of meaning to transparent allegory, x standing for y, and ultimately a misunderstanding that obscures why the books are so popular. No one I know loves the books and rereads them because "Harry is Jesus." A quick review of the final chapter and a longer look at its larger meaning will help explain what drives Potter-mania and why simplifying this meaning is to miss the power of the books.

Harry returns from King's Cross to the Forbidden Forest to find that Voldemort was laid out by the Killing Curse too. The Dark Lord rises, and Harry plays possum. Voldemort wants to know for sure that the Chosen One is dead; Narcissa Malfoy is pressed into action. She realizes Harry is alive and asks him if Draco is alive. When Harry says that he is, Narcissa's "nails pierced him"; she declares him dead.

The Dark Lord decides he must desecrate the dead, hitting Harry's supposedly lifeless body with *Crucio*, the Unforgivable Curse, and Harry is thrown in the air three times. Remarkably, "the pain he expected did not come."[18] In fact, throughout the chapter, the Dark Lord seems unable to hurt Harry or curse his enemies effectively, even to silence them for any period of time.

Harry is carried out of the Forest by Hagrid, an echo of his carrying Harry out of the Potter home when he was a baby. This time, alas, Hagrid believes Harry is dead and weeps and rages in alternation. Voldemort presents Harry's corpse to his followers in Hogwarts and offers them terms of surrender.

Neville, the loyal disciple, confronts Voldemort to get at Nagini, and because of his "need and valor,"[19] Neville is able to pull the sword of Gryffindor from the flaming Sorting Hat the Dark Lord had placed on his head to punish him.

> With a single stroke Neville sliced off the great snake's head, which spun high into the air, gleaming in the light flooding from the entrance hall, and Voldemort's mouth was open in a scream of fury that nobody could hear, and the snake's body thudded to the ground at his feet.[20]

Chaos has erupted as the giants, thestrals, centaurs, Buckbeak, and a host of families and Hogsmeade citizens join the fray. Harry chooses this moment to cover himself in the Invisibility Cloak in order to disappear and defend his friends with protective spells. The battle is taken into the Great Hall on a tide of combatants, including the house-elves of Hogwarts under Kreacher's leadership.

The battle is finally reduced to two duels: Bellatrix Lestrange against Molly Weasley and the feature battle between Harry Potter and Lord Voldemort. Molly defeats Bellatrix with the Killing Curse, and Harry reveals himself to the furious Dark Lord after shielding Molly Weasley from his rage.

And Harry tries to save the soul of Lord Voldemort.

He explains first how his self-sacrifice in the Forest has protected his friends; "I've done what my mother did." Then he dares
to call Voldemort by his given name and tutor him about Dumbledore's death on the Tower, Severus Snape's love for Lily and his
loyalty to Dumbledore, and finally about the Dark Lord's need for
remorse.

> "Before you try to kill me, I'd advise you to think about what
> you've
> done. . . . Think, and try for some remorse, Riddle. . . ."
>   "What is this?"
>   Of all the things that Harry had said to him, beyond any
> revelation or taunt, nothing had shocked Voldemort like this.
> Harry saw his pupils contract to thin slits, saw the skin around
> his eyes whiten.
>   "It's your one last chance," said Harry, "it's all you've got
> left. . . . I've seen what you'll be otherwise. . . . Be a man . . .
> try . . . Try for some remorse."[21]

This is beyond Voldemort's capacity to understand or act upon.
So Harry explains that he is the master of the Elder Wand because
he disarmed the previous master, Draco Malfoy, during the escape
from Malfoy Manor. Draco had disarmed Dumbledore on the
Tower, which made him, unknown to Draco and his family, the
Elder Wand's sovereign.

As dawn breaks over the enchanted ceiling of the Great Hall,
Voldemort hurls the death curse and Harry responds with his signature disarming spell. Harry is right; the Elder Wand refuses to
harm its master, and the Killing Curse rebounds to destroy the
Dark Lord.

The story ends with Harry, Ron, and Hermione in the headmaster's office. Harry asks Dumbledore's portrait for his advice
about the Hallows. Harry asks if it is wise to leave the Resurrection
Stone in the Forest but to keep his Invisibility Cloak. Dumbledore

applauds both ideas. Harry then renounces the Elder Wand, and after repairing his holly and phoenix-feather wand that Hermione had broken in their escape Christmas Eve, he pledges to put the Wand of Destiny back in Dumbledore's tomb. Close curtain. *Exeunt omnes.*

CHRISTIAN ECHOES AND SPIRITUAL MEANING
IN "THE FLAW IN THE PLAN"

You want Passion narrative and other biblical parallels and allusions? Step right up.

❖ As Narcissa's nails "pierce Harry's flesh" and she announces his death, we have the Crucifixion of Christ with nails to the Cross and his burial in the tomb.

❖ Voldemort desecrating Harry's body with the Cruciatus Curse is another Crucifixion reference, on the fly, for anyone who missed the first five or six.

❖ Hagrid carries Harry's body from the Forest, a picture like Michelangelo's *Pietà* and a reference to the women who came to the tomb to care for Christ's body.

❖ The Dark Lord's incapacity to hurt Harry or his friends is an echo of Christ's sacrifice having broken the devil's power over humanity.

❖ Harry's disappearance under the Invisibility Cloak at Hagrid's feet parallels the empty tomb discovered by the women and their announcement of same to the apostles.

❖ Neville's decapitation of Nagini as Harry comes to life is the victory over the Garden's serpent at Christ's Resurrection.

❖ Harry's use of a blackthorn wand and victory over Voldemort using a hawthorn wand points to the victory of *Christus Victor* via a crown of thorns and the Cross, not through individual triumph in arms.

❖ Harry's urging Voldemort to "try for some remorse" and sharing with him all he knows about the Elder Wand makes him the story shadow of Christ as the incarnate Truth waiting for the repentance of all sinners.

❖ Harry's rejection of the Elder Wand and Resurrection Stone resonates with the Christian victory via Christ's Resurrection over the temptations of power and over the fear of death.

With all these not-so-subtle parallels and echoes, though, aren't we supposed to think of Harry as Jesus? Isn't his return from King's Cross meant to be one more Hogwarts formulaic end-story resurrection, this time with Harry as a symbol of Christ himself rather than needing a phoenix, stag, or some other Christ symbol to fill that role?

Yes. And no.

Yes, the parallels and allusions are all right there: the cross, the nails, the spear, and death. Firenze the centaur is lanced in the side and lies wounded in the Great Hall during the battle of Hogwarts as an image of the Christ pierced on the Cross. The almost exclusively Christian nature of the English literary tradition makes what already leaps from the page undeniable. This is the work of a writer who knows how to use the images from Scripture and the symbols of the English fantasy literature tradition both with subtlety and openness as her story dictates.

I worry, though, that seeing Harry as Jesus rather misses the point. If Harry is anyone's real-world double, I suspect that he is each of us, including Rowling. Rowling's "struggle to believe," she has said, is evident in *Deathly Hallows*—and the only character who struggles to believe is Harry himself.[22] And as much as we tend to be postmoderns and skeptics about religious belief, we pray with the father in Scripture, "Help thou mine unbelief" (Mark 9:24, KJV).

The idea that Harry equals Jesus also cannot explain the popularity of the books; if anything, it makes the popularity of *Deathly Hallows* and the other books to which it is a fitting finale rather mysterious. It's pretty hard, after all, to suspend disbelief sufficiently that one can identify with a Jesus cardboard cutout and experience the catharsis alongside Christ on the Cross.

Harry is no saint—and no Jesus, either. Harry, like all of us, struggles to believe and overcome doubts about spiritual realities and the efficacy of religious belief. He struggles, but by the force of the example of people (and one house-elf) who believe and those who do not, he chooses the path of obedience, love, and sacrifice. The result is that Harry becomes a Christian Everyman who dies not as a perfect savior but to his own corrupted soul fragment.

Harry's transformation within Christ, not surprisingly, has strong parallels and echoes in his final transformation and victory over the evil within and without with the sacrifice and obedience of Christ in the Garden of Gethsemane and on Golgotha. However, this is not because he is an allegorical Christ but because his choices must be the same as Christ's.

Those decisions make Harry a hero with human doubts, failings, and temptations that every reader can identify with. The consequence of Harry's victory over the scar Horcrux and his internal triumph at King's Cross is his defeat of Lord Voldemort, the very real external foe whose power was broken on the Cross.

Reading *Harry Potter and the Deathly Hallows* as an allegory is tempting, but by interpreting an alchemical and spiritual drama with universal human meaning—especially for postmodern readers with doubts—into a denominational tract, the story's power and meaning are lost. Readers around the world love this book and the series that it closes in spectacular fashion because it encourages them and challenges them to make the hard, sacrificial, loving choices to overcome the Voldemort on the inside to get at the Voldemort on the outside.

And the first and hardest and most important choice is to believe in God. This choice means, if Harry's experience is our guide, enduring the agonies of the nigredo and the world before Nativity, the purification and illumination of baptism into Christ's death and Resurrection, and the crucible of dying to our fallen nature and confronting this evil in the world as well. If we choose to do this, because we accept it as both our design and destiny as essentially spiritual beings, we will not become Jesus; we will have some hope of being fully human, however, and experience some measure of the love, freedom, and joy available to us through the disciplines, graces, and sacrifices of an orthodox spiritual tradition. The Sufi master Frithjof Schuon tells us, "The human being by his nature is condemned to the supernatural."[23] It is in religious belief that this supernatural nature is perfected.

Conclusions

Deathly Hallows, then, is a spectacular spiritual finish to the Harry Potter series with "obvious" Christian content and edifying universal meaning. It is the destination to which the six previous books' literary alchemy, hero's journeys, doppelgängers, and traditional symbolism were only pointers and foreshadowing. Harry's decision in Dobby's grave to feel his remorse, experience the love that heals a splintered soul, and believe despite his doubts leads to his triumphs over the little bit of the Dark Lord within him and the very real extension of this internal evil in the "real world." We learn in *Deathly Hallows* that the choice to believe and the struggle with doubts are the first and most important choices for human beings to make. All spiritual choices are not equal; *Deathly Hallows* rejects the idolatry of materialism, the egotism and power lust of occult belief, and the superficial profundity of the New Age. Casting the alchemical stages in Harry's last adventure around and in the image of the Christian holy days of Nativity, Theophany, and the Resurrection of Christ, *Deathly Hallows* points to an orthodox belief in Christ as a valid path to spiritual transformation and fully human life without evangelizing or excluding other faiths as somehow invalid.

We learn, too, about the power of this inclusive spiritual artistry. Christian images, symbols, themes, and meaning are included in all the Harry Potter books, which, of course, have special resonance with Christian readers. For those readers who are not Christians, even those who have been immunized against anything with a Christian label, however, this use of traditional items from faith and the English "greats" is done with such a light hand that their universal and transcendent spiritual freight are delivered undamaged by their Christian forms. It is this freight that is the meaning driving Potter-mania; Harry Pottter, simply put, satisfies on an imaginative level the human need for religious, mythic, or spiritual experience. As a postmodern artist, Rowling satisfies this need like no other living writer.

As he leaves King's Cross, Harry asks Dumbledore if what he experienced in this limbo-like afterlife was real or "has this just been happening inside my head." Dumbledore responds, "Of course it is happening inside your head, Harry, but why on earth should that mean that it is not real?"[24] The real alchemy of Harry Potter is in our identification with Harry's struggle to believe and, via this suspension of disbelief, our transformation with him into a hero of sacrificial humility and love who is cleansed of his interior failings and thereby changes, even "saves," the world. It all happens inside the reader's head, of course, but the reality of this experience is so great, so foreign, and so near to our spiritual beings that, though only imaginative, it has the power to turn us right side up and orient us to that Light that shines in the darkness and in whom is our hope of eternal life. I doubt the twenty-first century will experience a more profound or more countercultural publishing event than Potter-mania, at least not until Rowling's next series of novels. Hasten the day!

20

FAQS

*The other big questions on the minds of
Harry Potter readers*

My father once worked on the New York Stock Exchange. As a joke or an experiment, I think, he once gave my college professor mother some money to invest in order to see if she could outperform the Wall Street professionals without any training or experience. She did quite well, if I remember correctly; over the course of more than a year the stocks she bought outperformed the portfolios of my father and the other all-stars with whom he worked.

The secret of her success? Mom didn't have a lot of time to invest in the project back when there was no Internet to ease research. So she kept it simple. She bought stock only in companies whose names she saw everywhere without an evident competitor. She "sold short" on those older companies with a rival that seemed to her to have a competitive edge. When I asked for an example of a company she liked, she told me she had a lot invested in Otis

Elevators. Sure enough, I noticed she was right; every escalator and elevator I entered in buildings and stores, very old or brand new, had the name Otis on its threshold.

If I had money to invest—well, let's not talk about laughable impossibilities. If I were advising people about where to invest their money based on my mother's model, I'd probably say, "Buy Wiley." Not the Coyote, the publishing house. They own the "For Dummies" series of books, and though there is some competition from the "For Idiots" how-to guides, I own a whole shelf of the yellow and black "For Dummies" helpers, and it's a rare day I don't reach for one for some help with chess or Microsoft PowerPoint or personal finance.

My favorite part of these books (and most likely the reason I own so many of them) is the closing chapter: "The Part of Tens." Here, no matter what the subject, the guru who has written the book lays out several lists of ten items that are usually very funny and, at the same time, some of the most helpful and interesting stuff in these information-filled treasures. My bet is this is where the subject matter expert throws everything that didn't fit into the neat outline the editors sent him or her.

Now that I'm at the end of this little book on the meaning that drives Potter-mania, I have two objectives that I think I can reach simultaneously. I want to start a conversation with you that I hope will continue in my future books and online, and I have a lot of information to share that didn't fit anywhere in the rest of *How Harry Cast His Spell*. I think I can knock down both these bird-problems with one chapter-rock by answering the ten questions I am frequently asked in my public talks at universities, churches, libraries, and bookstores.

This way, I get to download the information about Harry you most likely really want to know, while at the same time you get used to thinking of me as your friendly Harry Potter and English literature expert so you can write with your thoughts and questions, comments and corrections. My e-mail address is at the end of this chapter, and I sincerely hope you will use it to tell me what you think of *How Harry Cast His Spell*, to share with me your Harry Potter experience, and to ask the questions you may have about these and other books.

This kind of correspondence, quite frankly, is the best part of being a BNF ("Big-Name Fandomer") and Harry Potter SME (subject matter expert). The friends I have made via e-mail and my blog, HogwartsProfessor.com, are some of the best friends I have.

1. *What is the story behind Dumbledore being "gay"?*

It is a very long and very interesting story, the longer part of which you can read about at my blog.[1] I think there are three points to take away from this tempest in a teapot.

First, almost anything you read about Harry Potter in the mainstream media suffers inevitably from what I call the "Skeeter effect." If Rowling's portrayal of reporters in her novels and comments to the media are any indication, she herself believes that journalists distort the news they share to sell papers or television advertising and that they're just not very nice or thoughtful people. She has set up a Web site so she can communicate directly with her fans, an effort she has made and maintained presumably out of frustration with the misrepresentations of the media about her.

The Carnegie Hall "Dumbledore is gay" media event is an excellent illustration of the Skeeter effect. That week Rowling had finally discussed the religious symbolism in her books. It received almost no coverage. The same night Rowling talked about Dumbledore's sexual preference she also spoke about important plot and character points, for example, in praise of Molly Weasley as a stay-at-home mother. None of these points were raised in the media tsunami about Dumbledore the next day.

Second, Rowling didn't say, "Dumbledore is gay." She said, "I have always thought of Dumbledore as gay." What's the difference? To

Americans, at least, the word gay is used for homosexual men and women for whom their sexual preference is not only an important part of their identities but also the defining point of their public, private, and political ideas of themselves. The fact that Rowling said she "always thought of Dumbledore as gay" reflects that, while this was her idea of the headmaster's sexual orientation, this preference was not so much a part of the character's defining life that she needed to introduce it to the story line.

And it is nowhere in the story line. Dumbledore's fascination with Grindelwald, a man described as Dumbledore's "evil twin" (see chapter 5 on doppelgängers) is not sexually driven. Dumbledore's sexuality is never alluded to or touched upon anywhere in the books. What we need to take away from these facts is that while writing the books, Rowling had an artist's conception of the character that included his sexual preference but that this orientation was such an inconsequential part of Dumbledore's identity and relationships with students, teachers, Muggles, and family members that she never mentions it.

Why, then, should we make anything of it? It just isn't important to understanding the story. If it were, the author would have included it in the story.

Third and last, some Dumbledore notes and thoughts on sex in Harry Potter.

Christian critics of the series have, as you might imagine, made a big deal alongside the Rita Skeeters of the world about Dumbledore's being "outed" by Rowling. Both the journalists, who wanted nothing to do with the story of Rowling's discussing the explicitly Christian content of her books that week, and the Harry haters in Christian communities want Rowling and Harry Potter to remain in the "anti-Christian" pigeonhole. I hope after reading this book that you understand the absurdity of this position.

That the Harry-is-dangerous argument is being made now about a lead character's never-mentioned sexual orientation not only overlooks all the transcendent meaning and religious content of the books, it also neglects the sexuality that is in the books. All the characters in the books who are sexual in any way are openly heterosexual—and *mirabile dictu,* all the couples in the book who are not schoolchildren are on their way to the altar to get married (with the possible exception of Lord Voldemort and Bellatrix, not exactly the couple Rowling offers as a role model). If these books are the vehicle of a "gay agenda," as some of Rowling's critics have suggested, she has taken quite the obscure path to get there.

I confess when I heard the announcement that "Dumbledore is gay," I thought, That makes sense. He's an alchemist, and an accomplished one. As such, he is a philosophical Rebis, or androgyne. What better way of conceptualizing a character who is the "resolution of all contraries" including gender than as a gay or relatively effeminate man? I understood both why Rowling never included this very distracting point in the books and why it must have been helpful to her to think of him this way.

To the critics and journalists for whom Dumbledore being gay is now what they think of first and last when the subject of Harry Potter comes up, I would say only, "You missed a much more important point about Dumbledore—and one that is in the books." Rowling always thought of Dumbledore as gay, but she also thinks of him as the only character in the books who has explored and takes consolation in Christian Scripture. It is Dumbledore, after all, who chooses the inscriptions on the Godric's Hollow tombstones. Dumbledore's never-mentioned-in-text homosexuality is an interesting if not very important point; as Rowling has said, the Scripture passages epitomize the meaning of the whole series, so Dumbledore's faith and spiritual orientation is both interesting and important.

I'm not holding my breath for either group reveling in Dumbledore being gay to understand that point.

2. *At the end of* Half-Blood Prince, *Dumbledore orders Severus Snape to kill him. What's the difference between this and assisted suicide?*

Great question. The answer is, "Not much."

As I've discussed in my previous books about Harry Potter, one of Rowling's signature techniques is something called "narrative misdirection." In every book she restricts the point of view from which the story is told to "just above Harry's head." We think we know what's going on, but we never know what Dumbledore, Snape, Voldemort, or even Ludo Bagman are up to. At the end of the story, consequently, when we find out about something that has been going on outside of Harry's line of sight, we're blown away by what we missed (see chapter 6 for why Rowling does this).

What's the big surprise of *Deathly Hallows?* That Albus Dumbledore, greatest wizard of the age and Harry's de facto parent and mentor through most of the series, is all too human—and, to say the least, not always on target ethically. When Harry finds out from the likes of Rita Skeeter and Ron's batty aunt some of the things the headmaster never told him about Dumbledore's life, he realizes Dumbledore has told him almost nothing and begins the struggle to believe that largely defines the book (see chapter 17).

The two most disturbing things we learn about the headmaster both involve Severus Snape. The most dramatic thing is that Harry has been kept alive, not out of any grand love for Harry or the memory of his mother, but so he might die at the right time—in Severus's words, like a "pig to slaughter." As Rowling has said, Dumbledore has a strong Machiavellian streak, a side of planning and secretiveness that his brother Aberforth despised, and quite rightly.

The second thing we learn is that Dumbledore's death on the Tower was planned. There are apologists for this plan with interesting arguments:

❖ Dumbledore was already dead, so this was not murder or assisted suicide.

- ❖ By dying on the Tower as he does, Dumbledore saves Draco from having to commit the murder, Severus from failing to keep the Unbreakable Vow, and Snape's status inside Lord Voldemort's camp (i.e., it is a heroic and noble sacrifice).

- ❖ Snape has to kill Dumbledore in order to gain control of the Elder Wand and be safe from the Dark Lord's attack (this explains Dumbledore's plan and intention, but Draco's disarming Dumbledore ruins the plan, albeit providentially).

- ❖ As Dumbledore says to Snape, his being killed by his friend prevents the potentially horrible death he might otherwise suffer at the hands of the Death Eaters (he mentions the bloodthirsty Fenrir Greyback in particular).

All these defenses are decent arguments, but they fail ultimately on ethical grounds. Dumbledore is still alive on the Tower, and however justified, heroic, even Christlike the headmaster's sacrifice is, it still requires Severus Snape to kill an innocent, living man. As Mark Shea wrote in *First Things* magazine, "The fact remains that 'You shall not do evil that good may come of it.' It is evil to kill an innocent man, as Snape himself points out. Mercy killing isn't just wrong for Muggles. And 'I was just following orders' was shown to have limited traction in 1946."[2]

The point of *Deathly Hallows* is in large part coming to terms with the fact that the beloved headmaster and the greatest wizard of his age was not the man we thought he was and perhaps not even a very good man. Dumbledore apologizes to Harry with tears in King's Cross for just the failings we have mentioned and confesses that he has known for some time that Harry was "the better man."

How is Harry a "better man"? For some clues, look at his battle with Voldemort. That was no agape fest they were having in the Great Hall in the darkness before the dawn, but Harry is transparent in telling Voldemort what he knows and urging him to take the only path that had any hope of saving his atrophied, fragmented soul a life of eternal torment, i.e., feeling remorse. Voldemort is incapable of this, but Harry is obliged to call him to repentance because of the stakes involved and his obligation, for lack of a better phrase, to love his enemy. Voldemort kills himself, figuratively and literally, because Harry's disarming spell will only kill Voldemort if he is right about being the master of the Elder Wand. Voldemort disregards Harry's advice and tries to kill him.

Rowling offers Harry's love for an enemy and transparent service to the truth as the way to fight internal demons and external evils. Dumbledore's Hemlock Society Machiavellianism is what we must come to terms with to understand the headmaster; we are not meant, however, to embrace or defend the command decision that ordered another man to commit murder. As Dumbledore said at King's Cross to Harry, "Poor Severus."

3. *Harry uses an Unforgivable Curse — the Cruciatus Curse — on a Death Eater teacher at Hogwarts. Isn't this something only the Death Eaters do?*

I get a lot of mail about Harry Potter from concerned parents, and surprisingly little of it involves the "magic controversy." Most of it, believe it or not, turns on the misbehavior of the young characters. They say nasty things about adults, they break rules with impunity, they swear, and in *Deathly Hallows*, at least, they even use Unforgivable Curses. Let's talk about the general problem of the bad kids at Hogwarts first and then Harry's use of the Crucio curse against Amycus Carrow in *Deathly Hallows*.

First things first. I'm careful about what my older children read and even more discriminating in what I read aloud to my younger children. I am not a libertine or even a libertarian when it comes to parenting. I understand the concerns of parents about the quality of the books their children are reading.

I confess, though, to scratching my head about the fear and trembling about allowing children to read Harry Potter because the students in the stories break rules and are sometimes disrespectful to adults. They break rules like curfew because they are doing things like, well, saving the world from the return of the Dark Lord. They are disrespectful to adults and, specifically, some of their teachers, because those teachers are mean-spirited idiots or even borderline sadists.

And the times they break rules just to break rules, the way children do? They get a pretty sharp reward. In *Prisoner of Azkaban*, Harry sneaks out of the castle using the Marauder's Map despite the entire Ministry and Hogwarts faculty laboring to protect him. The reprimand he receives from Remus Lupin about putting at risk the sacrifice his parents made to save him for a joyride in the village shatters Harry and reorients him.

More devastating still, Harry disobeys Dumbledore's direction to study Occlumency. The consequence? The Dark Lord manipulates Harry into believing that he has Sirius as prisoner in the Department of Mysteries and is torturing him there. Harry, sans Occlumency and the means to protect himself from Voldemort's Horcrux games, falls for it, and Sirius dies in the battle at the Ministry that results. Does Harry feel the consequences of his disobedience? Forgive me the rhetorical question.

More to the point, effective storytelling requires some transformation in characters from the beginning of the story to the end. If everyone is little Lord Fauntleroy at the start, we're not going to see much change over the course of the drama. Harry blows up his already self-inflated Aunt Marge at the beginning of *Prisoner of Azkaban* because she says unkind things about his parents. By the end of the book, he shows mercy on the rat-man who betrayed his parents to Voldemort and all but killed them by this treachery. If we won't let our children see Harry angry and out of control with the drunken Aunt Marge, how are they going to appreciate Harry's transformation in the crucible of the Shrieking Shack to someone Christlike in his mercy?

To the specific concern of Harry's using the Unforgivable Cruciatus Curse in *Deathly Hallows*, look at the context. Amycus Car-
row has just physically threatened and spit in the face of Professor
McGonagall, Harry's head of house as a Gryffindor. Carrow and
McGonagall had been arguing about what they would tell the Dark
Lord when he arrived because they didn't have Harry Potter as
Alecto Carrow thought. Amycus's plan was to blame the students
and let Voldemort torture them. McGonagall told him that wasn't
going to happen and gave him the short course on right and wrong.
She gets spit on and threatened for her trouble.

And Harry blasts Amycus with an Unforgivable Curse.

Note two things about this: McGonagall's response in the
Ravenclaw common room and Harry's behavior later.

McGonagall reprimands Harry, not for using the Cruciatus
Curse successfully (which requires real hatred; she commends him
for being "gallant" in this regard), but for being "foolish" in revealing
himself.[3] She then uses an Unforgivable Curse, Imperio, on Amycus to disarm him and position him next to his sister for binding
with ropes. Voldemort's imminent arrival at the castle, the context
of both Harry's and McGonagall's use of the Unforgivable Curses,
means the Battle of Hogwarts has begun. Their use of the strongest
possible magical spells on the enemy is no more surprising or a
moral failure than Molly Weasley's using a Killing Curse on Bellatrix
at the battle's climax.

Incredibly though, Harry does not use any Unforgivable Curses in
the Great Hall after his execution in the Forest and his return to life
and action after a trip to the limbo King's Cross. He uses "jinxes and
curses" against the Death Eaters while under his Invisibility Cloak[4] and
a host of shielding charms to protect his friends. He doesn't run wild
with the Unforgivable Curses, however; he even uses a disarming
spell on Voldemort rather than the Killing Curse, Avada Kedavra!

Why? Because his sacrificial death and resurrection have
changed him. I don't think he's equal to the hatred necessary to use

those spells. He even seems to be loving to Voldemort in advising him to try to feel some remorse (see chapter 17).

The objection to Harry Potter books because they have wicked children in them—students who are disrespectful to adults and who break rules indiscriminately—is silly, perhaps even reason put into the service of prejudgment. These are books whose spiritual meaning and specifically Christian content are radically counter-cultural and cause for celebration. If you've been told these books have "questionable moral values," you've been misled. I'd urge you to sit down with your children tonight and enjoy some time with the most challenging and edifying books in recent or long-term memory. I did, and the family reading time with all the Potter novels are some of my clan's most treasured memories.

4. *Some critics say that Harry Potter is gnostic—should I be concerned?*

I don't think so. Michael O'Brien is a noted Catholic novelist and artist whose passion for fighting the good fight in the culture wars and against Harry Potter specifically has come to overshadow his excellent reputation as a writer and painter. He wrote an essay for LifeSiteNews a month after *Deathly Hallows* was published called "Harry Potter and 'the Death of God.'"[5] Father Alfonso Aguilar, LC, shared his thoughts in the *National Catholic Register* in a short piece called "Judging Harry Potter."[6]

Neither of these men read Harry Potter except in light of the culture war. They have prejudged Rowling as being on the side of the real dark lord in the battle of the white hats against the culture of death, and they use her books as opportunities to parade the offenses and mistaken beliefs of the forces they are resisting. It doesn't matter that she doesn't fit into the heretical pigeonholes they say she does.

Gnosticism is an excellent case in point. This is Father Aguilar's preferred point of attack, so I will focus on his claims and the deficiencies of his argument.

Father Aguilar argues that the Harry Potter books are essentially gnostic; that is, they are based on the idea that there is a secret knowledge that divides the adepts from the plebeians. He writes:

> Consider now the concept of man implicit in J. K. Rowling's narrative. Humans, called "muggles," are divided into three categories: ordinary "muggles" with no magical power who disdain the magic world (the despicable Dursley family); "muggles" who fancy the magic world but cannot reach it (Hermione Granger's parents); and the witches and wizards.

This is not the division of the magical world; Hermione's parents don't pine for the magical life, and Squibs are Rowling's "middle piece." Back to his point:

> The ideal is, no doubt, to become a good witch or wizard. What's the way? Train yourself to look into yourself to find the magical powers within you.
>
> Good training requires masters who help make you aware of the magical ("divine") forces in your spirit. These are the professors at the Hogwarts School of Witchcraft and Wizardry. Albus Dumbledore, the school headmaster, is the main spiritual guide.

"Train yourself"? Hogwarts professors training students to realize the divine forces in their spirits? The aloof Albus Dumbledore as the chief adept and spiritual guide? Father Aguilar is forcing the pieces of his argument with such disregard for the texts that I wonder if he has read the books as claimed or if he has only seen the movies.

> Year after year, through training and exercise, Harry Potter becomes ever more aware of his inner powers and can, thus, use more sophisticated spells and jinxes.

In the fourth installment, *Harry Potter and the Goblet of Fire,*
we read: "Harry had soon mastered the Impediment Curse,
a spell to slow down and obstruct attackers; the Reduc-
tor Curse, which would enable him to blast solid objects
out of his way; and the Four-Point Spell, a useful discovery
of Hermione's that would make his wand point due north,
therefore enabling him to check whether he was going in the
right direction within the maze."

Harry, of course, is something of a dullard among wizards,
especially compared with Hermione and Ravenclaw students. If
Harry becomes more aware of his "inner powers" to master "more
sophisticated spells and jinxes," it isn't betrayed in the books, least
of all this passage from *Goblet*. Harry is only able to master Occlumency, for example, when he is transformed by grief, which is to
say, by love. This isn't an occult epistemology à la Hermann Hesse,
as Father Aguilar wants to argue; it is an existential epistemology
in which character or purity of soul determines what one can and
cannot know. In his rush to force Rowling into culture war categories born of nineteenth-century historians of heresy, Father Aguilar
has this critical point almost exactly backward.

He continues with a parallel argument against the Star Wars
movies:

The Star Wars films follow a similar pattern.
There are humans and creatures who do not enjoy the
use of "the force." Only the Jedi, such as Luke Skywalker, who
was trained by masters Obi-Wan Kenobi and Yoda, obtain a
full control over "the force."
In both cases, the role of the human body is downplayed,
as if it were not an essential part of one's own personhood.
The spirit, where the realm of the magic or of "the force"
dwells, is the inner true self. This view of man sounds gnostic
to me.

If he were using the word *gnostic* as Saint Paul, Saint Clement, and Saint Simeon used it, he would be correct. But Father Aguilar is using the word *gnostic* to mean something like "New Age" or "occult." Would that the legionnaires of Christ read French Catholic theologian Jean Borella or the Palamite fathers in their years of study to understand the kinship of gnosis and theosis, of gnostic and saint.

> We come, finally, to the concept of the world. Harry Potter's physical universe is not explicitly viewed as a prison for mankind created by evil demons, as it appears in classical gnostic ideologies.
>
> Yet it is portrayed as less "real" than the wizard world—the fantastic realm of powers whose gate can only be opened by the key of esoteric knowledge. Doesn't the reader feel more "at home" at Hogwarts than in the boring material world of muggles?
>
> To me, the fact that only witches and wizards are able to see the Platform Nine and Three-Quarters at King's Cross station is meaningful. Those whose spirits are in the magic world can see "more" than ordinary people or muggles. They live in a spiritual (magical) dimension that frees them from the laws of the material world.

Again, have Aguilar and I read different Harry Potter novels? While there are objects in the world that Muggles cannot see, this is because of magic performed on these objects rather than a contrary "spiritual dimension." Witches and wizards are not freed "from the laws of the material world," or Fred Weasley would not have been crushed by a falling wall. This is projection onto a text or an experience from a movie rather than legitimate criticism. It's flat-out error and misrepresentation intended to raise conservative touchstones.

That Rowling divides creatures on planet earth into magical and nonmagical creatures, that she leaves the Muggles well off-screen for almost all the books, and that she gives all the "magical brethren" different powers and a hierarchical relationship born of metanarrative rather than these powers does not give us a gnostic view of man. It gives us a parallel universe in which we are meant to see a fantastic image of how men and women stand with respect to other men and women in the "real world." The image, though fantasy, because it acts as a Swiftian or, better, Cruikshankian mirror, has a sharp, satiric edge.

All of which art is lost on the legionnaire, who will find the "gnostic gnail" on which to wield his "gnostic ghammer," however inappropriate, uncharitable, and just plain wrong. No, I don't think we need be concerned with culture warrior concerns about gnosticism in Harry Potter.

5. *What books do you recommend so I can understand more about what you've written here? The alchemy, hero's journey, doppelgänger, and symbolism stuff is mind blowing.*

There are seven classic books by varying authors that I think are the most helpful in understanding Harry Potter: Dante's *The Divine Comedy*, Swift's *Gulliver's Travels*, Shakespeare's *Romeo and Juliet*, Dickens's *A Tale of Two Cities*, Austen's *Emma*, Stoker's *Dracula*, and Hughes's *Tom Brown's Schooldays*. All of these are available online and in every library. You cannot go wrong with this set. If you want to learn more about how Rowling's books work in addition to what you've learned here about why the world loves the books, please pick up a copy of my *Unlocking Harry Potter: Five Keys for the Serious Reader.*

The first nonfiction author on my recommended reading list is Mircea Eliade, late professor of the history of religion at the University of Chicago. His argument in *The Sacred and the Profane* that entertainments serve a mythic or religious function in a desacralized or secular culture is the foundation of the thesis of *How Harry Cast His Spell*. His *The Myth of the Eternal Return: Cosmos and History* is the best introduction to the hero's journey and its transcendent meaning in literature and human experience. If you want to understand more about doppelgängers and the defining polarity in human existence we are called to resolve or unite, Eliade's *The Two and the One* is the most challenging and edifying point of entry. Symbolism is covered by this man, too; check out *Images and Symbols: Studies in Religious Symbolism.* And alchemy? Eliade again: *The Forge and the Crucible: The Origins and Structures of Alchemy.* All these books are relatively short and repay all investments of time and thought with rich dividends.

Three other alchemy books that have been invaluable to me are *Alchemy: Science of the Cosmos, Science of the Soul* by Titus Burckhardt, *Darke Hierogliphicks: Alchemy in English Literature from Chaucer to the Restoration* by Stanton Linden, and *A Dictionary of Alchemical Imagery* by Lyndy Abraham. The very short and equally lucid *The Elizabethan World Picture: A Study of the Idea of Order in the Age of Shakespeare, Donne, and Milton,* if paired with Martin Lings's *The Secret of Shakespeare,* will go a long way to illuminating not only the never-failing power of Shakespeare but also literature and drama as spiritual exercise, even means to enlightenment of sorts. Lings's *Symbol and Archetype: A Study of the Meaning of Existence* is the best exposition of how symbols work and what they are. His clarity and profundity are a reflection perhaps of his study and friendship with C. S. Lewis.

Speaking of Lewis . . . those wanting to read fiction like Harry Potter, meaning novels with some substantial spiritual freight and compelling artistry, I urge to read the Space Trilogy by C. S. Lewis. It has been called "the Chronicles of Narnia for adults," but that doesn't get to the half of it. *Out of the Silent Planet* is a Wellsian science fiction piece and alchemical nigredo; *Perelandra* is part *Paradise Lost,* part epic fantasy, and perhaps the most openly alchemical work since Shakespeare; and *That Hideous Strength,* the trilogy's finale, is a spiritual Gothic horror novel and rubedo to keep you up way past bedtime.

I also encourage anyone wanting to understand how Harry Potter works and why readers love these stories to pick up Michael Ward's *Planet Narnia.* Ward explains the hidden key to the Narnia novels—their astrological symbolism—so cogently and clearly (not to mention "exhaustively") that Lewis's genius and Christological artistry will open up to the careful reader in life- and mind-changing fashion. Rowling's almost invisible alchemical structures, too, will make much more sense in light of Lewis's astrological stage settings and Ward's explanation of same.

And if you've read all those and want some lighter fare, I recommend two rather bizarre novels whose artistry and meanings I found simultaneously shocking, delightful, and strangely uplifting: *Jonathan Strange and Mr. Norrell* by Susanna Clarke and *An Instance of the Fingerpost* by Iain Pears. Not enough? Take a return trip through Jane Austen and Charles Dickens with stops at *Northanger Abbey* and *Martin Chuzzlewit.*

6. *J. K. Rowling has said recently that wands are "quasi-intelligent" magical objects. Wands are a big part of* Deathly Hallows. *Can you explain what makes wands intelligent and why I should care?*

Rowling was interviewed on The Leaky Cauldron's PotterCast program in December 2007 and made quite a few comments about wands. The core of the Elder Wand is a thestral hair, for instance, and that makes a sort of sense, given that the wand is supposed to have belonged to Death himself. The most interesting thing Rowling talked about, though, is the "quasi-sentience" of wands. Let's read what she said:

> Essentially, I see wands as being quasi-sentient. . . . They're not exactly animate, but they're close to it, as close to it as you can get in an object, because they carry so much magic. So that's really the key point about a wand.[7]

Wands are magical objects made of pieces of wood and magical cores. The woods are important to a degree, but it is their stuffing and its combination with the quality of the wood that seem to give wands their greater or lesser power. As we learned from Ollivander in *Philosopher's Stone* and again in *Deathly Hallows*, the "wand chooses the wizard" because of recognition (sentience), natural affinity, and correspondence. In August 2006, after a reading she gave with John Irving and Stephen King, Rowling answered some questions, including this one on wand cores:

> Q: In the wizarding world, there are many wand makers, Ollivander's being the one we're most familiar with. How come Ollivander chose the three magical cores for the wands he makes and decided these are the most powerful cores instead of other cores, such as Veela hair?
>
> ROWLING: It is true there are several wand makers. And in my notes I have many different cores for wands. Essentially, I decided Ollivander's was going to use my three favorites. So Ollivander has decided those are the three most powerful substances. Other wand makers would choose things that are particular to their country. Because countries in my world have their own particular indigenous magical species. So Veela hair is kind of obvious for Fleur's wand.[8]

What does this have to do with wand core quasi-sentience? To get that, we have to understand what Rowling's favorites and Ollivander's three most powerful substances have in common and what, if anything, this shared quality has to do with their power and sentience.

Unicorn hair, phoenix feather, and dragon's heartstring: not an obvious trio, perhaps, but if you'll look back at chapter 9, you'll see that the phoenix, or Resurrection Bird, and the unicorn are both symbols of Christ. What link, though, is there between dragon's heartstring and the Son of God?

We learn on Dumbledore's important Chocolate Frog card that he is an alchemist and that he discovered the twelve uses of dragon's blood. Hermione, of course, has them memorized, and Hogwarts thinks it's important enough that it's in the first year's curriculum (assuming Hermione is cramming for exams when she learns this rather than just showing off[9]). Dragon's blood, especially with the evident importance Slughorn, master potions maker, and Dumbledore, accomplished alchemist, give it in their curious asides to one another during cleanup in chapter 4 of *Half-Blood Prince*, is pretty important stuff.

How important?

Dragon's blood, according to Lyndy Abraham's *A Dictionary of Alchemical Imagery*[10] is linked in alchemical writings with the Elixir of Life. The elixir is the tincture of the Philosopher's Stone, a traditional symbol of Christ in poetry and drama because it offers eternal life and spiritual riches usually represented with gold. Here, then, is a connection between dragon's blood with the Eucharist, or specifically the blood of Christ, via alchemical symbolism. From dragon's blood, it is relatively easy to jump to dragon's heartstring because the heartstring will have been saturated with the blood.

So the three preferable wand cores are all symbols in some fashion of Christ. Rowling says Ollivander prefers feather, hair, and heartstring because he "has decided that those are the three most powerful substances." This makes all three wand cores pointers to Christ, even independent of the traditional symbolism of unicorn, phoenix, and dragon's blood/Philosopher's Stone.

Why?

The answer lies in Dumbledore's repeated explanations to Harry and expositions of the power of love. Love, quite simply, is the great mystery and power of Rowling's magical world and, by the way, of all traditional cosmology. God is love, as Saint John tells us (see 1 John 4), and the creative principle driving and sustaining creation is one of polarity resolved, hence the complementary opposites that define life on earth (male/female, night/day, hot/cold, contraction/expansion of heart, etc.). In Christian language, this principle is God's *Logos*, or Word, that becomes a man as Jesus of Nazareth, the Christ.

Back to wand cores.

What are the most powerful wand stuffers? Those that draw from or focus best the power that is the fabric of all things, seen and unseen. This power is love. What better way would there be to represent this in story than to use pointers to Love himself? We have that in Ollivander's preferences for phoenix feathers (the Resurrection Bird), unicorn hair (a traditional symbol in poetry, tapestry, and story for Christ), and via its connection with the dragon blood–red tincture of the Philosopher's Stone's elixir, dragon heartstrings.

And sentience? According to traditional epistemology, the only reason that anything material or conceptual can be known is because it is created and sustained by the logos, or creative principle, which principle is intelligible and the substance of our faculty of understanding. That the wand cores are all made from Christ/logos symbols would mean that their "quasi-sentience" and powers of choice (or at least recognition of affinity) are "logical." They have the substance of intelligence and intelligibility as their essence.

7. *Are you related to Hermione Granger?*

I am asked this question almost as often as "Have you ever met J. K. Rowling?" (See the introduction for the answer to that one.) If the person is joking, I play along and say I am her Muggle cousin, three times removed. I give the same answer to small children who ask.

Believe it or not, it has been suggested[11] that Rowling changed Hermione's middle name from Jane to Jean in *Deathly Hallows*[12] as a hat tip to me. Hermione in that chapter receives *The Tales of Beadle the Bard* in Dumbledore's will. The thought was, because beadle is a churchwarden and bard is often used to describe Shakespeare the alchemical dramatist, that Rowling changed Hermione's name to Jean because her job was to discover the meaning of a book with alchemical and Christian content. Like "John Granger."

Nice thought, but I think "typo" is a more likely explanation. As far as I know, Rowling has never heard my name, read my books, or discovered my blog. I'll stick with the Muggle cousin answer.

8. *Besides reading the books you have recommended, how can I continue this conversation? Is there a place on the Internet where serious readers talk about these things?*

There are at least ten thousand Web sites on which you can read about all the Harry Potter news as it breaks, discuss your favorite theories, post novel-length fan fiction, or keep up with your favorite Harry Potter–inspired rock groups, charities, and artists. You can even sign up for one of the five or six international conferences and fan cons held every year to discuss the meaning of the books and have fun with other readers.

I check three Potter Web sites with some regularity. The first is Accio Quote (http://www.accio-quote.org) and its Webmaster's Madam Pince home page (http://madam-pince.blogspot.com). This is the one-stop source for finding transcripts of everything Rowling has said in interviews from 1997 to the present—and I don't know how I'd live without it.

The second is a blog called the Hog's Head (http://thehogshead .org). Hog's Head is written by Travis Prinzi, and his perspective, charity, balance, and insights on all things Harry Potter, especially the philosophical and theological sides of things, are invaluable to me. I refer so often to his Web site on my own blog that I have called Hog's Head the sister site to Hogwarts Professor. Prinzi has also mastered the art of podcasting, which gives the site a very personal dimension. Most important to me, though, is the community of readers and comment-box writers at Hog's Head, all of whom write in a generous spirit and with a good sense of humor. They are also very smart.

The third site is my place, Hogwarts Professor (http://www .hogwartsprofessor.com), or HogPro, as most of the readers there call it. It is what the subtitle says it is: "Thoughts for the Serious

Reader of Harry Potter." We discuss Harry Potter, English literature, and the intersection of reading, spirituality, politics, and the signs of the times. If you enjoyed this book, you'll like HogPro. Please join us next time you're online.

9. *I keep reading that Pope Benedict XVI has condemned Harry Potter. What's up with that?*

A small group of Roman Catholics in the small town of Combermere, Ontario, run a Web site called LifeSiteNews that started this absurd Skeeter effect that won't go away. Three days before the release of *Half-Blood Prince* in July 2005, LifeSiteNews issued a press release online with the inflammatory headline "Pope Opposes Harry Potter Novels." A headline reflecting the reality described in the article would have been *"Vatican office sends polite thank-you to frenetic Harry-Hater."*

When he was still Cardinal Ratzinger, Pope Benedict received a copy of a book criticizing the Harry Potter novels, and he—or a page in his office—wrote a short response saying it was important to be discerning about what children read and that the author should contact a priest in the Vatican whose job it was to discuss these things (i.e., "Lady, I'm really busy"). The author contacted the priest named in the note, and he told her in a four-page, single-spaced letter how wrong she was. Being the model of humility she is, her response to this correction was to tell the world (with the help of her friends in the backwoods of Ontario) that the Pope was a Harry hater.

Sadly, the world as we have it is very much like Harry's world in that many people believe what the *Daily Prophet* tells them, however laughable. Even Rowling seems to believe that Cardinal Ratzinger had read her books and commented on them critically. The only things the Vatican has said about Harry Potter have been (1) at a news conference about a Vatican publication on the New Age, at which Father Peter Fleetwood said positive things about the series, (2) in an article in the Catholic News Service the week the LifeSite-News post was made ("New attention given to 2003 Cardinal

Ratzinger letter on Harry Potter"), which denied the Pope had taken a position on the matter, and (3) in January 2008, when *Deathly Hallows* was finally published in Italian, the Vatican newspaper, *L'Osservatore Romano,* "dedicated a full page to a Pro vs. Con debate on the merits of the Harry Potter series as a whole."[13]

The Vatican and the Pope do not waste their political and spiritual capital in the public square on issues people of good faith can disagree about without any violation of principle. That doesn't mean religious leaders won't discuss the value of books people read; the condemnation of Philip Pullman's children's books by Catholic bishops and other spiritual leaders in America comes immediately to mind. The Harry Potter books, however, have not been opposed, condemned, or criticized by any agency or person of authority in the Vatican (except, I'm told, by a loose cannon exorcist). The Pope certainly hasn't spoken on this subject.

The history of this whole it-would-be-funny-if-it-weren't-true illustration of the power of faux journalists with Web sites to create false impressions in the public mind has been written up at Hogwarts Professor as "Rita Skeeter Covers the Vatican."[14] Again, if you hear your friends talking about this subject, tell them the Pope doesn't oppose Harry Potter.

10. *Is Harry Potter a "Great Work"? Is J. K. Rowling a great writer like Shakespeare, Tolstoy, or Tolkien?*

I think it's hard to deny that Harry Potter is a Great Work or that Rowling is a great writer. I guess it's how you define these things that matters. When *Time* magazine made Rowling one of the runners-up in their Person of the Year issue at the end of 2007, they quoted a friend and English professor on just this subject:

> That is on top of the impact, even her critics acknowledge,
> of inspiring a generation of obsessive readers unafraid of fat
> books and complex plots. "They're easy to underestimate

because of what I call the three Deathly Hallows for academics," says James Thomas, a professor of English at Pepperdine University. "They couldn't possibly be good because they're too recent, they're too popular, and they're too juvenile." But he argues that the books do more than entertain. "They've made millions of kids smarter, more sensitive, certainly more literate and probably more ethical and aware of hypocrisy and lust for power. They've made children better adults, I think. I don't know of any books that have worked that kind of magic on so many millions of readers in so short a time in the history of publications."[15]

The three litmus tests I give a candidate for a great or classic book are: (1) Does it ask the big questions about what it means to be human? (2) Does the artistry of the book support the answers the author gives? and (3) Are the answers edifying and challenging? If the book is from the English literary tradition, I make this last question a lot simpler: "Are the answers Christian?" Not many books survive this trifold test. If you've read this book, you know that Rowling's Harry Potter novels do. The degree to which they exceed expectations on all three measures is the degree to which their popularity exceeds other books.

Audiences usually think I'm joking when I say Rowling compares favorably with Shakespeare, Tolkien, or Tolstoy. A lot of this, no doubt, is a reflection of Professor Thomas's "three Deathly Hallows for academics": The books are too recent, too popular, and too juvenile for people to take seriously (just as Shakespeare and Dickens were discounted by their contemporaries for being groundlings' fare). But a lot of it is a denial of the obvious strengths Rowling has in comparison with writers everyone admires and nobody reads.

❖ There are no great flights of eloquence and exalted prose in Rowling's books (if they're a long way from Goosebumps and even better children's literature on this count).

She is correspondingly more accessible to readers, young and old, however, and her message gets through. Considering the remarkable artistry and spiritual freight the books are carrying, this is no small thing.

❖ There is a lot of good humor and the occasional crude juvenile joke in the Harry Potter novels. A Tolkienite friend of mine once observed, "Y'know, there are no 'Uranus' jokes in The Lord of the Rings." That's certainly true. I'm not sure that is a significant advantage to the Hobbit novels when the seven books of Rowling's and Tolkien's series are put in the critical balance. The laughs of The Lord of the Rings can be a long time coming.

❖ J. K. Rowling delivers difficult truths to a postmodern audience in such a way that they accept as givens ideas they would otherwise reject, even laugh about. The existence of the soul? The importance of choosing to believe? The certainty of a life after death and a judgment of those with atrophied souls and darkened hearts? Rowling smuggles these golden wheelbarrows and quite a bit of Christian doctrine and ideas about the human person via her story line right past the most skeptical, even cynical, readers in history.

C. S. Lewis is supposed to have had much simpler measures of a book's worth. The first, shared in *An Experiment in Criticism*, was simply, "Do people read it again and again?" Lewis is said to have reread every Austen novel every year. He claimed her books "had only two faults, both of which are damnable; they are too few and too short." J. K. Rowling and Benjamin Disraeli are also said to have read Austen repeatedly; *Emma* twenty times in a row for the Harry Potter author and *Pride and Prejudice* seventeen times for the prime minister.

I have met readers who have reread the 4,100 pages of the series multiple times—and the last book hasn't been out for more than a year at this writing. I spoke at a bookstore when *Half-Blood Prince* was first released and learned that a mother and daughter in my audience had read the first five books fifteen times in anticipation of the sixth. They looked like normal people too. Harry Potter certainly passes what I'll call the "Austen repeater" test. As the shared text of at least three reading generations, readers have, as a rule, read the books more than once (and they own the movies, to boot).

C. S. Lewis also thought a book was great if you liked it very much and thought you were a better person for having read it. That may sound simplistic, even juvenile, but it is an acid test devoid of pretense. Does the book do what books and entertainment in general are supposed to do? Sidney said they were supposed to "instruct while delighting."

My hope, at the close of *How Harry Cast His Spell: The Meaning behind the Mania*, is that you will understand why readers around the world of all ages and beliefs love the Harry Potter novels. These books answer profound spiritual questions that are even more profoundly felt by a generation at least one step removed from traditional religious life. In an age of skepticism about the possibility of anything transcendent, our faculties of perception for greater realities than the stuff of matter and energy are, at best, atrophied for lack of exercise and more likely denied by our conscious minds.

Into this vacuum arrive the tales of our young wizard friend and his battle with the Voldemort inside and outside his person. J. K. Rowling, using the traditional symbols and artistry of faith and English letters, exercises the atrophied spiritual imaginations of her readers and enlarges their capacity both for love and for understanding of the world and themselves with a transcendent dimension.

She delights and instructs—and we are much the better people for this delightful instruction. I think the books are great. Please write and tell me what you think. Thank you for joining me on this adventure in reading and, in advance, for your first e-mail message. See you at Hogwarts Professor!

JOHN GRANGER
john@HogwartsProfessor.com

NOTES

INTRODUCTION
[1] "The Truth about Death," *Journal of Genetics* 58 (1962-1963): 463–464.
[2] *J. K. Rowling: A Year in the Life*, a documentary by James Runcie (December 30, 2007), ITV1
[3] Mircea Eliade, *The Sacred and the Profane: The Nature of Religion* (New York: Harcourt, 1957), 204.
[4] Ibid., 205.
[5] Ibid.
[6] *J. K. Rowling: A Year in the Life.*
[7] *Face to Face with J. K. Rowling* (December 7, 1998), http://www.accio-quote.org/articles/1998/1298-herald-simpson.html.
[8] See www.HogwartsProfessor.com.

CHAPTER 1
[1] Mircea Eliade, *The Sacred and the Profane*, 205.
[2] For more on the confusion between the psychic and the spiritual realms in our time and the dangers of occultism, please see Charles Upton's *The System of Antichrist: Truth and Falsehood in Postmodernism and the New Age* (Ghent, NY: Sophia Perennis, 2001), 134–137.
[3] See C. S. Lewis, *Prince Caspian*, chapters 7 and 12. Readers of the Narnia books remember from *The Magician's Nephew* that Aslan created that world with his song—as does the divinity in J. R. R. Tolkien's Middle Earth.
[4] C. S. Lewis, *Mere Christianity* (New York: Collier Books, 1960), 51.
[5] "Fundamentalism Afoot in Anti-Potter Camp, Says New-Religions Expert: Popular Culture Enjoys an Autonomy, Explains Massimo Introvigne," *Zenit News*, December 6, 2001, http://www.cesnur.org/2001/potter/dec _03.htms.
[6] Bishop Auxentios, *Orthodox Tradition* 20, no. 3 (2003): 14–26.

[7] See C. S. Lewis's *The Silver Chair* for this modern tragedy told in story form. *The Silver Chair* is a vibrant story of the confusion and modern enchantment with materialism or "life underground." Is there any Narnia moment greater than Prince Rilian's victory over the Emerald Witch in chapter 12?

CHAPTER 2
[1] Tom Shippey, *J. R. R. Tolkien: Author of the Century* (Boston: Houghton Mifflin Co., 2001), 147.
[2] Perry Glazer, "The Surprising Trouble with Harry," *Touchstone* (November 2003): 13.

CHAPTER 3
[1] David Colbert, author of *The Magical Worlds of Harry Potter*, thinks the formula is the universal hero pattern described by Joseph Campbell in his *Hero with a Thousand Faces*. Joan Acocella in the *New Yorker* magazine traces the pattern to Vladimir Propp's 1929 book, *Morphology of the Folk Tale*. Elizabeth Schafer believes Rowling is a fan of Carl Jung; she cites Lord Ragland's work on archetypal heroes, *The Hero: A Study in Tradition, Myth, and Drama*, as a guide to the formula Rowling follows.

CHAPTER 4
[1] For more information on alchemy and its use in classic literature, please read *Darke Hierogliphicks* by Stanton Linden, a history of alchemy and its usage in English literature, or subscribe to *Cauda Pavonis*, an academic journal on alchemy in literature.
[2] *The Tempest, Romeo and Juliet, Antony and Cleopatra, The Two Gentlemen of Verona, The Comedy of Errors, Love's Labour's Lost*, and *The Merchant of Venice* come to mind. In her book *The Art of Memory* (Chicago: University of Chicago Press, 1974), Dame Frances Yates demonstrated that Shakespeare built the Globe Theatre on alchemical principles for the proper staging of his alchemical dramas.
[3] Anne Simpson, "Face to Face with J. K. Rowling: Casting a Spell over Young Minds," *The Herald* (December 7, 1998).
[4] Lyndy Abraham, *A Dictionary of Alchemical Imagery* (Cambridge: Cambridge University Press, 1999).
[5] Ibid.
[6] Ibid.
[7] Ibid.
[8] Mircea Eliade and Stephen Corrin, *The Forge and the Crucible: The Origins and Structures of Alchemy* (Chicago: University of Chicago Press, 1979), 153.

CHAPTER 5
[1] For more on this, see the discussion of the spell in chapter 13 on *Prisoner of Azkaban*.
[2] J. K. Rowling, *Harry Potter and the Order of the Phoenix* (New York: Scholastic, 2003), 607.
[3] Ibid., 841.
[4] PotterCast 130 (December 2007), http://www.accio-quote.org/articles/2007/1217-pottercast-anelli.html.
[5] J. K. Rowling, *Harry Potter and the Half-Blood Prince* (New York: Scholastic, 2005), 511.
[6] J. K. Rowling, *Harry Potter and the Deathly Hallows* (New York: Scholastic, 2007), 710.

CHAPTER 6
[1] There actually is such a book, titled *Unlocking Harry Potter: Five Keys for the Serious Reader* (Zossima Press, 2007), and I recommend it to the literature geeks out there.
[2] See "Why *Half-Blood Prince* Is the Best Harry Potter Novel" at http://www. HogwartsProfessor.com.

CHAPTER 7
[1] Malcolm Jones, "Harry's Hot," *Newsweek* (July 17, 2000): 56 and David B. Caruso, "Harry Potter Case Illustrates Blurry Line in Copyright Law," Associated Press (April 19, 2008).
[2] J. K. Rowling, *Harry Potter and the Sorcerer's Stone* (New York: Scholastic, 1997), 297.
[3] Ibid., 299.
[4] J. K. Rowling, *Harry Potter and the Prisoner of Azkaban* (New York: Scholastic, 1999), 427–428.
[5] Rowling, *Order of the Phoenix*, 861.
[6] Ibid., 773.
[7] J. K. Rowling, *Harry Potter and the Goblet of Fire* (New York: Scholastic, 2000), 648, 653.
[8] Rowling, *Order of the Phoenix*, 814.
[9] Rowling, *Prisoner of Azkaban*, 247.
[10] Rowling, *Order of the Phoenix*, 836.
[11] Ibid.
[12] Ibid., 841.
[13] Ibid., 814.
[14] Ibid., 843–844.
[15] Ibid., 836
[16] Rowling, *Sorcerer's Stone*, 296.
[17] Rowling, *Deathly Hallows*, 328.
[18] Shawn Adler, "'Harry Potter' Author J. K. Rowling Opens Up about Books' Christian Imagery," *MTV*, http://www.mtv.com/news/articles/1572107/20071017/index. jhtml.
[19] Rowling, *Deathly Hallows*, 726.

CHAPTER 8
[1] See Aristotle's *Nicomachean Ethics*, book 2, for the longer definition.
[2] J. K. Rowling, *Harry Potter and the Chamber of Secrets* (New York: Scholastic, 1999), 333.
[3] Rowling, *Goblet of Fire*, 708.
[4] Ibid., 724.
[5] Rowling, *Sorcerer's Stone*, 108, and *Goblet of Fire*, 708.
[6] J. K. Rowling, *Chamber of Secrets*, 198.
[7] Rowling, *Sorcerer's Stone*, 59.
[8] Rowling, *Prisoner of Azkaban*, 415.
[9] Rowling, *Goblet of Fire*, 613.
[10] Rowling, *Deathly Hallows*, 362.
[11] Ibid., 713.
[12] Rowling, *Order of the Phoenix*, 34.
[13] Rowling, *Chamber of Secrets*, 333.
[14] Ibid., 317.
[15] Rowling, *Half-Blood Prince*, 512.
[16] See http://www.mugglenet.com/jkrinterview.shtml.

CHAPTER 9
[1] Martin Lings, *Symbol and Archetype: A Study of the Meaning of Existence* (Cambridge: Quinta Essentia), vii.

[2] Bishop Auxentios, "The Iconic and Symbolic in Orthodox Iconography," *Orthodox Tradition* 4, no. 3 (n.d.): 49–64. See also http://www.orthodoxinfo. com/general/orth_icon.htm.

[3] The symbolism springs from Plato's myth of the charioteer in the *Phaedrus* (246b, 254c-e) and its explanation in the *Republic* (441e–442b). The disciples of the apostles and of Christ "baptized" this doctrine in light of the Christian revelation in the first centuries AD.

[4] C. S. Lewis, *Abolition of Man* (New York: Collier Books), 28. See also 1 Thessalonians 5:23, where Saint Paul describes the whole person as a trinity of "spirit, soul and body."

[5] Rowling, *Chamber of Secrets*, 204.

[6] J. K. Rowling, *Fantastic Beasts and Where to Find Them* (n.p.: Bt Bound, 2001), 20.

[7] David Colbert, *The Magical Worlds of Harry Potter: A Treasury of Myths, Legends, and Fascinating Facts* (n.p.: Bt Bound, 2002), 107.

[8] Rowling, *Chamber of Secrets*, 334.

[9] Colbert, *Magical Worlds*, 109.

[10] Rowling, *Sorcerer's Stone*, 256.

[11] Rowling, *Goblet of Fire*, 436, 440–441.

[12] *Strong's Concordance of the Bible*, s.v. "unicorn."

[13] Colbert, *Magical Worlds*, 182.

[14] J. E. Cirlot notes that Carl Jung mentioned this symbolism with a reference to an author contemporaneous with the tapestries: "The very fierce animal with one horn is called unicorn. In order to catch it, a virgin is put in a field; the animal then comes to her and is caught, because it lies down in her lap. *Christ is represented by this animal, and his invincible strength by its horn.* He who lay down in the womb of the virgin has been caught by the hunters; that is to say, he was found in human shape by those who loved him." "Honoris of Autun, Speculum de Mysteriis Ecclesiae (Eyeglass of the Mysteries of the Church)," quoted in *Symbolism*, 357–358; emphasis mine. Not convinced? Paul Ford in his encyclopedic *Companion to Narnia* confirmed my memory and this interpretation. The unicorn, he reports, is "a mythological beast with a single horn in the center of its head. It variously symbolizes purity, chastity, and even *the Word of God as brought by Jesus Christ*" (emphasis mine). See Paul Ford, *Companion to Narnia* (San Francisco: HarperSanFrancisco, 1994), 430.

[15] J. E. Cirlot, *A Dictionary of Symbols* (New York: Dorset Press, 1991), 254; Allan Kronzek and Elizabeth Kronzek, *The Sorcerer's Companion* (New York: Broadway Books, 2001), 188; Colbert, *Magical Worlds*, 82.

[16] Rowling, *Prisoner of Azkaban*, 424.

[17] Ford, *Companion to Narnia*, 440.

[18] See Cirlot, *Dictionary of Symbols*, 308–309. "Its symbolic meaning is linked with that of the tree of life . . . inexhaustible life, and is therefore equivalent to a symbol of immortality . . . because of the resemblance of its antlers to branches. It is also a symbol of the cycles of regeneration and growth. . . . The stag . . . came to be thought of as a symbol of regeneration because of the way its antlers are renewed. Like the eagle and the lion, it is the secular enemy of the serpent . . . [and acts] as [one of the] mediators of heaven and earth. . . . In the West, during the Middle Ages, the way of solitude and purity was often symbolized by the stag, which actually appears in some emblems with a crucifix between its horns."

[19] Rowling, *Prisoner of Azkaban*, 385.

[20] Ford, *Companion to Narnia*, 358.

[21] C. S. Lewis, *The Last Battle* (New York: Collier Books, 1960), 193.

[22] Lewis didn't see the horse, the centaur's driving part, as a passionate creature, but as the desires (or belly) in alignment and in service to will and spirit (chest and head), especially when hosting a human rider. The centaur,

"a semi-divine being with the head and chest of a man and the body of a horse," the embodiment of horse and rider, represents the reconciliation "of our spiritual and physical nature." "For Lewis, the Centaur represents the harmony of nature and spirit." See Ford, *Companion to Narnia*, 102, 235.

23 Rowling, *Deathly Hallows*, 733.

24 For the full story, see Colbert, *Magical Worlds*, 113–116.

25 Allan Zola Kronzek and Elizabeth Kronzek, *The Sorcerer's Companion: A Guide to the Magical World of Harry Potter* (n.p.: Bt Bound, 2001), 109.

26 Cirlot, *A Dictionary of Symbols*, 149.

27 Titus Burckhardt, *Alchemy: Science of the Cosmos, Science of the Soul* (Baltimore: Penguin Books, 1972), 18.

28 C. S. Lewis, *The Lion, the Witch and the Wardrobe* (New York: Collier Books, 1970), 104.

29 Burckhardt, *Alchemy*, 91.

30 Rowling, *Sorcerer's Stone*, 292.

31 See "But Obviously Dumbledore Is Not Jesus" at http://www. HogwartsProfessor.com.

32 This is how C. S. Lewis described the effect that the works of George MacDonald had on him. See *George MacDonald: 365 Readings* (New York: Macmillan Publishing, 1986), xvi.

CHAPTER 10

1 Donna Farley, private correspondence.

2 For more on Helena Blavatsky, see *The Theosophical Enlightenment* by Joscelyn Godwin (Albany, N.Y.: The State University of New York Press, 1994). This book is a remarkable introduction to a woman whose wild ideas still, alas, influence our world.

3 Francis Bridger, *A Charmed Life: The Spirituality of Potterworld* (n.p.: Image Books, 2002), 19.

4 Linda McCabe, private correspondence.

5 Rowling, *Chamber of Secrets*, 31.

6 See http://ww2.netnitco.net/users/legend01/weasel.htm.

7 Rowling, *Prisoner of Azkaban*, 74.

8 A correspondent from Iceland, Sigurdur Arni Thordarson, taught me that lilies are held by the archangel Gabriel at the Annunciation in Western iconography; the dead hold the lilies like Gabriel in anticipation of Christ's coming again to earth.

9 When *Book* magazine, a publication of Barnes and Noble, featured a mug shot of Rowling on their June 2003 cover to herald the arrival of *Harry Potter and the Order of the Phoenix*, they had no trouble finding five American men named Harry Potter, all of whom told the same tale of crank calls and new friends delighted to "meet the man himself." Rowling was sued in New Jersey by a children's book author whose story featured a hero named Harry Potter. Better than these examples, Netflix released two mock-horror, B-movie gems, *Troll* (1986) and *Troll 2* (1992), in which the family resisting Torok the troll's attempt to take over the world is led by a dad and son both named Harry Potter. Harry Potter Sr. and Harry Potter Jr. were all over the movie and HBO screens for two or three years; how meaningful was that? (Not very.) Thanks to Dan Rees of Joplin, Missouri, for Harry's first encounters with trolls.

My favorite instance of Harry sightings pre-Rowling comes from Monty Python. In a send-up strangely echoing the beginning of *Philosopher's Stone*, we hear Harry is about to be attacked: It was a day like any other and Mr. and Mrs. Samuel Brainsample were a perfectly ordinary couple, leading perfectly ordinary lives—the sort of people to whom nothing extraordinary ever happened, and not the kind of people to be the centre of one of the most astounding incidents in the history of mankind. . . . So let's forget about them and follow instead the destiny of this man. . . . (Camera pans off them; they both look disappointed; camera picks up instead a smart little business man, in bowler, briefcase and pinstripes.) . . . Harold Potter, gardener, and tax official, first victim of Creatures from another Planet. See http://www.ibras. dk/montypython/episode07.htm. I learned of this early Python sketch from Kia, a friend of Linda McCabe's.

[10] Edinburgh "Cub Reporter" press conference, *ITV* (July 16, 2005).

[11] Bloomsbury Live Chat with J. K. Rowling (July 30, 2007), http://www. bloomsbury.com/jkrevent.

[12] "To me [the religious parallels have] always been obvious," Rowling said. Shawn Adler, "'Harry Potter' Author J. K. Rowling Opens Up about Books' Christian Imagery," http://www.mtv.com/news/articles/1572107/20071017/ index.jhtml.

[13] Saint Dorotheos, "On the Fear of God," *Dorotheos of Gaza* (Kalamazoo, Mich.: Cistercian Publications, 1977), 110–111.

CHAPTER 11

[1] Rowling, *Sorcerer's Stone*, 256.

[2] Ibid., 258.

[3] See chapter 1 of Saint John Climacos, *The Ladder of Divine Ascent* (Mahwah, N.J.: Paulist Press, 1988).

[4] Rowling, *Sorcerer's Stone*, 270.

[5] See Aristotle's *On the Soul*; William Wallace, *The Elements of Philosophy* (n.p.: Alba House, 1977), 62; and the relevant articles on "soul" in the *New Catholic Encyclopedia*.

[6] See Aristotle's *Nicomachean Ethics*, book 3, chapter 4.

[7] Rowling, *Sorcerer's Stone*, 300.

[8] Ibid., 291.

[9] Ibid., 299.

[10] Alexandre Kalomiros, *River of Fire* (Montreal: Monastery Press, 1982), 18.

[11] Ioannes Romanides, *Franks, Romans, Feudalism, and Doctrine* (Brookline, Mass.: Holy Cross Orthodox Press, 1982), 46.

CHAPTER 12

[1] Rowling, *Chamber of Secrets*, 335–336.

[2] Ibid., 340.

[3] Rowling has admitted that Lockhart has a real-world model. My guess is Philip Pullman, author of the Dark Materials trilogy. Certainly there are sufficient points of correspondence between Pullman and Lockhart to merit serious consideration of the link: (1) as we know, Rowling likes to name characters in her books after characters from other famous books (see chapter 10), and one of the lead characters in multiple Pullman books is Sallie *Lockhart*; (2) Philip Pullman is a public atheist and despiser of organized religion—and admits freely in interviews that he proselytizes his worldview in his children's books; (3) Pullman is called the "UnLewis" in the UK because of his public disdain for C. S. Lewis's Narnia books and the values they represent.

[4] Rowling, *Chamber of Secrets*, 320.

CHAPTER 13

[1] Rowling, *Prisoner of Azkaban*, 187.

[2] Ibid., 188, 247.

3 Ibid., 189.
4 Ibid., 245.
5 Colbert, *Magical Worlds*, 125.
6 Rowling, *Prisoner of Azkaban*, 385.
7 Ibid., 376.
8 Ibid., 412.
9 Ibid., 415.

CHAPTER 14
1 Thanks to Eileen Rebstock for her help in understanding the rebirthing party in *Goblet of Fire*.
2 Rowling, *Fantastic Beasts*, 32.
3 Rowling, *Sorcerer's Stone*, 294.
4 Rowling, *Goblet of Fire*, 255.

CHAPTER 15
1 Rowling, *Order of the Phoenix*, 856.
2 Ibid., 862.
3 Abraham, *Alchemical Imagery*, 135.
4 Ibid., 136.
5 Rowling, *Order of the Phoenix*, 822, 850, 855.
6 Thanks to Dr. Amy Sturgis of Belmont University for pointing out the meaning of Moody's Disillusionment Charm.
7 Rowling, *Order of the Phoenix*, 810; *Half-Blood Prince*, 602.
8 Rowling, *Deathly Hallows*, 593.
9 Rowling, *Order of the Phoenix*, 843.

CHAPTER 16
1 Rowling, *Half-Blood Prince*, 513.
2 Ibid., 358.
3 Ibid., 511.
4 Ibid., 497.
5 Ibid., 498.
6 Compare to *Half-Blood Prince*, 511.
7 Ibid., 509.
8 Rowling, *Order of the Phoenix*, 733.

CHAPTER 17
1 *The Literary Impact of the Authorized Version* (London: Athlone Press, 1950), 22, http://www.biblicalstudies.org.uk/pdf/kjv_lewis.pdf.
2 Rowling, *Deathly Hallows*, 29.
3 Ibid., 152–153.
4 Ibid., 185.
5 The Leaky Cauldron interview (July 2005), http://www.mugglenet.com.
6 Rowling, *Deathly Hallows*, 351.
7 Ibid., 362.
8 Ibid., 364.
9 Ibid., 365–366.
10 Abraham, *Alchemical Imagery*, 52.
11 Rowling, *Deathly Hallows*, 366.
12 Ibid., 441.
13 Deborah Chan ("Arabella Figg") at the HogPro boards first pointed out that Dobby is the model Christian of the series.
14 Rowling, *Deathly Hallows*, 478–479, 483.

[15] Ibid., 484.
[16] Ibid., 563.
[17] Ibid., 713.

CHAPTER 18

[1] Shawn Adler, "Harry Potter Author J. K. Rowling Opens Up about Books' Christian Imagery" (October 17, 2007), http://www.mtv.com/news/articles/1572107/20071017/index.jhtml.
[2] Rowling, *Deathly Hallows*, 332–333.
[3] Ibid., 323.
[4] Ibid., 325.
[5] Ibid., 328.
[6] Ibid., 342.
[7] Ibid., 370.
[8] Ibid., 368.
[9] Rowling, *Sorcerer's Stone*, 118.
[10] Rowling, *Goblet of Fire*, 177.
[11] Conversation with the author at Prophecy 2007, a Harry Potter conference in Toronto, Canada (August 2007).
[12] See Saint Clement's *The Paedagogus*.
[13] A. N. Williams, *The Divine Sense: The Intellect in Patristic Theology* (Cambridge: Cambridge University Press, 2007), 72.
[14] Rowling, *Deathly Hallows*, 384–385.

CHAPTER 19

[1] Rowling may have chosen to read "The Silver Doe" to her Carnegie Hall audience in late 2007, but she has said that it isn't the most meaningful chapter of *Deathly Hallows* for her. That honor is reserved for the chapter paralleling the Garden of Gethsemane, the carrying of the Cross, and Calvary (chapter 34, "The Forest Again").

KRISTY: What was your favorite scene to write in *Deathly Hallows*?

J. K. ROWLING: Chapter 34: The Forest Again.

(Bloomsbury Chat, July 29, 2007, http://www.bloomsbury.com/jkrevent/content.asp?sec=3&sec2=1).

J. K. ROWLING: I really, really, really cried after writing chapter 34, which is where Harry walks back into the Forest for what he thinks will be the last time. Because I had to live that with Harry and feel the weight of his disillusionment and his fear because he believes he's being sent to his death by Dumbledore who he thought wanted to keep him alive. So that was massively moving to me to write.

Dateline (July 26, 2007).

MEREDITH VIEIRA: Overall, the loss of which character brought you to tears?

J. K. ROWLING: Definitely the passage that I found hardest to write of all of them in all seven books and the one that made me cry the most is chapter 34 in this one. But that was—and that was partly because of the content and partly because it had been planned for so long and been roughed out for so long. And to write the definitive version felt like a—a huge climax.

MEREDITH VIEIRA: And can you tell us what was in 34?

J. K. ROWLING: It's when Harry sets off into the Forest. Again. So that's my favorite passage of this book. And it's the part that when I finished writing, I didn't cry as I was writing, but when I finished writing, I had enormous explosion of emotion and I cried and cried and cried.

Today (July 26, 2007).

[2] Rowling, *Deathly Hallows*, 699.

[3] Ibid., 700.

[4] Ibid., 699.

[5] Ibid., 697–698.

[6] Ibid., 698.

[7] Ibid., 700–701.

[8] Ibid., 686.

[9] Ibid., 703.

[10] Ibid., 698.

[11] *Bloomsbury Chat* (July 29, 2007), http://www.bloomsbury.com/jkrevent.

[12] Rowling, *Deathly Hallows*, 720–721.

[13] Ibid., 722.

[14] Ibid., 723.

[15] Ibid., 722.

[16] Ibid., 706–707.

[17] *Bloomsbury Chat* (July 29, 2007), http://www.bloomsbury.com/jkrevent.

[18] Rowling, *Deathly Hallows*, 727.

[19] Ibid., 689.

[20] Ibid., 733.

[21] Ibid., 741.

[22] Rowling has compared her own faith to that of Catholic author Graham Greene: "Like Greene, my faith is sometimes about if my faith will return. It's important to me" (Stephen McGinty, "Life After Harry," *The Scotsman* (January 2006). Even more recently, in her post–*Deathly Hallows* interviews on MSNBC with Meredith Vieira, she expanded on this idea:

MEREDITH VIEIRA: Harry's also referred to as the Chosen One. So are there religious—

J. K. ROWLING: Well, there—there clearly is a religious—undertone. And—it's always been difficult to talk about that because until we reached book seven, views of what happens after death and so on, it would give away a lot of what was coming. So . . . yes, my belief and my struggling with religious belief and so on I think is quite apparent in this book.

MEREDITH VIEIRA: And what is the struggle?

J .K. ROWLING: Well my struggle really is to keep believing.

Dateline/Today (July 26, 2007).

Turning to the text of *Harry Potter and the Deathly Hallows*, Rowling herself seems to be up front about this subject-author connection:

LUKAS, 9: Is Harry Potter based on anyone that you know?

J. K. ROWLING: No, Harry is entirely imaginary. Erm, so I suppose that must mean that he comes from me a bit as well.

Dateline/Today (July 26, 2007).

[23] Frithjob Schuon, *Echoes of Perennial Wisdom* (Bloomington, IN: World Wisdom, 1992), 43.

[24] Rowling, *Deathly Hallows*, 723.

CHAPTER 20

[1] The October 21, 2007, post at my blog, "I always thought of Dumbledore as gay [ovation]," is an excellent place to start for the details about what really happened and what was said at Carnegie Hall (see http://hogwartsprofessor.com/?p=198). The October 23, 2007, post "Taking Stories More Seriously than the Author," is a good follow-up for the literature perspective (see http://hogwartsprofessor.com/?p=199).

[2] "Harry Potter and the Christian Critics" (September 13, 2007), http://www.firstthings.com/onthesquare/?p=844.

[3] Rowling, *Deathly Hallows*, 593–594.

[4] Ibid., 734.

[5] "Harry Potter and 'the Death of God'" (August 20, 2007), http://www.lifesite.net/ldn/2007/aug/07082003.html.

[6] "Judging Harry Potter," (September 2, 2007), http://ncregister.com/site/article/3663.

[7] PotterCast 131 (January 2, 2008), http://www.the-leaky-cauldron.org/2008/1/2/pottercast-131-j-k-rowling-interview-transcript.

[8] An Evening with Harry, Carry and Garp (August 1, 2006), http://www.accio-quote.org/articles/2006/0801-radiocityreading1partial.html.

[9] Rowling, *Philosopher's Stone*, 229.

[10] Abraham, *A Dictionary of Alchemical Imagery*, 29.

[11] http://hogwartsprofessor.com/?p=138.

[12] Rowling, *Deathly Hallows*, 125.

[13] Agency France-Presse, "Good vs. Evil Debate on Harry Potter in Vatican Mouthpiece," http://www.abs-cbnnews.com/storypage.aspx?StoryID=105571.

[14] http://hogwartsprofessor.com/?p=26.

[15] http://www.time.com/time/specials/2007/personoftheyear/article/0,28804,1690753_1695388_1695436,00.html.